APPRENTICESHIPS

Adult Care

Lead Adult Ca Worker

and

BTEC Diploma in Adult Care

Handbook

LEVEL 3

Published by Pearson Education Limited, 80 Strand, London, WC2R ORL.

www.pearsonschoolsandfecolleges.co.uk

Text © Pearson Education Limited 2018
Typeset by PDQ Digital Media Solutions Ltd.
Original illustrations © Pearson Education Limited 2018
Picture research by Integra
Cover illustration © Pearson Education Limited 2018

The rights of Carolyn Aldworth, Colette Burgess, Andrew Carter-Whiting and Siân Lavers to be identified as authors of this work have been asserted by them in accordance with the Copyright, Designs and Patents Act 1988.

First published 2018

21 20 19 18
10 9 8 7 6 5 4 3 2 1

British Library Cataloguing in Publication Data
A catalogue record for this book is available from the British Library

ISBN 978 1 292 27990 9

Printed in the UK by Bell & Bain Ltd, Glasgow

Acknowledgements

The author and publisher would like to thank the following individuals and organisations for permission to reproduce copyright material:

Photo credits: (Key: T-top; B-bottom; C-centre; L-left; R-right) **123RF:** Alexraths 214; **Alamy Stock Photo:** ALAN EDWARDS 197; **Carolyn Aldworth** 178; **Care Quality Commission**: Logo of Care Quality Commission, used with permission 14; **Getty Images:** Simon McGill/Moment 5b; **Shutterstock:** Monkey Business Images 5t, Magicoven 175; **Pearson Education Ltd:** Clark Wiseman. Studio 8 1, 25, 34, 55, 56, 64, 82, 87, 88, 98, 111, 128, 153, 154, 155b, 155t, 157, 166t, 166b, 167tl, 167tr, 167bl, 167br, 170, 171, 172, 174, 177, 179, 185, 189, 193t, 193b, 194, 196, 201, 203, 209, 237, 242, 248; Lord and Leverett 15; Stuart Cox 20;

Text credits: 69: Code of Conduct for Healthcare Support Workers and Adult Social Care Workers in England, © 2013, Skills for Care & Skills for Health; **97:** Pease, Allan and Barbara, The definitive book of body language, Orion Publishing Co, ISBN 9780752861180, © 2004, Orion Publishing Co; **99:** Advocacy QPM Code of Practice Revised 2014, QPM, National Development Team for Inclusion, © 2014, QPM | National Development Team for Inclusion; **98:** Care Act 2014, Independent advocacy support, retrived from http://www.legislation.gov.uk/ukpga/2014/23/part/1/crossheading/independent-advocacy-support/enacted: Contains public sector information licensed under the Open Government Licence v3.0; **102:** Data Protection Act of 1998, and the General Data Protection Regulation, Contains public sector information licensed under the Open Government Licence v3.0; **113:** What is abuse and neglect?, Birmingham Safeguarding Adults Board, © 2017 Birmingham Safeguarding Adults Board, Retrieved from https://www.bsab.org/what-is-abuse/definitions-of-abuse/; **122:** Care Act 2014, retrieved from http://www.legislation.gov.uk/ukpga/2014/23/pdfs/ukpga_20140023_en.pdf: Contains public sector information licensed under the Open Government Licence v3.0; **123:** The care certificate safeguarding adults, Standard10, The Care Certificate Workbook © 2010, Skills for Care & Skills for Health; **133:** The Care Certificate, Work in a Person-Centred Way, Standard 5, The Care Certificate Workbook, © Skills for Care Ltd, Retrieved from https://www.skillsforcare.org.uk/Document-library/Standards/Care-Certificate/Standard-5-2.pdf; **136:** Public Interest Disclosure Act 1998, retrieved https://www.legislation.gov.uk/ukpga/1998/23/pdfs/ukpga_19980023_en.pdf: Contains public sector information licensed under the Open Government Licence v3.0; **138:** A Guide To PIDA- Public Interest Disclosure Act 1998, Contains public sector information licensed under the Open Parliament License v3.0; **143:** The Mental Capacity Act 2005 Policy Adult Care Service, ©2018 Crown copyright, Contains public sector information licensed under the Open Government Licence v3.0; **146:** Code of Conduct for Healthcare: Support Workers and Adult Social Care Workers in England, Department Of Health, © 2017 Workforce Development Trust; **173:** Health and safety Executive, Contains public sector information licensed under the Open Government Licence v3.0; **186:** World health organization. Reprinted from Clean Care is Safer Care. Retrieved from http://www.who.int/gpsc/clean_hands_protection/en/; accessed on 11/10/2018; **190:** Health and Safety Executive 2018, retrieved from http://www.hse.gov.uk/msd/manualhandling.htm: Contains public sector information licensed under the Open Government Licence v3.0; **199:** Alternative measurements: instructions and tables, 'Malnutrition Universal Screening Tool'. Retrieved from HYPERLINK "https://urldefense.proofpoint.com/v2/url?u=https-3A__www.bapen.org.uk_pdfs_must_must-5Ffull.pdf&d=DwMFAg&c=bMxC-A1upgdsx4J2OmDkk2Eep4PyO1BA6pjHrrW-ii0&r=sh9PMrbSM8sX1sRhE9D0NAXJ7Vb9J59Q0FSh1kPX2El&m=dNDRSzKmq-g19jrb1wKK0KvvgnSwgv4oltghzK-UgrNE&s=9hTZq9RKc0tkDic-bCH5LN7KiO7YV68y9yC11b4EC7E&e= https://www.bapen.org.uk/pdfs/must/must_full.pdf. Used with permissions; **199:** BMI calculation chart. Retrieved from: https://bmicalculator.mes.fm/bmi-chart, © 2013 Math Easy Solutions.

Websites
Pearson Education Limited is not responsible for the content of any external internet sites. It is essential for tutors to preview each website before using it in class so as to ensure that the URL is still accurate, relevant and appropriate. We suggest that tutors bookmark useful websites and consider enabling students to access them through the school/college intranet.

Note from the publisher
Pearson has robust editorial processes, including answer and fact checks, to ensure the accuracy of the content in this publication, and every effort is made to ensure this publication is free of errors. We are, however, only human, and occasionally errors do occur. Pearson is not liable for any misunderstandings that arise as a result of errors in this publication, but it is our priority to ensure that the content is accurate. If you spot an error, please do contact us at resourcescorrections@pearson.com so we can make sure it is corrected.

Contents

About this book

This book is designed to support you through your on-programme learning as part of your apprenticeship for the *Lead Adult Care Worker Level 3* and as you prepare for your *End Point Assessment (EPA)*. It is structured around the standards for the apprenticeship while all the information comes from the essential knowledge for the mandatory units in your BTEC Level 3 Diploma in Adult Care. While you work through the book you will see it highlights the attitudes, values and behaviours that you will need to demonstrate in your day-to-day work.

Practical help for you in your role

It is a privilege to work in the Adult Care sector – helping to support individuals with their health and social care needs to achieve their personal goals and live as independently and safely as possible. As a Lead Adult Care Worker, you assist in enabling people to have control and choice in their lives – which is the heart of person-centred care. You will ensure that the most appropriate care and support is provided for users of service, so they can maintain their independence, dignity and control. Therefore, when an individual is faced with physical, practical, social, emotional and/or intellectual challenges, your input can make a positive difference to their life. But your role also extends to leadership and management of team colleagues. As a Lead Adult Care Worker, you will delegate responsibilities for care and may supervise the work of other care workers. By exercising autonomy and accountability, you will be able to lead and support others to comply with expected standards and behaviours.

Although this book will help you in your studies, and through your learning journey as an apprentice, it is also designed to help you in a practical way. All the activities and examples are taken from a range of adult care settings and feature different roles so that you can relate them to your own experiences and learn to grow within your job role – and particularly in taking on the Level 3 role. We hope you will be able to use the book as a professional tool long after you have gained your apprenticeship.

How to use this book

This book has been designed and structured around the Apprenticeship Standard for Lead Adult Care Workers. There are pages that cover the knowledge 'what you must know and understand' followed by the skills you will need to put that knowledge in place 'what you must be able to do'.

In this way you will be able to see how what you *do* relates to what you *know* – and the other way around.

Features of the book

To make your learning easier and to help you prepare for your EPA this is what we have provided:

Introduction to the start of each section to explain what is covered.

Summary text on the knowledge pages to help you focus on what you need to know. 

Key terms – important words are **highlighted** and defined so you know how to use them in the context of your work. The first time they appear in the book they will be explained. If you can't quite remember the definition, look in the Glossary afterwards. They are all listed there. 

Activity – a range of different activities helping you put your knowledge into practice and which you may also use to help plan assessment for your BTEC. These are mainly found on the skills pages. 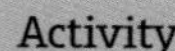

Scenarios and case studies – we have provided lots of these to help you relate the content to the work you do. They include reflective questions.

Qualification mapping – so you know how the information and activities in the book relate to the BTEC Level 3 Diploma in Adult Care. 

Reflective activity –this will help you to make sense of your work and improve the care and support you give.

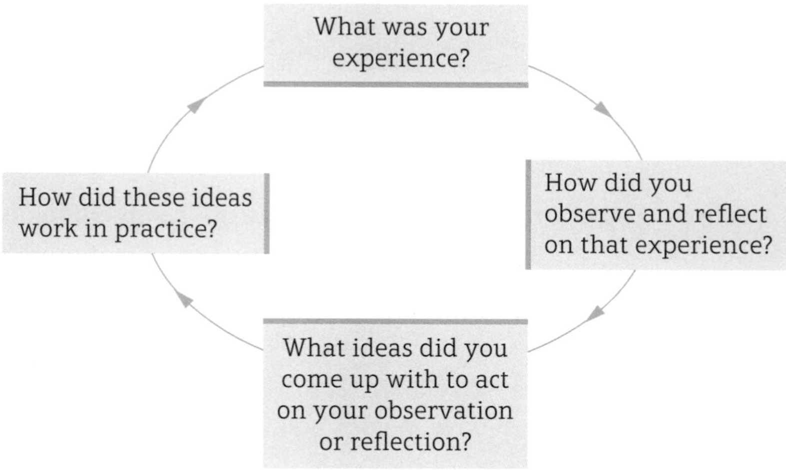

The Kolb learning cycle

Personal attributes and behaviours

There are important particular personal attributes and behaviours expected of everyone working as a Lead Adult Care Worker. These are the 6Cs – Care, Compassion, Courage, Communication, Competence and Commitment. Throughout the book you will find them highlighted in two ways:

Professional working – this is an important feature that highlights the attitudes, values and behaviours that a Lead Adult Care Worker needs to show at work. 

6Cs – how your work relates to the 6Cs which you will have covered in your Care Certificate. 

Linking content – to show where the Topics link. 

Linking the standards to the qualification

You will find a section included in the ActiveBook version of this book showing exactly how the Pearson BTEC Level 3 Diploma in Adult Care (England) maps to the Apprenticeship Standard for Lead Adult Care Worker, so you can find your way around both. You can access the ActiveBook using the code under the scratch panel at the front of this book.

Specific help for your End Point Assessment

Throughout your programme, you will have been gathering evidence from work activities so that you can demonstrate your knowledge, skills and behaviour in your Lead Adult Care Worker role. All of these will have been reviewed and you will have been given feedback to assist you in the final preparation for the EPA.

Your End Point Assessment is the opportunity for you to show what you have learnt.

Component 1: Situational Judgement Test

Component 2: Professional Discussion (supported by a range of evidence sources)

The Situational Judgement Test is an onscreen test that will assess your underpinning knowledge and your knowledge of the skills required across the Apprenticeship Standard. The Test consists of some short scenarios together with multi-choice questions and only one right answer.

The Professional Discussion is a planned, structured discussion between you and the independent end-point assessor. The primary purpose of the Professional Discussion is to assess how well you carry out your role as a Lead Adult Care Worker

The Professional Discussion gives you the opportunity to showcase – using a range of real work-based evidence – your ability to use the relevant skills, behaviours and underpinning knowledge effectively to undertake the duties within your role.

To help you practise and prepare we have provided activities in the book based on these assessment types.

- Practice for professional discussion activity – an opportunity for you to think about this part of your EPA.
- Situational judgement practice – questions at the end of each topic which are similar to the questions you will have in your online test. The answers to these questions can be found at the end of the book.

Tips to help you during the Professional Discussion

Key tips

- Speak slowly and clearly – do not interrupt or talk over the other person.
- Listen carefully to questions. Do not be afraid to ask for something to be repeated if you do not hear or understand – do not let your attention drift.
- Avoid jargon or acronyms as your listener may not understand.
- Ask yourself questions as you listen in case you need to clarify anything.
- Take notes if this helps you – in case you need to revisit a point.
- Be confident – you've done a great job so far to get to this stage.

About the authors

Carolyn Aldworth is a qualified nurse who works in a rehabilitation hospital for older people. She finds working with older people is very rewarding, especially supporting people to regain their health and mobility and to be able to return home. Carolyn spent 28 years working in further education and led a care and early years team for ten years before returning to nursing. She has been an author since 2007.

Colette Burgess trained as a nurse and now works as a college lecturer – supporting learners studying to work in the health and social care sector or to further their studies at university. She also works with apprentices, their assessors and the teacher education and first aid teams at the college. Colette says that the best part of her job is seeing the successes of her learners who work hard and who will be the health and social care practitioners of the future. Colette has written many books and other resources for students and tutors delivering health and social care courses.

Andrew Carter-Whiting began teaching in 1999 at St Clare's College in Oxford. At this time, his subject interest was art history and photography. After he had worked as a volunteer in South Africa, supporting children born with HIV, his interest turned to social care. He trained as a social worker and worked in sexual health for different voluntary organisations. Since then, he has worked in different areas of social care in the statutory and voluntary sector. Andrew went back to teaching eight years ago and has taught as an Associate Lecturer at Oxford Brookes University, Ruskin College and is now Senior Lecturer in Applied Social Science at City of Oxford College. He is also self employed as a professional practice assessor working with social work students in placement in and around Oxfordshire.

Siân Lavers is a registered nurse who spent much of her clinical career in operating theatres. She has worked in further and higher education since 1996, teaching Health and Social Care at Levels 1 to 5 and on undergraduate nursing programmes. She enjoys supporting students to develop their skills and knowledge to become effective and confident practitioners. Siân has contributed to more than 20 textbooks on health and social care since 2000 and has also been involved in the development of BTEC Health and Social Care specifications. She currently works in higher education as a Practice Education Lead for a paramedic science degree programme and is Programme Manager for a Foundation Degree for Assistant Practitioners in a college of further education.

A

Job role and responsibilities

Do you know where your role fits in with others who also support users of your service? You all have different roles and responsibilities but you have the same aims to provide a high quality, personalised and safe service to all those who you support. You will work together with the individual to draw up and review care plans, ensuring that the best possible care is given. In your role as a lead adult care worker, you will guide and supervise junior colleagues as well as working with your manager to ensure smooth running of the service. This topic will cover the following areas:

- job roles of yourself and others
- professional boundaries at work
- standards of behaviour and codes of practice
- what duty of care means in your area of work
- how to create, develop and review care plans for individuals according to their needs
- how to support others to adhere to regulations, policies and procedures.

You will also learn about the skills you will need so that you can apply this knowledge in the care setting where you work.

Your job role

Qualification mapping

Unit 6 LO 1 AC 1.2

Adult care work, and therefore the job roles of lead adult care workers, are so varied because of the wide and diverse needs of individuals who use the service. You must have a good understanding of your own role as well as the roles of others so that you can work in partnership to ensure positive outcomes for all users of the service.

Key terms

Statutory – provided by the state, for example, National Health Service, school education

Private – services that are run as a business and paid for by the user of the service, for example, private residential home, counsellor

Voluntary – services that are provided by charities or individuals and are not run for profit, for example, befriender, food banks

Where do people work in the adult care sector?

There are many different work settings and places where support is provided, just as the ages and the needs of individuals who use services will be very different (see Figure 1). Services may be **statutory**, **private** or **voluntary**.

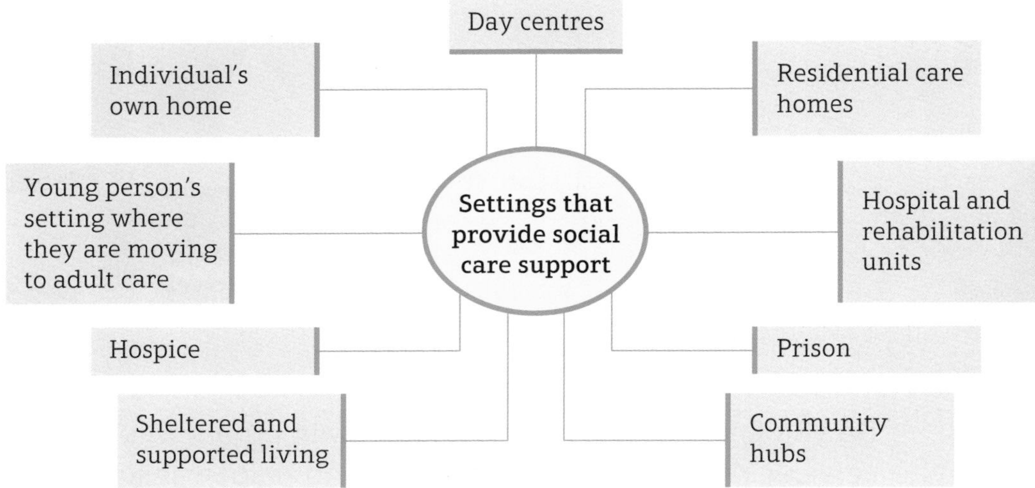

Figure 1: Many different settings provide adult care

Individuals will access adult care for a variety of different reasons; for example, they may have difficulties supporting themselves. This might be because of:

- learning disabilities
- a decline in their physical health, for example, because they are older
- cognitive impairment, for example, head injury or dementia
- socialisation needs
- mental health issues
- their being young people moving into adult care
- end-of-life care needs.

A range of social care workers with specialist roles are required to meet the needs of different individuals. As a lead adult care worker, you may have several different roles within your organisation and you are likely to work with other professionals from other organisations. Knowing the roles of those who work in adult care will help you understand where you fit into supporting the individuals who use your service.

Roles in adult care

Social worker

Social workers support individuals of all ages and are registered with the Health and Care Professions Council. They work with vulnerable people and help them through difficult times. Social workers often signpost individuals to different services in order to help meet their needs.

Adult care worker (ACW)

Adult care workers deal directly with users of the service to help meet their holistic needs. The ACW may help with personal care, eating and drinking, offering emotional support and encouraging individuals to engage in social activities.

Lead adult care worker (LACW)

The lead adult care worker makes a positive difference to individuals who need support. They often give direct support themselves but also lead and supervise other care workers to ensure that users of services have positive outcomes. LACWs are actively involved in improving the delivery of care and support.

Care and support manager

The manager's responsibility is to ensure that the organisation runs smoothly and meets its aims and objectives.

Occupational therapist

The occupational therapist's aim is to support individuals who are having difficulties to independently carry out everyday activities. This can often involve special aids and adaptations.

Professional working

Occasionally there can be a crossover of roles; for example, a manager of a small organisation such as a care home may deliver some direct individual care to users of the service.

Counsellor

Counsellors help to guide the individual when they are experiencing personal difficulties.

You may also think of many other roles in your workplace that support adult care work.

Each role and setting will be different but there is one thing that all the individuals have in common: as a lead adult care worker they are actively involved in making a positive difference to the individuals that they support. They are highly skilled in making judgements and acting upon them. Many have supervisory responsibilities and support junior members of staff. Lead adult care workers may also support managers to help them in the smooth running of the organisation.

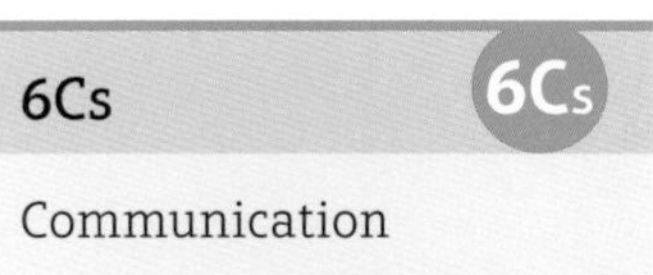

The roles of lead adult care workers vary between settings and organisations. The individuals in Figure 2 are all lead adult care workers; see how different their roles are.

I work in a residential care home and support people with everyday activities such as personal care, eating and drinking and socialising. I assess needs and complete risk assessments. I often lead the team to make sure that things run smoothly and everything gets done.

I plan stimulating social activities for individuals.

My job role includes supporting people who have learning disabilities. I help them to be as independent as possible. I work with the individuals and liaise with other professionals to help plan how they will achieve their goals.

I work in a setting that provides intermediate care for people leaving hospital and prepare them for safe discharge home. I help individuals to be as independent as possible, keep a close eye on monitoring their health and communicate with specialists from the hospital and community.

Every day is different for me at the addiction drop-in centre: assessing and supporting individuals' immediate and ongoing needs, including helping them to be successful in rehabilitation programmes.

In my role, I help people who have nowhere to live to access benefits, housing and other services. I also put them in touch with job centres and help with applications.

Figure 2: The varied roles of lead adult care workers

Summary

Your role as a lead adult care worker is an important one that contributes to the wider adult social care sector workforce. Each professional's role within it is equally important. Knowing about other roles will help you to know where your role fits into providing overall support for users of the service.

Working together

Have you ever wondered what makes your organisation successful in what it does? It is probably because you are all aware of your own roles and responsibilities, and respect those of others. Effective team work plays an important part in good working relationships.

Qualification mapping 

Unit 6 LO 1 AC 1.1 and 1.2, LO 3 AC 3.1

Working with others

When you consider the range of different individuals who contribute to the support of one user of your service it is likely to be quite a few different workers. Sometimes it is easy just to focus on what you do and not think about the contribution of the wider team.

Case study: Mrs Clarke's care

Mrs Clarke lives in The Beeches; a residential home for older people. Last week she had a stroke and the emergency services were called. The paramedic took Mrs Clarke to hospital. Mrs Clarke is making a good recovery. The result of the stroke has left Mrs Clarke with some weakness on one side and some swallowing and speech difficulties. The manager visited Mrs Clarke in hospital to carry out an assessment to make sure that they could give her the support that she needs and plan for her return. The occupational therapist visited The Beeches with Mrs Clarke to see if any adjustments were required to help her to be independent, for example, bath rails. The lead adult care worker gathered information, completed risk assessments and updated her care plan. Care staff have supported Mrs Clarke with personal care. Mrs Clarke has had visits from the physiotherapist assistant to help her to regain mobility. The speech and language therapist has supported her with speech as well as her swallowing difficulties; he has also supported care and kitchen staff in advising the best consistency for her food in order to prevent choking. Mrs Clarke has been prescribed lots of medication and the pharmacist makes sure that they are supplied and do not interact with each other. Mrs Clarke is making a good recovery.

- Can you identify how many professionals have been involved in supporting Mrs Clarke?
- What are their roles?
- Could anyone else be involved in her care and support?

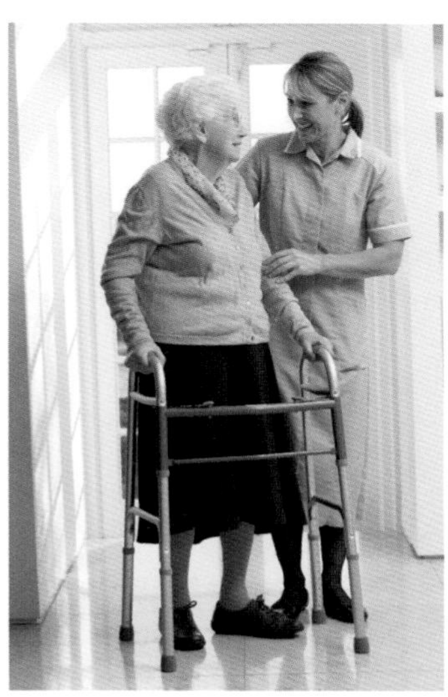

Mrs Clarke has many professionals to support her

Mrs Clarke's situation is not unusual. Many different professionals work together to help support her; there are also, for example, activity leaders, dieticians, kitchen staff and nurses. If the professionals did not work effectively with each other, Mrs Clarke's care would not be so positive. For example, if the kitchen staff did not help the care staff in presenting food in an attractive way, Mrs Clarke might not wish to eat her meals and this would impact on her physical health. She could lack nutrients and energy – making her less likely to mobilise, hindering her rehabilitation and possibly leading to complications such as poor circulation and pressure sores.

The cook takes time to make the food look appetising even when it is pureed to avoid a choking hazard

Link 

Topic F: Professional working and professional development

Professional working

Have you heard of the phrase 'mood hoover'? This is used to describe a person who is negative and tries to suck the energy and enthusiasm out of the team. Don't let a mood hoover drag your team down. Stay positive together.

6Cs

Communication

Different working relationships

Successful team working is about working to a common goal and having mutual respect. You may work closely with individuals in your workplace, you may even be friends, but it's important that you remain professional in your work. You can find out more about professional relationships and boundaries on page 10.

You will have different types of working relationships: with colleagues and co-workers; supervisory; and with external professionals and agencies, as shown in Figure 3.

You

Supervisory
For example, between you and your manager, who will lead, guide and monitor your performance. You may be a supervisor to junior colleagues. Respect and value their work and remember to be honest and give praise as this will enhance your working relationship.

Colleagues and co workers
Individuals who you work with, who may be in the same role as you but sometimes not; for example, you may work alongside kitchen and maintenance staff. Recognise the value of their role as they will with yours.

External professionals and agencies
You may work with external professionals such as advocates, physiotherapists and counsellors. Their expertise and contribution is crucial to the care and support of the user of the service.

Figure 3: Different working relationships

What makes a good team?

You have learned that you cannot work on your own to meet all the needs of individuals, it is a team effort. The team can be large or sometimes small with just a few members. No matter what the size of the team, a successful one will have the characteristics shown in Figure 4.

- Plan and work to achieve the overall aims ✔
- Well led ✔
- Focused and organised ✔
- Communicate effectively with each other ✔
- Respect each other's contribution ✔
- Everyone does their fair share ✔
- Supportive to each other ✔

Figure 4: An effective team will tick these boxes

Are you a team player?

An effective team is only as good as its members. All areas of care work rely on good teamwork. How can you make sure that you make a positive contribution? You can:

- be willing to contribute
- communicate with others in the team
- complete agreed tasks
- be honest if you can't do something
- be supportive of others
- be reliable
- have a positive attitude.

Summary

You cannot support users of your service on your own: you need to work with others. Professionals from other organisations are going to be involved too. You will all have your roles but will work together as an effective team.

Supporting others

In order to support individuals according to their personal care plan you need to work effectively with others as part of a team. This will include workers within your organisation as well as a wide range of external professionals.

Qualification mapping

Unit 6 LO 1 AC 1.2, LO 3 AC 3.1

Activities

Supporting individuals according to their support plans

Your role is about making a positive difference to people's lives especially when they are vulnerable and face difficulties. Choose three of the scenarios below and describe your responsibilities, think about who else may be involved and explain how you would carry out necessary tasks.

You might need to find out more about specific areas as you progress with the task, for example cultural differences and health difficulties, such as Parkinson's disease.

Social activities

Wheatfield is a day centre for individuals who have memory difficulties such as dementia. Those who attend have different interests and hobbies. Consider your role and those of others in planning, organising and delivering **social activities**.

What tasks would you have to carry out?	What would be your responsibilities?	Who else might be involved and what would be their role?
Find out what individual's hobbies are	*Build relationships with each person*	*Adult care workers will give practical support*

Monitoring health

A local rehabilitation unit supports individuals who abuse substances. Physical and mental health is often unstable and needs to be monitored. Consider your role and those of others in monitoring the health of individuals.

What tasks would you have to carry out?	What would be your responsibilities?	Who else might be involved and what would be their role?
Record vital signs such as blood pressure and pulse	*Contribute to the development of care and support plans*	

Eating and drinking

Adequate nutrition is crucial to health. You will advise users of your service and colleagues on good practice and how to promote independence while eating and drinking.

What tasks would you have to carry out?	What would be your responsibilities?	Who else might be involved and what would be their role?

Discuss the differences in the lead adult care worker's role in supporting the following individuals: Abi supports Cara who has anorexia, while Josef helps Bill who has had a stroke.

Mobility

Being active and mobile is good for everyone; it promotes not only physical but also mental health and wellbeing. But keeping mobile is not easy for everyone, especially if individuals have problems with movement and balance. Some individuals might not even want to move and this can pose other problems for you as the lead adult care worker as well as for the user of the service.

What tasks would you have to carry out?	What would be your responsibilities?	Who else might be involved and what would be their role?
A moving and handling risk assessment		*Moving and handling trainer; they will guide staff in how to move and handle safely*

Personal care

Good personal hygiene is not only important to reduce infection spread, it is also essential for a person's self- esteem. Think about how you could support the following individuals with their hygiene:

- You are a personal assistant to Parand who has developed depression. She does not want to shower or bathe or wash her hair. Parand follows the Muslim faith.
- Raymond has Parkinson's disease.

What tasks would you have to carry out?	What would be your responsibilities?	Who else might be involved and what would be their role?
Parand *Raymond*		

Refer to the individual's care/support plan

Think about an individual who you support. Write an account that shows how you support the individual with each part of their care plan. Describe your role in guiding others to support individuals in accordance with their care support plan.

Remember not to disclose the individual's identity.

Working with others to support individuals

It is likely that individuals who use your service are supported by a range of professionals from both inside as well as outside your organisation. Select an individual who you support. Copy the following mind map and use it to indicate the range of professionals involved and their supportive roles.

Professional [other workers]

How do you work in partnership?

Professional [other workers] – The dentist: checks the health of the mouth and teeth, and will treat disorders if necessary

How do you work in partnership? I remind 'A' that a check -up appointment is due and help him to book an appointment; I will accompany him to the dentist if he wants me to

Professional [other workers]

How do you work in partnership?

Working with others to support individuals

Professional [other workers]

How do you work in partnership?

Professional [other workers]

How do you work in partnership?

Professional [other workers]

How do you work in partnership?

Who's who in the team

Your team probably consists of lots of different individuals: for example, manager, different colleagues and external professionals.

- Create a mind map that shows you and your team members. Describe their roles.
- Which team members are supervisors and who do they supervise?
- Who are the immediate co-workers in your workplace that you work directly with?
- Who are external professionals?
- Explain why it is important to work in partnership with others.

Qualification mapping

Unit 6 LO 1 AC 1.2, LO 3 AC 3.1 and 3.2

Supporting individuals with complex care needs

You must be able to demonstrate that you can support individuals who have complex care needs; for example, people with dementia or whose needs have changed.

Obtain a witness testimony from your supervisor or manager and try to include the following areas:

- support given is according to their care/support plan
- you work with others to help achieve the individual's aims and goals.

Qualification mapping

Unit 6 LO 3 AC 3.2

Professional boundaries and limits

Qualification mapping

Unit 6 LO 1 AC 1.1, LO 2 AC 2.1 and 2.3

Professional working

If you are unsure about whether a situation would lead you to over step boundaries, it is best to err on the side of caution and hold back. Think about how your actions could affect the relationship with the individual. Supervision with your manager is a good time to discuss concerns, difficulties and dilemmas at work.

A relationship of trust is important in care work but knowing your professional boundaries and the limits to your training and expertise is crucial. Working outside your limits and contracted duties is dangerous and unprofessional.

Building a rapport and maintaining a trusting relationship with colleagues at work is important in adult care work but boundaries are vital too. Boundaries are about establishing acceptable behaviour, and knowing the limit of what is appropriate and what is not.

The ways in which you behave and interact with friends and family will be different from the way you behave with service users and colleagues. On page 12 you will learn more about how professional relationships can turn into inappropriate friendships.

The way you dress, the language you use and your physical behaviour can affect the boundaries between yourself and those you work with. You may not intend it, but boundaries can be crossed if you are not careful.

Look at the examples below. Are there any areas that would concern you about boundaries and professional distance?

Jack is a support worker in a substance rehabilitation centre. He formerly had a dependence on alcohol.

Jack shares his past experiences in relation to how his own addiction affected him and his family. He feels that sharing his experiences helps him to build relationships with users of the service.

Hayley works in a residential care home. The manager prefers care workers not to wear a uniform. Hayley often wears figure-hugging skimpy tops. Some residents have started making suggestive comments and request for her to support them with personal hygiene.

Toni is a domiciliary worker. She has been asked to visit and provide care and support to a new user of the service. When she arrives, Toni realises that it is her aunt who she hasn't seen for over a year because of a family disagreement. Toni is looking forward to trying to mend the family relationship while she is supporting her.

Aria works in a day centre. One of the users of the service told Aria that she can no longer look after her dog and that she will need to re-home him. Aria says that she will take the dog so the individual won't need to worry about her pet.

6Cs

Communication, competence, courage

The workers above have unintentionally compromised professional boundaries. When boundaries are broken, individuals can feel that they have a special relationship with the worker and this can affect the care and support that is given to them and to others. For example, wearing revealing clothes at work can give the impression of relaxed informal boundaries so you should always stick to the dress code in your work setting.

Limits to your training and expertise

Earlier, you learned about the wide range of roles in adult care. As a lead adult care worker, you were employed to carry out the duties stated in your contract and you must fully adhere to policies and procedures. Working in this way will keep you and users of the service safe. On your job description, it is impossible to list every single task that you can do so it will often state 'and any other duties commensurate or appropriate to the role'. These extra duties should reflect those that someone at your level would do. If you are unsure if the extra duties are outside your role, ask your manager for an explanation or seek advice from outside your organisation; for example, from a union. Never agree to be responsible for a task that is beyond your job role and do not ask others to work outside their role as this could put the individual, yourself and/or the organisation at risk.

Do not overstep your role

The examples below describe activities that you should not do unless you have had specialist training.

- Offering counselling advice when you are not a trained counsellor.
- Advising about over-the-counter remedies for individuals.
- Cutting the toe nails of an individual who has diabetes (this should be done by a chiropodist or podiatrist).
- Giving a vulnerable individual contraceptive and sexual health advice; this should be given by a trained professional.
- Advising specific exercises for musculoskeletal problems; this is the role of a registered specialist, such as a doctor or physiotherapist.
- Offering financial and legal advice.
- Diagnosing and giving treatment advice to individuals for physical and mental health problems.

Training will help you to carry out your job confidently and competently, but it is possible that there may be parts you still do not feel sure about. The ways in which we do things regularly change and develop over time; for example, you may need to use new systems and equipment. Supervision and appraisal meetings will help you to assess your performance and plan your development. You will learn more in Topic F about personal development and SWOB analysis. Remember that even the most experienced worker will find some areas challenging. See Figure 5 for some ideas about how to build your skills.

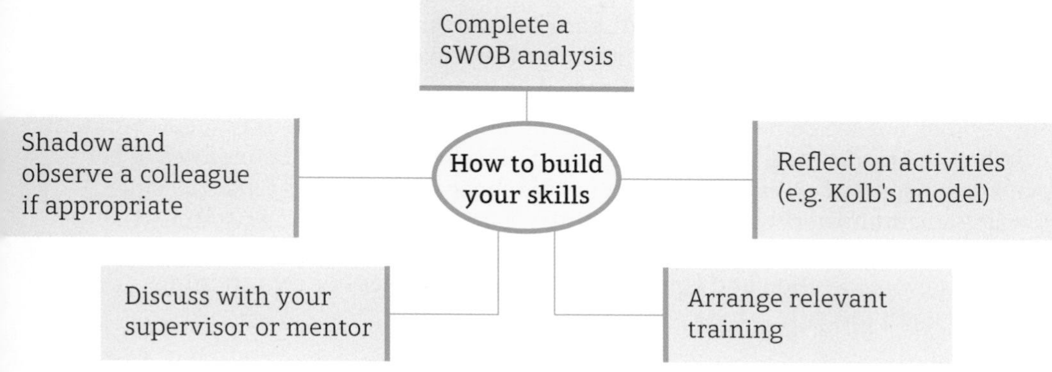

Figure 5: There are different ways to enhance your skillset

Professional working

In your role you may supervise others. You and the organisation could face legal action if a person is harmed while working outside their contracted role. As a lead adult care worker, you may have to advise and guide others about boundaries and limits to training and expertise. Include these areas in the induction programme for new workers and revisit them during team events. Also, check policies and procedures to support safe ways of working.

Qualification mapping

Unit 6 LO 2 AC 2.1

Link

Topic F: Professional working and professional development

Summary

Maintain professional boundaries to keep working relationships safe and appropriate. Your job role is likely to be wide and varied but be mindful of the limits to your training and expertise, so that you keep yourself and others safe.

Boundaries and limits: recognise and access help

Qualification mapping

Unit 6 LO 2 AC 2.1 and 2.3

It is important to recognise your boundaries and limits. If you are not confident or skilled in any aspect of the role you are undertaking you will need to access help, for your own safety and that of the individuals you are supporting. This might require you to have further training.

Activities

Professional working

You can learn about different ways of working if you shadow an expert; they can demonstrate how to carry out a task and then let you try. As they are supervising you, they are taking full responsibility for the activity. For example, an adult care worker in a nursing home might wish to find out how to record blood pressure. They could do this under direct supervision of the lead adult care worker or the nurse but they could not carry out the task unsupervised.

Boundaries and professional relationships

Imagine you are helping to plan the induction process for some new members of staff. They need to know about boundaries and professional relationships. You think that it will help to link your training to realistic examples that they may come across in your area of work.

Create two realistic fictitious (not real) examples relating to your area of work to help new staff to understand about boundaries and professional relationships.

Use the following plan as a guide for each example:

- a short scenario that explains how boundaries have been compromised
- details of how it happened
- what the possible consequences could be.

Workplace policies and procedures, and boundaries

New workers should be made aware of safe boundaries and professional relationships, for example around the receipt of gifts. Read and review your related workplace policies and procedures and answer the following questions:

- Which policies and procedures relate to boundaries and professional working?
- Can you summarise what they say?
- Are they accurate and easy to understand for all staff who work in your organisation? If not, suggest to your supervisor or manager how they could be made clearer.

Recognising when you are not skilled in the role

Maryam is a lead adult care worker and works in the community; she has been on holiday for two weeks. Maryam visits Cynthia who she has supported for some time. During the last week, Cynthia's lung disease has worsened and she was prescribed regular medication to be given via a nebuliser (a special machine that delivers medication directly to the person's airways).

Maryam has not seen a nebuliser before, let alone used one, and does not feel confident to deliver the medication that was prescribed. Maryam knows the boundaries of her own knowledge and skills and contacts her manager who arranges for a colleague to visit and administer the medication. While Maryam was on holiday, staff had been given training on using the specialist equipment in preparation for Cynthia's new medication and equipment. Maryam arranges her own training to use the equipment.

- Was Maryam right to speak up about the limits to her training and expertise around using the new equipment? Explain your answer.
- What would you have done if you had been unable to make contact with your manager in this situation?
- As a lead adult care worker you may delegate work and tasks to others. How could you have prevented this happening to one of your junior colleagues?

Limits of your job role

In order for you to be a safe lead adult care worker, you must be aware of and work to the limits of your job role. For this activity, give a range of examples of what is in your job role and list those tasks that are beyond your training and expertise.

Tasks that are within your job role	Tasks that are beyond the limits of your training and expertise

Areas of your job where you are less confident

There will be many parts of your job that you are confident about but it is likely that there are some areas where you feel less confident.

Make a note of areas of knowledge and skills that you need to build on and indicate how you plan to do this.

Remember to include any changes in legislation that will affect you and others at work.

Copy and complete the table below with your notes. You could add the information on to your personal development plan (see Topic F).

Areas that you need to develop	How can you gain competence and confidence?

Is Crystal an expert?

Crystal is a lead adult care worker and supports young people who are transitioning into adult care. Crystal supervises a group of adult care workers. One worker approaches Crystal because she is finding it difficult to support Elli who has started experiencing severe anxiety and is also depressed.

Crystal has a daughter who has also struggled with anxiety and depression. She feels that she could offer some personal and expert help and support, by giving examples of what has helped and hindered her.

- Is Crystal the right person to offer specialist advice and support to the care worker and Elli? Explain your answer.
- Has Crystal worked within her professional boundaries? Explain your response.
- What would you do if a junior colleague asked you for advice that you felt that you were unable to give?

Statutory standards and codes of practice

Qualification mapping

Unit 6 LO 2 AC 2.2 and 2.3

Professional organisations have agreed specific standards of work and behaviour that each user of service will receive when accessing social care. By working to these standards, you will feel confident in the standard of care you give.

Care Quality Commission (CQC)

How would you describe good quality of care? You might get a different response from each person you ask. Perhaps you have been around when your organisation was last inspected so you are aware of what the inspectors are looking for. Inspection means that organisations are being checked to make sure that agreed standards are met. Social care organisations are checked by the Care Quality Commission (CQC).

The Fundamental Standards were introduced to improve quality of care nationwide following the publication of the Report of the Mid Staffordshire NHS Foundation Trust Public Inquiry in February 2013. The report was about failings in care within the Trust. Robert Francis QC, the author of the report, made 290 recommendations for the improvement of care nationally.

The CQC inspections focus on five areas. They check that the organisation is:

1. safe
2. effective
3. caring
4. responsive to people's needs
5. well-led.

Within these areas there will be a range of further questions that the CQC will investigate, which enable the inspectors to make a judgement. Each area is awarded a rating:

- outstanding
- good – meets expectations
- requires improvement – the organisation will be told how they must improve
- inadequate – very poor performance, an action plan will be put in place.

You can access CQC inspection reports on its website

After each area is rated, an overall rating is given. Inspection reports are public documents and can be viewed on the CQC website. You can access the report for your organisation. Individuals who are looking for a provider may look at the inspection reports beforehand.

How can you help to make sure that your organisation provides a good service?

You do this by working to policies and procedures and ensuring that those who you supervise do so as well. Become familiar with what good quality care is as well as the statutory standards that you need to meet. Everyone should aim to give an outstanding service to individuals. Support your manager in maintaining high standards and if you notice anything that is not acceptable, you must challenge it

– even if it is a potentially difficult situation. It's a team approach, so you should all take pride in ensuring the quality of the service.

You will work with junior members of staff, give feedback on their work and praise good practice but you should always challenge poor practice. Policies and procedures, such as moving and handling, and infection prevention and control, are in place to ensure a safe and effective service. As a lead adult care worker you must ensure that you work in a way that complies with policies and procedures, and support others to do so as well. New staff will need guidance and will have lots to learn, so support them in their training and let them observe your good practice on a day-to-day basis.

CQC audits will take place but do not wait for them. Make a point of involving individuals who use the service; ask for their opinions and ways in which the service could be improved. This can be done on an everyday basis: encourage colleagues and individuals that you supervise to ask for feedback on the care and support that they are given.

Get into the habit of asking for feedback – 'How did I do today?'

The 6Cs

The 6Cs of compassionate care were developed following observation of care that was not compassionate or caring. You will find out more about the 6Cs in Topic B (Values and behaviours). They are also referenced throughout this book because your behaviour should *always* reflect care, compassion, communication, commitment, competence and courage. More junior adult care workers may need guidance, which is why it is so important to model good practice and give feedback on how they work. Mentoring, supervision and feedback on day-to-day activities will help application of the 6Cs to become natural to them too. Having the courage to speak up if a colleague has concerns can be especially difficult for less experienced staff, so you should help to create an environment where you are approachable, listen and act on concerns that are raised.

Professional working

Organisations and individuals who provide a regulated activity, such as personal care or accommodation for individuals who need treatment for substance misuse, must register with the CQC. Those who have a private arrangement, such as personal assistants and day centres, may not need to register. More information about registration with the CQC can be found at www.cqc.org.uk – follow the links for registration. Your local authority website will also be a good source of information.

Professional working

Policies and procedures are updated from time to time so keep ahead of changes and current ways of working. You should also support others to do so in their work. Individuals who do not follow their workplace policies and procedures may face disciplinary measures. Use mentoring and supervision meetings to inform safe current ways of working. Keep records to evidence the support and advice you have given to junior colleagues.

Link

Topic B: Values and behaviours

Professional working

You might be asked to support others in their qualification; for example, by providing a junior member of staff with a witness testimony to help them show evidence of competence. You must make sure that you are clear about what the standards are.

Occupational standards

Skills for Care is an organisation that works closely with the CQC and employers. It knows about the support that people need and the skills that workers must have to meet their needs. Skills for Care have developed National Occupational Standards for the care sector. These standards specify the knowledge and skills that are required for those who work in the care sector. Your qualification in care will be based on the national occupational standards; these are standards that are expected of an individual working in your sector and at the level of the role that they are working at. When your assessor states that you are competent in particular criteria they are measuring you against the National Occupational Standards.

Code of Conduct for Healthcare Support Workers and Adult Social Care Workers

This is your code of conduct as a lead adult care worker. It states the expected standards of behaviour and attitude of individuals who work in the health and social care sector. It will help you to provide a high standard of care. It was developed together by Skills for Health and Skills for Care. Both sectors require high standards of behaviour and a positive attitude. All workers in the sector are expected to support individuals in a respectful and dignified way. Working effectively with others is also an important part of the code and you are accountable for what you do: this means that you must be able to answer to and justify what you do, as well as what you do *not* do.

Familiarise yourself with the code of conduct and support others to work to it as well. It is a good base for discussion during supervision meetings. Junior members of staff may not be so familiar with the code so make a point of referencing to it while mentoring and supervising them.

Case study: Elisha uses her judgement

Elisha is a lead adult care worker in a residential care home for older people. Elisha is responsible for supervising a small team of care workers. One day, Jo asked Elisha if she could leave early so that she could take her daughter to a doctor's appointment. Elisha looked at the off-duty rota and who was working the shift, as well as what work needed to be completed. Elisha felt confident that Jo leaving early would not compromise the safe and effective delivery of care. Elisha knew that she was accountable for her actions and made a professional judgement that it would be ok for Jo to leave early.

- What information did Elisha look for before she made the decision as to whether Jo could leave early or not?
- Did Elisha make the right decision? Explain your response.

Professional working

Decisions that you make could be challenged, for example, by other professionals, so always think actions and decisions through carefully.

As a lead adult care worker, you may be given responsibility for making professional judgements. You might make decisions without having to ask your manager each time; you are also accountable for your actions. This does not mean that you should never allow for something out of the ordinary to happen, like allowing Jo from the scenario above to leave early. Always use all the information, knowledge and experience that you have in order to make informed decisions.

National Institute for Health and Care Excellence (NICE)

The National Institute for Health and Care Excellence (NICE) aims to improve health and social care and provide evidence-based guidance. NICE guidelines can help organisations to develop ways of working and procedures in the confidence that they are evidence-based.

Case study: Audit at The Firs

The Firs is a residential home and forms part of a larger organisation of five care homes. The organisation carries out internal audits of each of the homes in which managers inspect each other's care home as if they were an external inspector. This helps them to monitor and maintain standards of care. The focus for this audit was to find out if staff were fully aware of their own duties and responsibilities, and those of others. Staff did not know they were to be inspected so it was a realistic 'snapshot' of everyday work. This is what they found:

- All staff could give examples of their own and others' roles and responsibilities and gave examples of how they work together.
- One care worker explained how she approached her lead adult care worker for advice when she was worried about a resident and didn't know what to do.
- Lead adult care workers gave examples of the boundaries of their role; for example, one resident has a complex wound which needs to be dressed by a community nurse.
- Residents said that they were offered choice and treated respectfully.
- Staff followed professional guidelines, for example, NICE guidelines, to prevent and control the spread of infection.
- Lead adult care workers gave direct care to residents as well as successfully managing other junior workers in their role; the shift was well organised.

Following the audit, the staff were given feedback and complimented on their practice. All were clear about their duties and responsibilities and those of other workers. It was felt that the organisation was providing excellent standards of care and support.

- What other suggestions would you make for such an audit?
- How do you think this would compare with your own organisation?

Qualification mapping

Unit 6 LO 2 AC 2.4

6Cs

Communication, care, compassion

Summary

Individuals who you support have the right to receive a good standard of provision. Your organisation will strive to ensure that this happens, however, they cannot do this unless you and others work to a high standard.

Guide others with their duties and responsibilities

Qualification mapping

Unit 6 LO 3 AC 3.2

As a lead adult care worker, part of your role is to guide, mentor and contribute to the development of colleagues as they carry out their duties and responsibilities at work.

Activities

Care Quality Commission (CQC) inspection

The Care Quality Commission (CQC) inspects health and social care services. Everyone who works for the organisation has a responsibility to contribute and help to ensure that the organisation meets the required standards.

Familiarise yourself with the CQC website. You can access it at www.cqc.org.uk Imagine that you are looking for a provider of care for a friend or family member. Decide on the type of service that you are looking for, then:

- follow the links to inspections, research different providers in your area and read their reports
- suggest which provider you would choose based on the inspection reports
- answer the question: Are all providers carrying out their duties and responsibilities adequately? Explain your answer.
- if your organisation is inspected by the CQC, access the most recent report and make a note of any actions that need to be improved upon
- explain your responsibilities and those of others in addressing them.

Qualification mapping

Unit 6 LO 2 AC 2.4

Duties and responsibilities of workers

Your organisation is committed to raising and maintaining high standards of care. Your manager has asked you to complete an internal audit of your organisation (like that at The Firs on the previous page) to find out if workers fully understand their own duties and responsibilities, and those of others.

- Choose three different workers, such as adult care workers of different levels; for example, lead and adult care workers, activity leaders, administrators etc.
- Ask them to describe their own role and that of two different ones. Are their responses accurate?
- Observe general work practice as if you were an external visitor. For example, are individuals offered choice and is the environment clean and tidy?

Accountability of a lead adult care worker

Hari is a lead adult care worker. The team like working with Hari as their supervisor because he is relaxed. The team work hard and also quickly because they know that if they finish their work a few of them can leave early; they take it in turns. Yesterday was no exception. The team finished their work early and some individuals left early.
One difference, however, was that yesterday a user of the service went missing and there were not sufficient staff left to deal with the situation. The missing individual was later found but had suffered some injuries and required hospital treatment.

- Do you think that how Hari chooses to lead his team is right? Explain your answers.
- Hari is accountable for his actions. How do you think he could justify his actions on that day?
- What do you think the outcome will be for Hari and those who went home that day?

Access and read the Code of Conduct for Healthcare Support Workers and Adult Social Care Workers and answer the following questions:

- Did Hari work to his code of conduct? Explain your answer.
- Explain how Hari should have worked as a lead adult care worker and what Hari's duties and responsibilities were in relation to his accountability for his actions.

Spreading the word about the 6Cs

The 6Cs are integral to all care and support that should be given by everyone who works in your organisation. You want to raise awareness so have decided to create a display for all staff to show how the team work in a way that supports the 6Cs.

You are going to create a 6Cs tree, as shown in Figure 6, by drawing a tree trunk and cutting out hand shapes to be the leaves. Ask each team member to contribute to growing the tree. (Don't forget to include everyone such as the housekeepers, kitchen and maintenance staff, for example. If appropriate, you could involve users of the service to compliment the practice of staff if they have gone out of their way to be kind and caring.)

By creating the tree and sharing good practice you will support others to know what good practice is and work in a way that will raise and maintain standards. You must make sure that personal and identifiable information is not disclosed on the display.

Figure 6: Small acts of kindness can mean a lot

Contribute to the development of colleagues with their duties and responsibilities

As a lead adult care worker, you will help to develop others in their work.

Think of a time when you actively supported an individual to work to statutory standards. You may have assisted the individual to understand the standards, or their code of conduct, and then helped them to apply knowledge to their work role and practice.

Obtain a witness testimony or write a self-reflective account of when this happened.

Practice for professional discussion

Prepare for a 10-minute professional discussion around how statutory standards and codes of practice help to maintain and raise standards of care. You could include the following information:

- What statutory standards must be adhered to in your workplace?
- How do they comply with the standards?
- How can you help others to contribute to raising standards of provision?
- Assess how you apply your code of practice in your everyday work.
- Evaluate how statutory standards and your code of practice maintain and raise standards of care.

Duty of care

Qualification mapping

Unit 4 LO 1 AC 1.1, 1.2 and 1.3

You have a legal and moral obligation to act in the best interest of the individuals that you support and ensure that they are safe: this is duty of care. It is not always easy and you may need to help to overcome some conflicts and difficulties. You might also need to support junior colleagues.

There have been many incidents of poor care and safeguarding omissions over the years where there have been serious failings in duty of care. Some individuals suspected poor practice but did not act upon their suspicions. As a lead adult care worker, you need to be particularly vigilant in exercising duty of care because the individuals who you support are vulnerable and may be unable to speak up for themselves or maintain their own safety.

Who has duty of care responsibilities in your workplace?

Look at some of the examples in Figure 7.

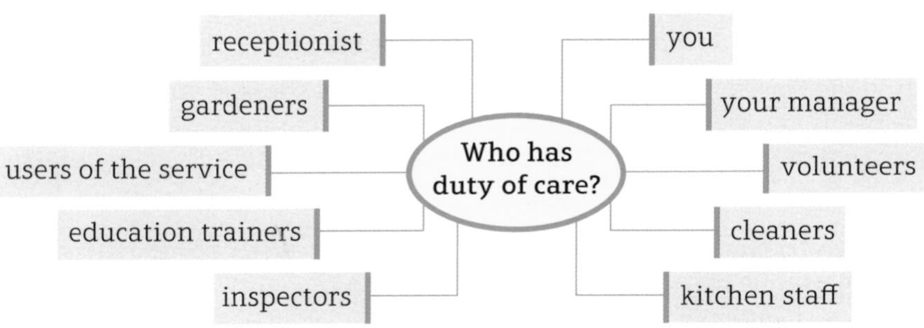

Figure 7: Many workers have a duty of care to users of service

Do you raise the alarm or ignore it? Duty of care is everyone's responsibility.

Duty of care is not only for people who work in health and social care. Imagine if you noticed a fallen live power cable blocking a road or an unattended bag in a public place, such as an airport. Both of these could pose a serious problem to others. It would be your duty of care as a member of the public to report such events.

Case study: Fran

Fran is a lead adult care worker in a residential care home. Today Fran is leading the shift. The team receive handover and Fran delegates team members their responsibilities. She asks if anyone has any concerns about what they have been asked to do. Fran gives direct care support to residents and supports them in a way that is agreed in their care plans and risk assessments. Fran ensures that her team have a break.

Fran has exercised duty of care in her role as a lead adult care worker. She supported individuals as she should and made sure that staff to whom she delegated work were, to the best of her knowledge, competent and confident in what they were doing. Fran also made sure that the staff had adequate breaks.

- How do you exercise duty of care in your everyday work?

6Cs

Care, courage, competence

What does duty of care mean to you in your role?

As a lead adult care worker, it is likely that you will have direct contact with users of the service but you may also have a supervisory role where you support junior colleagues and delegate work. You will be responsible for giving and receiving information. To ensure that you uphold duty of care in your work role, you must make sure you:

- check you are working to your code of conduct
- keep your knowledge and skills up to date
- always provide high quality care
- maintain consistent excellent record keeping
- do not **delegate** work to others unless you are confident they can do what you have asked
- adhere to all agreed ways of working
- work within the law
- maintain confidentiality, but disclose if there is a safeguarding concern
- speak up and raise any concerns you have.

What does it mean to your manager and supervisor?

Managers and supervisors have the same responsibilities as listed above but they also have a duty of care towards the people they manage. Managers and supervisors must also:

- ensure that workers can do their job safely and have the necessary resources
- make sure that staff feel confident to speak up if something is wrong or unsafe
- seek guidance from their own supervisor if unsafe situations arise that they are not able to deal with themselves.

Duty of candour

Occasionally mistakes can happen or things can be forgotten. All adult care workers have an obligation to be open and honest when this happens. In the past, there were failings where it was claimed that mistakes were hidden from users of the service. It was then formalised that all workers have a duty of candour, which means being open and honest to the individuals concerned.

Case study: Fran and duty of candour

One care worker tells Fran that she has accidentally given a resident a meal that contains gluten and she is gluten intolerant. Fran thanks the care worker for telling her then Fran discusses this with her manager and they explain to the resident what has happened. The resident was given the prescribed medication to relieve symptoms. The incident was documented.

Accidents do occasionally happen and the care worker was honest about the mistake. Fran and the manager were also open and honest and told the resident; this is duty of candour. The situation was dealt with safely and properly. If the resident was cognitively impaired, the next of kin would have been informed.

- Why do you think that it is important for the user of the service to know that a mistake has been made?

Key term

Delegate – give someone else the responsibility of doing a job or task

Professional working

Workers who are registered with a professional body, such as the Nursing and Midwifery Council or Health and Care Professions Council, and those who are members of professional associations, such as the British Association of Social Workers, can access professional advice about safe ways of working. Registered practitioners are required to evidence fitness to practise. This means that they are in good health, have appropriate skills and knowledge and are of good character. If there is concern about fitness to practise and duty of care concerns they may be unable to remain on the register and subsequently be unable to practise as a registered practitioner.

Summary

Working in the adult care sector means you need to be vigilant about duty of care on a day-to-day basis because you are supporting vulnerable people. Duty of candour means that you must be honest if a mistake has been made.

Support others to comply with regulations and policies

Qualification mapping

Unit 4 LO 2 AC 2.1, 2.2 and 2.3

Adult care work can be complex and some environments are challenging to work in. Exercising duty of care is often not easy or straightforward. As a lead adult care worker, you will need to lead and support others to do the right thing. This also requires you to be compliant with regulations and the policies and procedures of your organisation.

Your work in adult care is complex and you will probably find that you deal with difficulties around duty of care on a regular basis. Everyone might take minor risks from time to time. Users of the service have the right to take risks, but the important thing is to be fully aware of what is involved and the possible consequences of taking the risk.

Users of your service have the right to make choices too, but you have the responsibility to protect them. This is where conflicts can arise between your need to protect individuals and their right to make choices. The case studies in this section provide examples of lead adult care workers who have managed conflicts in their work.

Case study: The drop-in centre

Marek works in a drop-in centre for substance users that Josef attends. Josef is trying to quit using substances and is on an established rehabilitation programme. Marek reviews his progress and Josef says that he has not used any illicit substances between the last visit and today. Marek asks for a urine sample before he sees the doctor for his prescription.

Josef's urine sample is positive for illicit substances. Josef denies using the substance and begs Marek not to tell the doctor. He then admits using the substance because of a one-off stressful situation and says it won't happen again.

Marek sensitively explains that he must inform the doctor of the result. Josef's treatment plan was reviewed and records updated.

- Why do you think that Josef did not want the doctor to know about his result?
- Why did Marek have a duty of care to tell the doctor?

All adult care workers will aim to give high quality care, meet everyone's support needs and protect them from harm but it is not always easy. As a lead adult care worker, you may be faced with many challenges and conflicts, for example:

- a user of the service refuses to take their prescribed medication
- a physically ill individual, being supported in their own home, refuses to discard the 'out of date' food in their fridge
- two individuals who have learning disabilities wish to have a physical (sexual) relationship
- an individual in a woman's refuge says that she wants to see her abusive partner again.

You want to maintain the safety of the individuals but can see the potential dangers around the choices the individuals make. However, you also need to be respectful of their decisions.

Managing conflicts

These are some tips for managing conflicts:

- Explain why you consider the activity unsafe (ensuring that the individual understands what you are saying).
- Suggest an adjustment or an alternative.
- Seek specialist advice.
- Weigh up the risks with the user of the service.
- Ask colleagues if they have dealt with a similar situation and how they dealt with it.
- Refer to policies and procedures.
- Document the incident and any decisions made.
- Complete or update the individual's risk assessment.

How policies and procedures can help

It is often not the day-to-day work that you and others might find challenging; it is usually the more complex situations, such as what to do if a person refuses to take medication, goes missing or even dies unexpectedly. This is where policies and procedures will help guide you. By following the correct policies and procedures you will be confident that you are doing the right thing and working in a safe way. Make a point of referring to procedures when working with junior colleagues. This lets them know that you are working in the correct way and will help them to understand that there are some things in the job that you need to seek information about.

Challenging poor practice

Sometimes duty of care towards users of the service can mean that you need to challenge poor practice; for example, if you see staff not washing their hands properly, not engaging in conversation with individuals they are supporting, not offering choice or putting dirty linen on the floor. It can be difficult to challenge other workers but if you ignore the situation, the poor practice will continue. It is also likely to get worse and could lead to abuse and neglect.

It can be hard to get your message across when you observe poor practice, especially as you want to maintain good working relationships. You may also worry that you were seen to be critical of others.

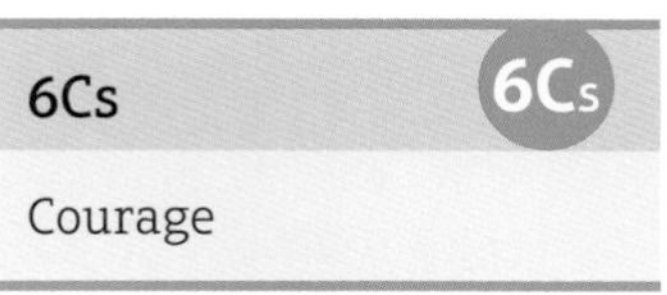

Professional working 

If a situation was dangerous or abusive you would need to deal with it straightaway. Refer to Topic D (Safeguarding) for more information.

Case study: Being ignored

Bernie works in a residential care home as a lead adult care worker. A trip was organised for the residents to go to the local park. Bernie noticed when they were there that one of the adult care workers, Jo, was on her phone and laughing, while the individual appeared to be bored and ignored. Bernie has observed Jo using her phone a lot and wonders if this is getting in the way of her giving good care.

Bernie felt it necessary not to ignore the situation but did not want to cause arguments or conflict between them. She took a moment to think how best to handle it rather than rushing in and confronting Jo. Bernie wanted Jo to be aware of what she was doing but wanted to deal with it in a friendly, non-threatening way; after all, Jo might have had a good reason to be using her phone.

When Jo put her phone away, Bernie asked if she could have a word with her. Bernie asked if everything was OK because she had noticed her on her phone while she was with the resident. It was Jo's friend and they were organising a night out. Jo realised straightaway that what she had done was wrong.

Bernie tactfully managed the situation without causing conflict and arguments. Sometimes all it takes is for the person to become more self-aware about what they are doing and to know that others have noticed what they are doing.

- Can you think of any other examples of poor practice that would need to be challenged?
- What would you have done in Jo's situation?

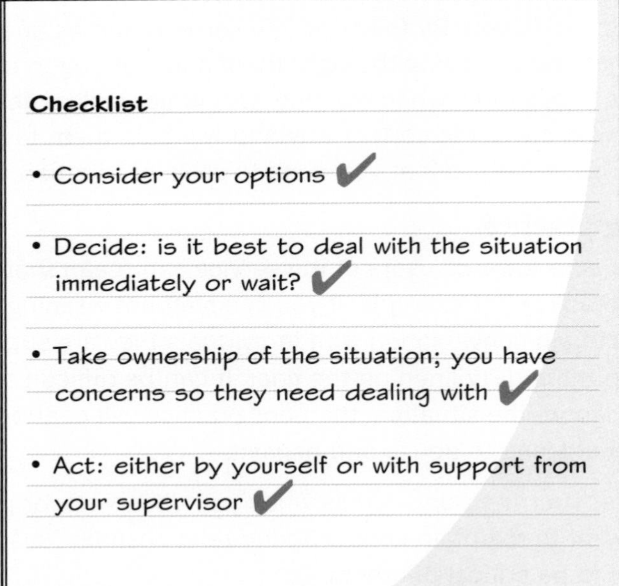

Figure 8: Tips that can help when challenging poor practice

If you supervise individuals, it is an important part of your role to ensure that they follow policies and procedures. If you find that individuals are not following correct policies and procedures it is often because they do not realise that the policy or procedure exists, or the importance and relevance of it. Either way it is your role to make sure that they do know.

I have found that doing it like this works well

I wasn't taught to do it that way, I was told that this was the way we need to do it because ...

I couldn't help noticing that you did ... can you explain why?

Figure 9: Try to express your concerns tactfully

Professional working 

When dealing with conflicts to duty of care, remember to be sensitive and empathetic. Be careful not to come across as patronising.

Complaints

Occasionally users of the service are not satisfied with an aspect of the service that they have received or decisions that have been made. You have a duty of care to take their feelings and comments seriously and not ignore them. Each organisation will have a procedure around what to do if an individual wishes to complain (see Figure 10 for one suggestion). You should be familiar with the procedure and ensure that any workers you supervise are familiar with it as well. Users of the service have a right to comment or complain.

Complaints should not be viewed as negative; feedback helps the organisation to improve on what they are doing.

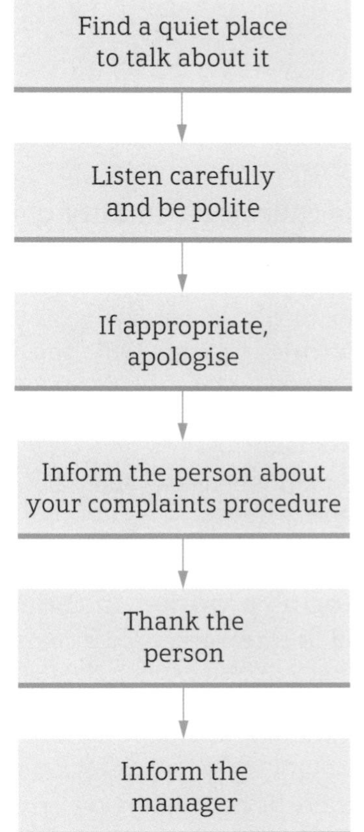

Figure 10: What to do if a person complains

It's your role to make sure others know about policies and procedures

6Cs 

Care, compassion, courage, communication, competence

Summary 

Exercising duty of care is not always straightforward: there can be conflicts and difficulties. Usually it is possible to resolve conflicts and achieve a positive outcome. If the user of the service is not satisfied with an outcome they have a right to complain.

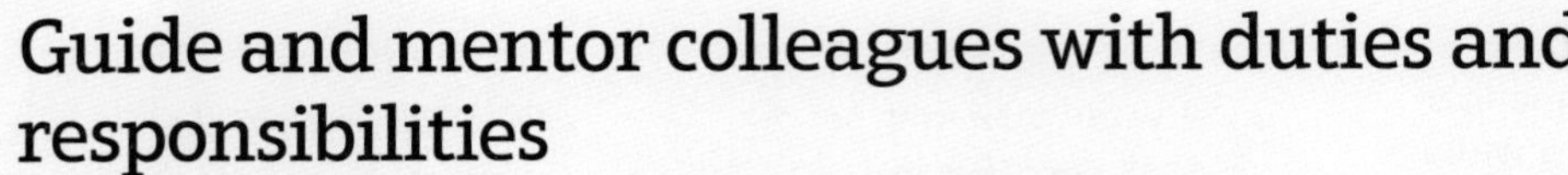

Guide and mentor colleagues with duties and responsibilities

Qualification mapping

Unit 4 LO 1 AC 1.1, 1.2, LO 2 AC 2.1, 2.2, 2.3, LO 3 AC 3.1 and 3.2

As a lead adult care worker you and your team are likely to face challenges around duty of care. You will need to help and guide others to do the right thing as they carry out their duties and responsibilities.

Activities

Guide colleagues in duty of care

A large and important part of the responsibilities for all adult care workers is to exercise duty of care and know your limitations. Your code of conduct is clear around what you must do.

- Work with a colleague who you are mentoring or supervising and access your professional code of conduct together. Find out what it says about your responsibilities around duty of care and link to what it means in your own work environment.
- Mind map some ideas about how you each exercise duty of care in your own workplace duties.

Mentoring a worker in their roles and responsibilities

A new adult care worker, Jodie, joins your organisation. You are her mentor; she is shadowing you. You explain the tasks that you undertake. Although Jodie has been in a lead role in another organisation, the manager realises that it was a different situation, which is why she is shadowing you. There are tasks such as doing off duty and using specific computer systems that Jodie is not familiar with.

- Describe the help that is available in your setting for new lead adult care workers.
- Explain how you would help to guide and mentor a new lead adult care worker in their roles and responsibilities in your setting.

Conflicts around duty of care

It is not always straightforward to exercise duty of care. Often you must make professional judgements but you still have to work within policies and procedures in your work setting.

Make a list of conflicts about duty of care that you have faced at work. Copy and complete the table below, explaining how you managed these conflicts.

Conflict	How was it managed?	Was it successful? If not, suggest how it could have been resolved

Duty of candour

Have you ever made a mistake? Just about everyone has!

Being open and honest about mistakes or errors that you make at work is important. This is duty of candour. Think about a time when a mistake was made – you don't have to write about what it was – and answer the following questions.

- Why do you think that it was important to own up to the mistake?
- What could have happened if you had not been open about the error or mistake?
- Why do you think that being honest about mistakes is part of your duty of care?

You may wish to keep the responses to the first two questions private.

Reviewing the complaints procedure

Read and review your workplace complaints procedure.

How would you explain the complaints procedure to a user of the service or a new member of staff?

Make some notes and then write your own explanation of the complaints procedure. Keep it safe in case you need it in the future.

Challenging poor practice

Think about a potential area of poor practice that you may witness as a lead adult care worker. For example, this might include observing a member of staff not promoting an individual's independence or a worker with a poor handwashing technique.

Consider and make notes on how you would deal with the poor practice that you have observed.

Copy and complete the table below to explain how you would deal with the situation.

Area of poor practice	How you would manage the situation in a professional and non threatening way

Take the initiative when faced with different duties at work

Qualification mapping

Unit 6 LO 2 AC 2.1 and 2.3

6Cs

Commitment, courage, competence

Your normal day-to-day work will involve repetition of some tasks and you will probably feel confident in your approach. However, occasionally you will be faced with things that are very different, so you will need to use your initiative. Situations like this will require you to use your wider skills.

It takes time to become confident in what you are doing and sometimes you will be faced with a new challenge, a different situation from the one you are used to, such as the examples given in Figure 11. Your first response might be 'I can't do this' because it's unfamiliar. You may even refer the situation to your supervisor. However, it's possible that you need to stop and think before you say that you cannot deal with the situation. Throughout your experience, work and training, you have gained many valuable skills that are transferrable and now is the time to put them to the test.

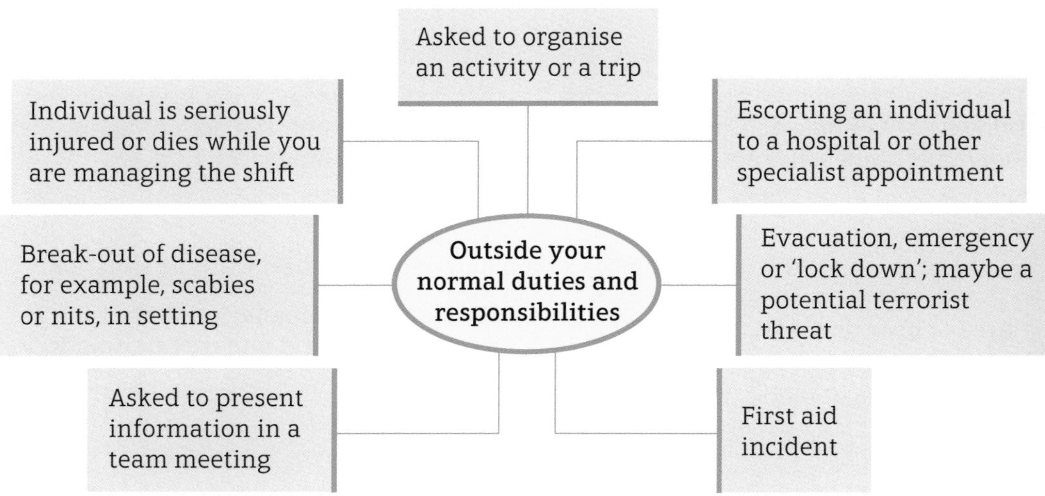

Figure 11: You could face some potentially unfamiliar situations

Key term

Transferable skills – different skills and abilities that you have and can use in various situations

You have probably had training for 'out of the ordinary' events such as fire and first aid. However, dealing with a real situation will require you to use your initiative and act decisively. Initiative is about using common sense, seeing what needs to be done and getting on with it. This is not always easy: you will need to draw on your knowledge and the **transferable skills** that you have gained through your experience, such as those shown in Figure 12.

Some situations you could face will be completely unexpected and you will need to use your professional judgement and act fast.

Case study: What would you do?

Jess is a domiciliary live-in adult care worker and was off duty. She went to a local pub for a drink with her partner. There were a group of individuals out for the evening and it became evident that they were adult care workers also providing domiciliary care but from a different provider than the one that Jess works for. The group began talking about events that had happened at work, individuals who they liked working with and those they didn't. Then one of them spoke about an individual who was morbidly obese. She was judgemental about the individual and many of the group joined in to say, 'how could anyone get so large?'. They laughed and joked.

But Jess knew exactly who they were laughing at: it was Maureen, a user of her service. Two individuals are needed to help move Maureen and they use a domiciliary provider to supply another care worker; it was one of them who spoke unkindly of Maureen that evening.

Jess was not sure at first what to do but she bravely spoke to the individuals and said that she knew the person they were talking about and it was unprofessional to speak in this way. The crowd became quiet and changed the subject.

Jess spoke to her manager who took the incident further. This event was outside her normal duties but Jess used her initiative and drew upon her skills and confidence to deal with the situation in a professional way.

- What do you think you would do in a similar situation? (Be honest.)
- How else could the situation have developed?

6Cs

Commitment, courage, communication

Professional working

After any unfamiliar event or anything out of your normal duties and responsibilities, do the following things:

- Reflect on the event or activity; identify what went well and what you need to do to develop your knowledge or skills.
- Debrief – especially after emergency situations.
- Use supervision to discuss the event.
- Be proud of your achievements.

What transferable skills could you use?

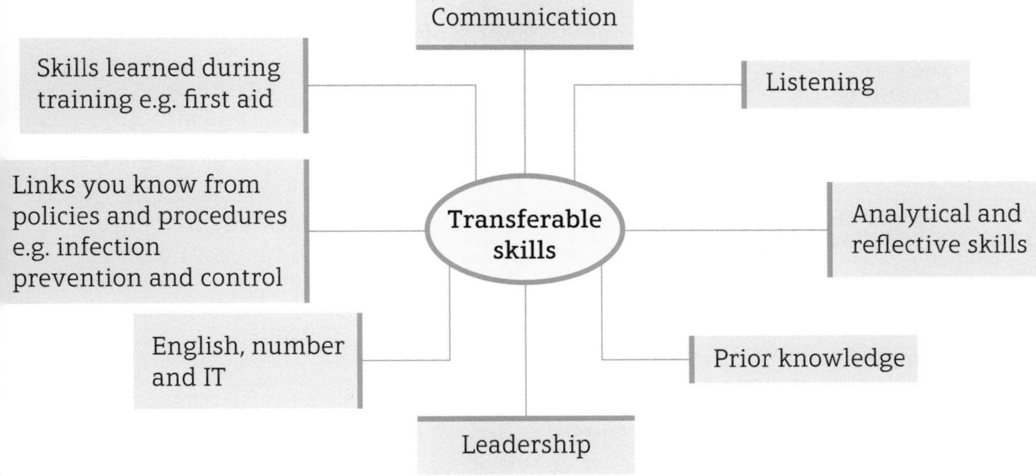

Figure 12: There are different transferable skills you could use in an unfamiliar situation

After the event, reflect on the situation and make judgements about what happened and how you did. By doing this, you can learn a lot and gain valuable experience from these unusual situations. You can gain confidence even if the outcome was not positive. For example, if you were on hand to support an individual who collapsed and you performed basic life support but it was unsuccessful, at least you tried and did your best for the individual.

Professional working

Most of the time, your work will be familiar to you and you will feel confident in what you are doing. However, sometimes you will be faced with situations that are outside your normal duties and responsibilities; these may be unfamiliar situations. Have confidence in yourself and draw on the transferable skills that you have.

Use your wider skills when in unfamiliar situations

When you are faced with unfamiliar situations at work that are outside your normal duties and responsibilities, you will need to use your wider skills.

Activities

Working outside your normal duties and responsibilities

You will feel confident on a day-to-day basis about what you do. However, sometimes you may be faced with unfamiliar situations that are outside your normal duties and responsibilities.

What unfamiliar situations could you face at work?

List five examples.

Using your transferable skills

Sometimes your first response to an unfamiliar situation is resistance or concern that you cannot deal with it. This is when you need to have confidence in yourself and your role. Your experience as a lead adult care worker will have equipped you with many skills and qualities – probably more than you realise.

Think carefully about your skills and qualities. These could also have been gained away from work; for example, time management and organisational skills to get things done at home. Copy and complete the table below to give examples of how you have used your skills and qualities.

Skills	Give an example of how you have used transferable skills in unfamiliar situations
Transferable knowledge e.g. first aid and infection prevention	I am familiar with safe disposal of waste and reducing the spread of infection. When an individual cut their arm and was bleeding a lot, I used my knowledge of infection prevention in a different way.
Communication	
Reflective skills	
Organised	
Calm	
Leadership	
English, number and IT	
Other	

Taking the initiative when working outside normal duties

Try to recognise and look positively at your transferable skills. You will have more than you realise. Initiative is an important skill for a lead adult care worker: being able to do things without being told.

Look at the scenarios below and think about each situation. Suggest how the lead adult care worker could take the initiative when working outside their normal duties and responsibilities. What transferable skills could they apply in each situation?

- Markus is a shift leader at a large residential home. A phone call has been taken that indicates there is an explosive in the building. The staff have heard and there is panic across the setting.
- Cara is a lead adult care worker at a supported living complex for individuals who have learning disabilities. Cara is new in the supervisory role. While leading the shift yesterday, a care worker approached Cara and was very distressed because she had discovered an individual who had taken their life in their room. The parents were in the lounge waiting to visit.

Professional working 

Witness statement: Obtain a witness statement from your supervisor or manager to provide evidence of how you have successfully used your initiative when faced with an unfamiliar or emergency situation.

Skills to develop initiative

As a lead adult care worker, you will need to use your initiative to get things done. You need to foresee jobs that need doing and identify problems before they arise. You will often be the person who junior care workers will go to with questions. You can build skills to help develop initiative.

Individuals with lots of initiative possess many of the characteristics below. Which ones relate to you? Ask your supervisor or assessor to look at the list and identify the characteristics that they think you possess.

Notice what needs doing before it is obvious	Hardworking	Notice potential problems before they arise
Creative	Do more than is asked of you	Speak up with new ideas
Always seek solutions to problems	Strive for good results	Energetic
Calm	Confident	Do things without being asked
Use every opportunity to show your skills	Keen to progress	Aware of what is going on around you

Building your skills

Use your personal development plan to address areas that you could develop.

This will help you to build skills so that you feel prepared to manage situations that are out of your normal duties and responsibilities.

Make a list of the skills you need to develop.

A person-centred approach to create and develop a care plan

Qualification mapping

Unit 7 LO 1 AC 1.1, LO 2 AC 2.1

The individuals you work with have the same right of choice about their lives as you have but they might need some additional support to make it happen. They should be actively involved in a personal care/support plan that will clearly show their wants and needs. This is a person-centred approach to planning care.

Who decides for you what you do, and where you go? The answer is probably you. You can likely manage most or all parts of your life, for example your physical needs, going to work, relationships and social life, without anyone's help. You work with vulnerable people who do need some help in parts of their life. The individual might be able to manage some parts without any help but will need support in others. An assessment of their wants and needs will be carried out.

The assessment and plan of care will be written down; it is documented either in written or electronic form so that the individual knows what should happen. This also helps care staff to know how to support the individual. As the needs of an individual change so will the care plan. The care plan should be reviewed at regular intervals with the individual being supported and others who are involved in their care.

Care plans do not look the same in all organisations, so you will need to become familiar with what is used where you work. Care plans are tailored to meet the needs of the individual but they will all follow a similar outline to that shown in Figure 13.

Professional working

A detailed care plan will be created and will include risk assessments, such as the likelihood of falls or pressure sores. These documents can be lengthy and will often be filed into a folder. A 'one-page profile' such as 'This is me' is sometimes created so a person's preferences and needs can be seen at a glance.

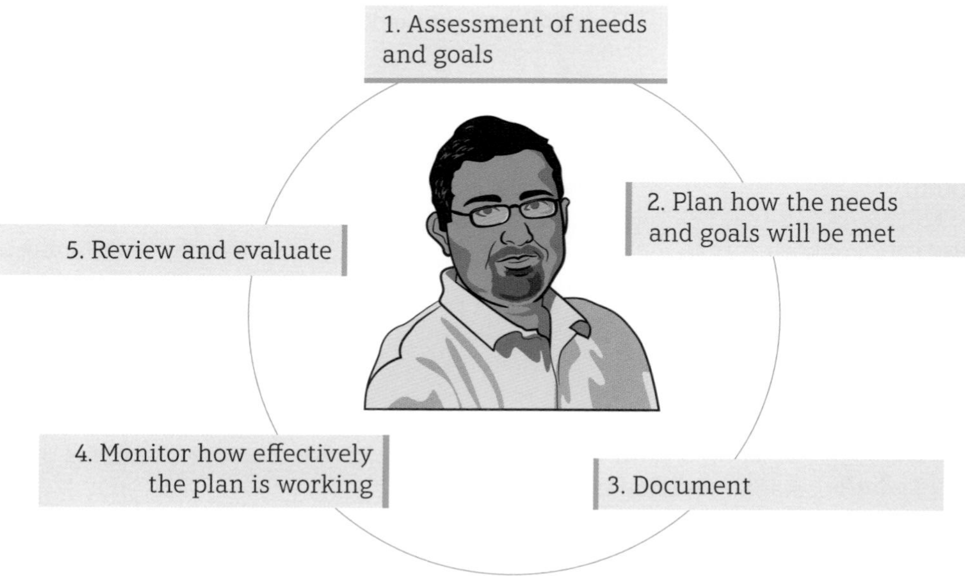

Figure 13: The structure of care planning

Users of the service should be actively involved in every step of the plan, which should be person-centred and service user led. When supporting individuals in adult care, you must apply person-centred values, as shown in Figure 14.

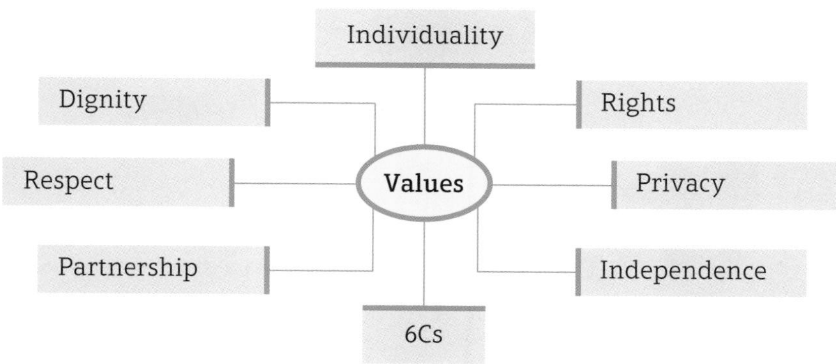

Figure 14: Person-centred values are essential for the care-planning process

;upport the care planning process

'hink about how you would want to be involved in deciding how to live your life. Jsers of your service should be the ones deciding for themselves. You can help by 'eveloping a trusting relationship with them.

)evelop a trusting relationship

;ommunication is the key to developing any relationship. If you develop a good ·usting relationship, the person is more likely to feel valued as well as comfortable bout sharing their needs and wishes. Spend time to find out about them as a ·erson, and what their preferences and goals are.

Vould the individual like someone else involved?

he individual might want to have someone else with them during the care planning ·rocess. Having a family member or friend present to help them express their noughts and ideas may make service users feel more comfortable. It should not be ssumed however, so always ask them first. In some situations the individual may ·refer to be alone, especially if you are discussing sensitive or embarrassing subjects. .lso, some people can be too over powering and dominant which is not helpful.

:hoices and options

ind out what the individual wants. For example, do they want to be supported in neir own home rather than residential care? Would they like to have someone do neir shopping for them or someone to help them to do their own shopping online? Vould they like someone to call early or do they prefer to sleep in later? It is often ossible to accommodate an individual's choices with a little thought. Remember nat you must respect an individual's choices even when they are not decisions that ou might make.

Qualification mapping

Unit 7 LO 2 AC 2.1, 2.2, LO 4 AC 4.3, LO 5 AC 5.1, LO 6 AC 6.3

You must involve users of the service in every aspect of the care-planning process

Holistic support

When assessing an individual's needs, you need to consider the whole person, not just their needs in isolation. For example, a person who requires physical support while undergoing treatment for cancer should also have their emotional and spiritual needs considered. Holistic assessment takes into consideration the needs shown in Figure 15.

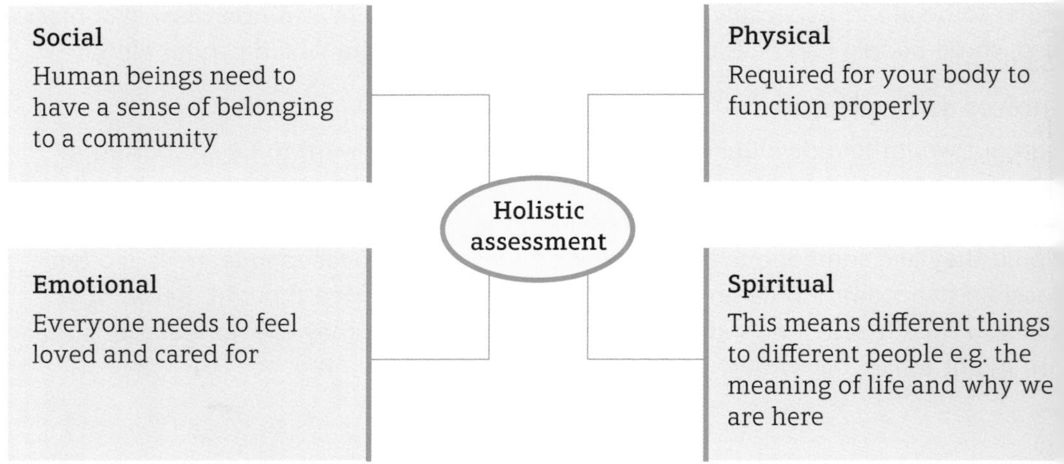

Figure 15: Holistic assessment considers the many different needs an individual may have

Case study: Lana and substance misuse

Emmie is a lead adult care worker specialising in substance misuse support. She supports Lana who injects substances. Eventually Lana would like to quit substance use but she does not feel ready at the moment. Lana is vulnerable, so she is supported to access services to help keep her safe. Emmie considers Lana's holistic needs.

Physical	Lana is at high risk of developing blood-borne diseases such as hepatitis B. Access to a needle exchange programme reduces this risk. Temporary housing means that she is not on the streets and vulnerable to physical attacks.
Spiritual	Music and meditation are important to Lana, helping her to connect with her mind.
Emotional	Lana needs a lot of emotional support. Talking and counselling helps get to the root of her problem with addiction and helps her to move forward.
Social	Friends are important to Lana but she can see how her current social circle is not helping with her addiction. She doesn't want to leave them but since attending the drop-in centre she has built friendships with other people trying to quit substance misuse.

- Why is it important to consider Lana's wider holistic needs as well as her physical needs?
- How successful do you think she would be in her aim to be free of substance misuse if Emmie only helped with her physical needs? Why do you think this?

6Cs

Care, compassion, communication

Professional working

It should be made clear at the beginning what the service is able to offer, so the individual can make a judgement about whether they wish to use it. For example, a small residential home with ten residents might not have fitness and gym facilities.

Summary

It is essential to take a person-centred approach when care planning and to consider the individual's holistic needs. Empowering individuals to make choices will enable them to be actively involved in the whole process.

Development and review of care plans

Qualification mapping

Unit 7 LO 1 AC 1.2, LO 2 AC 2.1, LO 4 AC 4.3, LO 5 AC 5.1, LO 6 AC 6.3

An important part of your role will be to contribute to the development and ongoing review of the care plans for the individuals you support. This will involve taking into account all their different needs and preferences, and encouraging individuals to participate in the way their care is delivered.

Activities

Developing a support plan

For this activity and the one that follows you will need a copy of your workplace assessment and care-planning documents, as well as any specific guidance materials. Documents differ between organisations so it's best to learn from your own. If your documents are electronic, see if you can print a paper copy to use.

First, read through the assessment and guidance materials.

Then create your own imaginary character and make notes about the person. You should include the following details:

- personal history: their age, who they live with, family members
- a little about their background; for example, where they work (or used to work), their interests and preferences, such as what time they like to get up and go to bed, and any leisure activities they like to pursue
- support needs: physical, emotional, spiritual and social.

Based on the character you have made up, complete an assessment using your workplace template.

If this were a real individual in your setting, explain how you would provide the individual with information so they could exercise choice in how they are supported. How would you actively involve them in the assessment process?

Show your assessment to your supervisor or assessor for feedback.

Meeting needs and goals

Now that you have identified the individual needs of your character, you must work with the care team to agree how the needs and goals will be met while respecting their individual choices.

Create a mind map of ideas on the options and choices that you think your character might wish to make and consider.

Document their choice on the care plan, with additional notes as required.

Show the care plan to your supervisor or assessor and ask for feedback.

- Would it be easy to follow?
- Does it consider the holistic needs of the individual: physical, emotional, spiritual and social?

Different preferences and needs

Often individuals have similar needs but, because of their circumstances and preferences, the ways in which their needs are met can be very different. Read about Charlie and Bert below. Imagine you were a lead adult care worker in the settings and, using the information, prepare a plan of care for them both.

In a real situation, the individual would actively participate in the process and involve significant others.

You may wish to be creative and can add extra detail to the case studies.

Charles	Bert
Charlie is 84 years old and has arthritis. He has limited mobility but can get about using a walking frame. Charlie has no family nearby. He loves the company of others and led the dominoes and crib teams at his local pub. He also likes gardening; he has tended to his church grounds voluntarily for years. Charlie is mostly independent but needs a little help with personal care and struggles with the household chores. Charlie has decided to move into a local residential home where he won't have the worry of paying bills and shopping. He wants to enjoy life without the responsibility and worry of running his own home. You are Charlie's adult lead care worker and have been asked to prepare a care plan with him.	Bert is 82 and recently had a fall. He is recovering well and can walk independently using a frame. Bert needs some support with everyday tasks. Bert's wife died five years ago and he can still get very upset. He believes that when he dies, they will be together again. Bert has a strong faith. Bert is a keen gardener and bird watcher. He also likes to visit his local club where he sees friends. Bert has lived in his home for nearly all of his life. He likes gardening; he grows vegetables and gives them to his friends and neighbours. Bert has chosen to stay in his own home. You are Bert's adult lead care worker and have been asked to prepare a care plan with him.

Involving the individual in the support plan

For this activity, you need to carry out an assessment and plan care/support for a real person; this individual should be a user of your service. You must maintain confidentiality by disguising personal details and remember to gain consent from the individual.

You may wish to ask your supervisor to support you during this activity.

- How did you prepare for the assessment?
- Explain how you actively involved the individual in the assessment process, respected their views and choices, and encouraged their participation.

Encouraging the individual to participate in their care plan

Molly attends a day centre. She has Down's syndrome. Molly is supported with independent living skills, such as shopping and cooking. While at the day centre Simone, her key worker, has actively involved her in decisions around how Molly wishes to be supported. Molly wants to be able to shop independently in the supermarket but asks Simone to wait near the checkout in case she needs help. Molly's support requests and needs are clearly documented in her care plan.

Sometimes Molly will change her mind and ask Simone to go around the supermarket with her. Simone asks each time to make sure that the level of support she gives is what Molly wants at that time.

- Why is it important that Simone actively involves Molly in how she wishes to be supported?
- Think of the support that you give to users of your service. Obtain a witness testimony that shows how you have encouraged an individual to actively participate in how their care and support is delivered.

Reflecting on assessment of needs

Carrying out an assessment of an individual's needs requires a lot of skills; for example, communication, information gathering and documenting. Now that you have completed an assessment, reflect on how you did.

Refer to Kolb's model of reflection along with the instructions on page v. Use the model to reflect on how you did.

If you have identified further learning needs during the process, note them down; you can discuss this at a supervision meeting and include it in your personal development plan.

Person-centred values in care planning

Revisit what is meant by person-centred values. Think about the care-planning process and answer the following questions.

- How can the care-planning process promote person-centred values?
- Why are person-centred values important to consider when planning care?
- What difficulties could you face around applying any of the person-centred values when care planning?
- Go online to research 'best practice' in care planning. Do you have any ideas on how the methods used in your organisation around assessment and planning care could be improved upon?
- Overall, what conclusions can you draw from the responses to the above questions? Why?

Specialist assessment and support

Assessing a person's needs can be straightforward if you can both understand each other, but what if the user of the service has difficulties with communication, expressing themselves or has a support need that is out of your expertise? In these cases, more skilled support will be needed.

Qualification mapping

Unit 7 LO 2 AC 2.1, 2.2, LO 4 AC 4.1

On page 36 you looked at social, physical, emotional and spiritual needs. But how can you assess these needs? It can be especially challenging when an individual has specific complex needs, such as cognitive, sensory and physical difficulties and disabilities. Assessment is not always straightforward and you want to make sure that accurate information is gathered so that the support fully meets the person's preferences and needs. You will need to use excellent communication skills. Refer to Topic C (The importance of communication) to remind yourself what they are. Remember the 6Cs and show care and compassion; you will need to be patient.

6Cs

Care, compassion

How to support assessment

Allow plenty of time

The assessment process may take longer if the individual has specific needs. The process cannot be rushed otherwise the trusting relationship that has been built will soon be broken and the assessment will be unsuccessful. The user of the service may be nervous and apprehensive as well as unsure what to expect; you are there to make it easier for them.

Actively involve the individual

The individual should be at the centre of the planning process but must not feel alone in it. Information should be given in a way that they can fully understand so that they can choose how they would like to be supported.

Involvement of others

Ask the individual if they would like anyone else involved such as family or friends. You may need to use specialist communication methods to find this out. Other people may be involved, but they may not all be able to attend the assessment:

- The medical team, such as doctor, nurse, occupational therapist, can contribute their views in relation to supporting the individual. You might discuss current or planned treatment and how this could affect the individual; for example, some medication can affect a person's physical and emotional health.
- Specialists, such as end-of-life and dementia practitioners, will have expert information to offer and can contribute their knowledge of best practice.
- The social care team: the individual may have a social worker who is signposting to other agencies, such as housing and benefits. They will be able to contribute to supporting the assessment of the individual's physical, emotional and social needs.

Professional working

When assessing and planning care, it is vital that the individual is at the centre of the whole process and that they know exactly what they are agreeing to when decisions are being made.

- Previous providers might be involved. The individual might have used a different service previously. For example, for an individual with dementia, who is leaving hospital following hip surgery, the discharge planning team is likely to be involved.
- Family and friends: they know the individual well, so their contribution can be valuable in assessing emotional and spiritual health and needs. They may also give insight into what social activities the individual enjoys.
- The individual might also have an advocate who they would like to help with decisions; for example, they might have a solicitor to help deal with their financial affairs.

Why are some assessments more difficult than others?

Some individuals find communication and expressing themselves difficult. This means that it is more challenging to assess and help to meet their needs. Individuals who have cognitive, sensory and physical impairments and difficulties, such as those shown in Figure 16, may need more support through the assessment process.

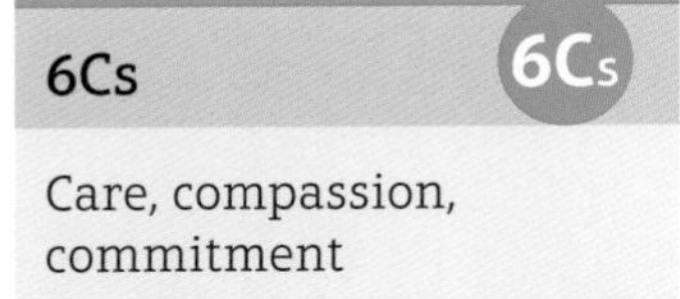

6Cs

Care, compassion, commitment

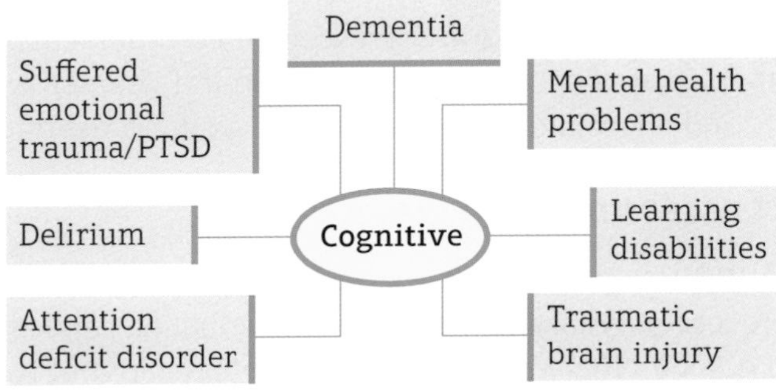

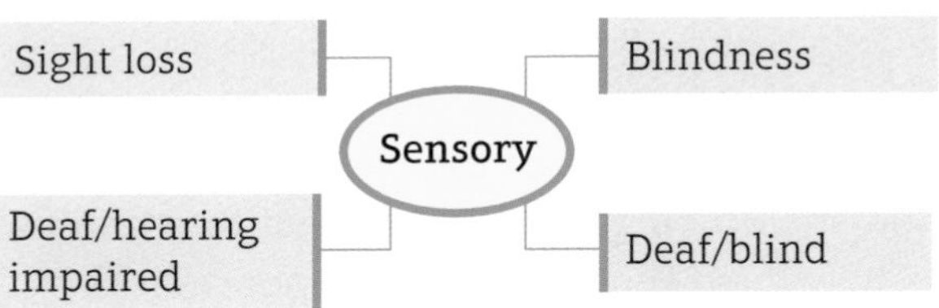

Professional working

Some individuals might experience specific difficulties that can make the assessment process more challenging. It may take more planning and input from others. It is important to make time to get the assessment accurate.

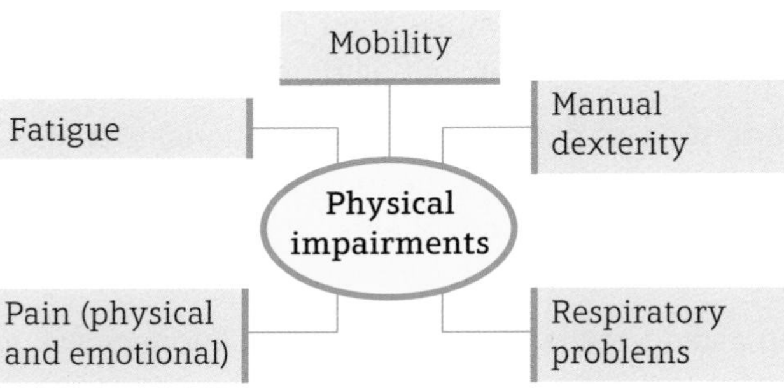

Figure 16: Some individuals may need more specialist support during the assessment process

Case study: Rahi

Rahi is a new lead adult care worker and is now becoming involved in assessments. Rahi is familiar with the range of different individuals who need to participate and recognises that the user of the service should be at the centre of the process. Rahi can understand how a person's physical, social and emotional needs can be assessed but was unclear about spiritual needs because these can be different for everyone. Rahi asked some individuals what spirituality meant to them; this is what they said:

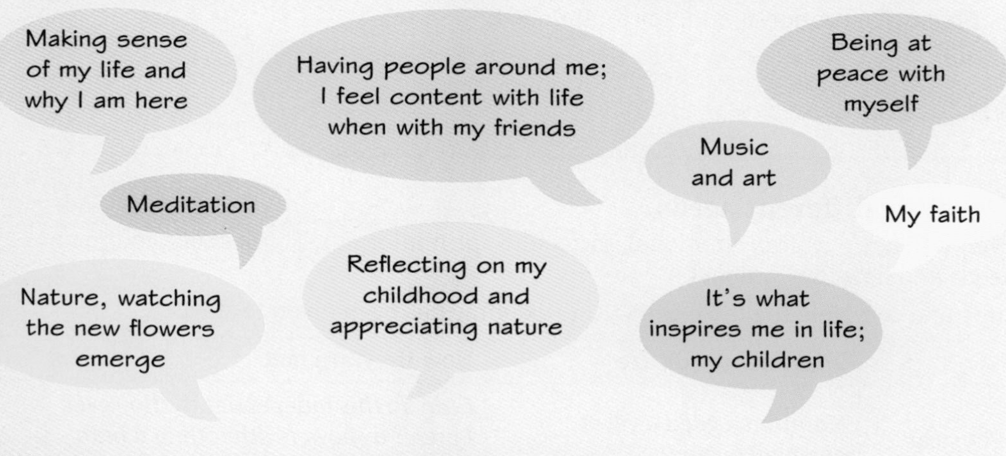

- What would you add to these thoughts on spirituality?
- What would you say to Rahi?

As a lead adult care worker, you might be the person who organises the assessment, so you will have to think about some practical things:

- The time: is the time of the assessment suitable for the user of the service? Some individuals find they think better in the morning and become tired as the day goes on. Make sure that there is sufficient time allocated and remember that a break might be necessary.
- The environment where the assessment is taking place: is it accessible and suitable?
- Should refreshments and water be supplied for all the participants?
- Have all individuals been informed of the assessment? If any cannot attend, do you have relevant information from them?
- Are all documents available and will computer equipment and the internet be needed?
- Think about the transport and travel arrangements for those who attend.

Specialist assessment for different needs

Part of your role might be to help with the specialist assessment of individuals with cognitive, sensory and physical impairments in order to meet their social, physical, emotional and spiritual needs.

Activities

Qualification mapping

Unit 7 LO 2 AC 2.1, 2.2, LO 4 AC 4.1, 4.2, 4.3, 4.4, LO 6 AC 6.3 and 6.4

Meeting different needs

Everyone has physical, emotional, social and spiritual needs. Think about your own needs and how they are met.

Copy and complete the table below. One example has been given to start.

	What my needs are	How they are met
Physical	*Maintain a good level of personal hygiene*	*I can do this independently. However, I prefer a shower rather than a bath because I have an arthritic hip*
Emotional		
Social		
Spiritual		

Supporting individuals through the process

Some people find the assessment process difficult and challenging. For example, it can be overwhelming for some individuals to be faced with lots of questions from people that they don't know particularly well, especially as some questions can be quite personal and private. In such situations, it can be easy to lose sight of what the individual's choices are and what they want.

Think about the individuals who access your service and their different personalities and needs.

- Explain why some individuals who you support might find the assessment process difficult.
- How could you help create an environment that is supportive to them?
- Explain how you could make sure that they are given sufficient information to make choices about their care and support.

Write a self-reflective account that shows how you have helped an individual with specific needs, for example, an individual who is sight, hearing or cognitively impaired, to actively participate in decisions about how they wish their care and support to be given.

Assessing specific needs

The individuals below have specific needs relating to memory, communication and physical difficulties. Suggest how you could support the assessment of their physical, emotional, social and spiritual needs.

A few examples have been given.

Ken is 75 and has difficulty with his memory; he has dementia.	Choose a time when Ken is more likely to be more alert. See if Ken has a relative or friend who knows him well who could be involved.
Tahira is 45 and has problems with her sight; she has limited vision.	
Bessie has had a stroke and has lost the use of one side of her body; her speech is also slurred.	

Assessment of complex needs

Pam is a personal assistant to Lin. Lin has struggled with her breathing for some time but just needed a little help from Pam for some day-to-day support. But last week Lin was diagnosed with advanced lung cancer.

Lin is devastated about the diagnosis and is struggling to think about what the future holds; she can't think clearly and is struggling emotionally. Lin's daughter lives nearby. She is very worried about her mum and fears that she might be depressed.

Lin's needs have now become more complex as she is approaching the end of her life. Lin and her daughter recognise that they need to make plans for the future.

- What do you think are the concerns for Lin and her daughter?
- What do you think will be part of their plans?
- Who will be involved in the assessment and what are their roles?
- What skills do you think the individuals involved in the assessment will need to have?
- What should be considered about the place and the environment of the assessment?
- How could you ensure that Lin is actively involved in all decisions about how she is to be supported and that her choices are fully respected?

Witness statement for specialist assessment

Use your skills to prepare and implement a specialist assessment for a user of your service.

Remember you must maintain confidentiality.

Obtain a witness statement from your supervisor to evidence when you have planned for a specialist assessment.

Ask them to include how you prepared in advance, who was involved, how you actively involved the individual and your role in the process.

Then reflect on the feedback that you were given, using Kolb's model of reflection on page v.

Informed consent

Qualification mapping

Unit 7 LO 3 AC 3.1, 3.2 and 3.3

Individuals must know what they are agreeing to when receiving care and support. You must get permission from the individual, as you need to be sure that they know what they are agreeing to. Decision-making should be based on information that has been given and fully understood. A person who lacks mental capacity could make unsafe and dangerous decisions so might need to have some of their right to liberty removed.

When you need to make a decision, you usually gather information beforehand and then decide what to do. For example, if you were asked to take part in a food-tasting research project that was testing gluten-free products, the researcher would need to tell you if there was a possibility of other allergens being present, such as fish or nut products. You would then use this information to judge whether to consent and go ahead or not.

Help individuals to make informed decisions

An individual is offered a flu jab because they have diabetes and asthma. The nurse explains that if a person who has breathing problems such as asthma gets flu, there is a higher risk of serious and sometimes fatal complications, such as pneumonia. The practitioner will also explain the risks; for example, serious side effects of the flu jab are not common but your arm can be sore afterwards and you might experience a mild fever. Also there is no guarantee that it will protect against all flu strains but if you do get flu it should not be so severe.	An individual has been staying at a residential care home while recovering from a broken hip. Her mobility has improved and she uses a frame to get about. Recently, she has requested to move back to her bungalow rather than stay at the care home. Her social worker has suggested that she would benefit from the support of care workers. Her social worker and a neighbour who knows her well discussed with her the positives and negatives of consenting to have a care worker. The individual had time to think through and make her decision, after which she decided to have a care worker support her at home.
Both individuals were given the information to make an informed decision. The benefits and risks were outlined.	

When it comes to consenting to an activity, the individual must have sufficient information in order to decide whether to agree or not. As a lead adult care worker, you will need to gather relevant information to give to the individual in order for them to consider consent. You may have to find further information if you are not sure about questions that they might ask during your conversation. You will also need to give the individual time to process the information fully. If a person does not have sufficient information they could inadvertently consent to something that they did not understand that they were agreeing to.

Case study: Drug rehabilitation centre

Rushd is a substance misuse worker. He works at a drug rehabilitation clinic where individuals are trying to quit drug addiction by undertaking a detox plan which involves taking prescribed medication as a replacement for the harmful drug. The agreement of the programme includes not taking the harmful drug; if they do, it will compromise their ability to remain in the programme.

At each appointment, they must confirm that they have not used since the last clinic visit and consent to giving a urine sample to test for substances. They are informed of this on their initial visit. If they refuse to give consent or substances are found in the sample, they will not be given their alternative prescription medication.

The individual will then make an informed decision to either give consent to the urine sample or not.

- Give an example of when a user of your service has given consent for an activity or treatment (for example, a new medication or treatment plan is being suggested).
- Were they given information beforehand, for example, information on possible side effects, so that they could make an informed decision as to whether to agree or not?

The individual needs to be supported to make informed decisions about their care and support. There are some factors that can influence an individual's full ability to express consent:

- **mental impairment**, for example, depression, bi-polar disorder, dementia
- **physical illness**, for example, stroke, motor neurone disease, unconsciousness
- **learning disabilities**, for example, Down syndrome
- **language barriers**, English may not be the individual's first language.

When you give information, you need to consider whether the individual can understand you. Have you expressed yourself clearly and avoided jargon? Do they need a translator or interpreter if English is not their first language? This would be especially important if consent was needed for important decisions, such as medical treatments. When big decisions are being made and written consent is needed, interpreters will be used but what about the day-to-day activities, such as helping with hygiene? You cannot expect to have an interpreter around every time you need to ask permission to help a person to wash.

Gaining consent

Everything that you do with users of service requires consent. It demonstrates respect and it keeps the service user in control. For example, asking an individual if you can help with personal hygiene gives them the opportunity to respond, 'No, not at the moment. I didn't sleep well. Can you help me later on this morning?'

Verbal consent is acceptable when supporting individuals in everyday activities. If a person does not verbally respond to you but they nod in agreement, or hold out their hand to receive medication, that is acceptable and is considered to be implied consent. However, if you do not get any positive response then you do not have consent. So what can you do? Some tips are shown in Figure 17.

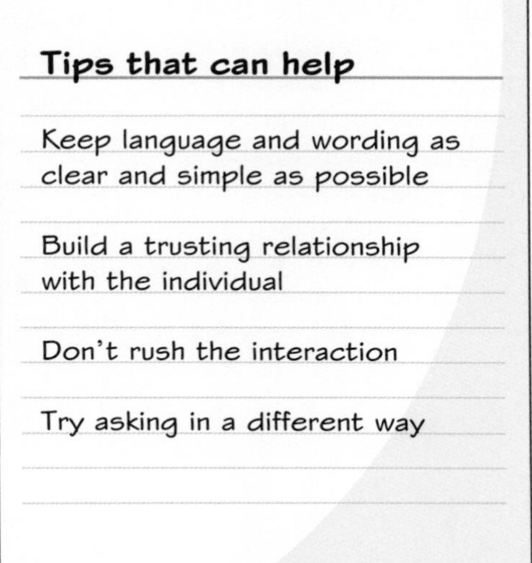

Figure 17: Tips to help with informed consent

6Cs 

Care, compassion, competence

- Do not just walk away from the situation.
- You might need to explain more clearly or in a different way.
- The individual might be worried about the activity or about something else. Be sensitive and try to find out what is worrying them.
- They might not feel happy to undertake the activity at this moment in time but will do a bit later.

Usually, after sensitive and empathetic conversation, the individual will consent to the activity. It is not that you are forcing them to do something they do not want to do, but sometimes people need more explanation and time to process what you are asking of them.

Case study: Assisting Bill

Josh is a lead adult care worker in a residential care home. Bill has dementia; he is 85 and is confused at times.

One morning Josh goes to assist Bill with his personal hygiene. Josh asks if he can help him to wash. Bill refuses. Josh wonders if it was because he was standing up, he might have appeared to be overpowering and his direct question might have confused Bill. He sat down and calmly engaged in conversation about how he was feeling and what he would like to do today. Bill said that he would like to have a wander around the garden later so Josh then asked if he would like help to have a wash so he could go out later. Bill then agreed.

Josh's change of approach was supportive and the outcome was positive.

- What do you think Josh would have done if Bill had refused again to have a wash?
- Can you think of an example from your own practice when a user of your service did not give consent to an activity? What did you do to ensure a positive outcome?

Professional working 

Always gain permission before you carry out an activity. You may need to adapt how you ask the person. If an individual does not have the mental capacity to make safe decisions they may have their right of liberty taken away, but a thorough assessment must be carried out beforehand and be clearly documented.

The Mental Capacity Act and Deprivation of Liberty Safeguards

The Mental Capacity Act is a law about making decisions and what must happen if an individual cannot make decisions for themselves. Each user of your service is presumed to have the mental capacity to make their own decisions until proven otherwise. Individuals who lack mental capacity are vulnerable and need protecting. The Deprivation of Liberty Safeguards form part of the Mental Capacity Act. Liberty is about having the freedom to do what you want (as long as it is within the law). Some people who lack mental capacity need to have this right removed in order to keep them safe. For example, if an individual is in a dangerous physical state because they have anorexia, it would be in their best interest to be kept safe and given fluid and nutrition.

There are policies and procedures that must be followed, with accurate documentation at each stage, to ensure that the law and regulations are followed.

Support others with informed consent

In your role as a lead adult care worker you need to lead and support colleagues to understand how to establish informed consent when providing care and support for individuals.

Qualification mapping 

Unit 7 LO 3 AC 3.1, 3.2 and 3.3

Activities

Different decisions

Making decisions is part of life for everyone. Some decisions are major and could be life changing, while others have less of an impact on your life; for example, what you would like to wear or eat that day.

Without naming the people involved, make a list of decisions that individuals who you support might make. You could copy and complete this table.

Important decisions that could impact on their life e.g. where to live	Day-to-day decisions

Gaining informed consent

Paulo is a new domiciliary adult care worker and is shadowing Leila, a lead adult care worker. Leila is guiding Paulo on how to support the users of the service with day-to-day activities. Paulo and Leila are visiting Cliff who has had a stroke. Although Cliff is regaining his speech, he often finds it difficult to verbally respond and conversations can be challenging. Paulo and Leila plan to help Cliff with personal hygiene, by washing, shaving and dressing him and giving him his routine medication. Cliff does not always agree to take his prescribed medication. Before they leave, they plan to prepare some lunch for Cliff.

Although Cliff's speech is slow and slurred he has full mental capacity.

- If you were Leila, how would you explain to Paulo how to establish informed consent for the various planned activities?
- As Cliff's verbal communication is restricted, how would you explain how his actions could indicate implied consent?
- How would you explain to Paulo the importance of informed consent before carrying out activities?

Establishing consent

You will carry out many activities in your role as a lead adult care worker for which you will need consent. You will also need to lead and support others in this role.

- Make a list of the activities that you carry out in your workplace where you need to gain consent.

Some activities might be more life affecting, such as whether the individual consents to taking medication, while others are less life changing, such as assisting the individual with personal hygiene.

- Explain how you gain consent to undertake the various activities.

Sometimes it can be difficult to gain consent; for example, the individual might have communication or memory difficulties, or physical or mental health problems.

- How would you establish consent for day-to-day activities?

Supporting junior staff

As part of your role as a lead adult care worker, you may guide junior staff in how to carry out the tasks that they are required to do. You are updating the induction teaching materials and want to create some 'true' and 'false' flash cards to help junior staff learn about informed consent.

Use the example below as a guide and create 10 more cards: five true statements and five false.

On one side write the statement and on the other the correct answer (true or false).

Try to link your statements to examples that could relate to your workplace.

The following are examples of appropriate consent:

The person nods when you ask if you can help them to take off their soiled jumper and replace it with a clean one	TRUE
The care worker sensitively explains that she will help the individual to eat their breakfast	FALSE

Practice for professional discussion

Prepare for a 10-minute professional discussion on the issue of consent.

You may wish to consider:

- what you understand about informed consent
- the different factors and circumstances that could influence an individual's ability to express consent.

If an individual refused to give consent for an activity that you consider important, for example, taking vital medication such as. In your role as a lead adult care worker, what would you do and why?

Care plans and changing needs

Care plans have to be monitored and reviewed within specific times and it might be your responsibility to make sure that this happens. If the needs of an individual change, you must make sure that the care plan is updated to reflect the changes in their preferences and needs.

Qualification mapping

Unit 7 LO 2 AC 2.3, LO 4 AC 4.1, 4.2, 4.3, 4.4, LO 5 AC 5.1, 5.2 and 5.4

Monitor and review

Care plans are formally reviewed within the first three months and then at least once per year. This does not mean that the care plan is not altered until the next review; it is a working document. But much can happen in a year so, as a lead adult care worker or key worker, it may be your responsibility to monitor or check the plan regularly and update it in response to any changing needs. It may also be your responsibility to prepare for the formal review.

The review is a formal assessment of how the plan is working. It looks in detail at the care plan with those involved in meeting the individual's needs. Each part will be assessed to consider what is working well and what is working less well. Person-centred values must be applied at all times so that the individual is at the centre of the process. For example, their rights, dignity and independence should be respected as you work in partnership with others to meet the individual's holistic needs.

Suggestions and adjustments to the care plan will be made that are based on the result of the discussions. Whatever the outcome, it is crucial that the user of the service knows what they are agreeing to; that is where your presence is valuable because you will have built a trusting relationship with them.

Professional working

Junior members of the team may be responsible for documenting the care and support they give to the individual on a day-to-day basis. Make a point of letting others know how important the accuracy of their records and reporting are so that you can ensure the care plan fully meets its purpose.

Does the plan still meet the individual's needs?

It is important to monitor the care plan and check that it still meets the needs of the individual. An individual's health or circumstances can change and the care plan should reflect any changes. Similarly, 'one-page profiles' can change; for example, an individual might have developed a new interest. The user of the service must always be at the centre of the monitoring process but other individuals are also likely to be involved. It may be your responsibility to organise and facilitate the review meeting. This includes the practical requirements, such as letting individuals know when and where it will take place.

Involving key people

The review meeting will involve: the user of the service; family, friends or carers; health care professionals; social workers and key workers.

As a lead adult care worker, you are likely to have regular direct contact with the individual and are more likely to be the one to know if the plan will meet their needs or to see significant changes, such as those shown in Figure 18.

Professional working

Do not ignore or treat lightly any concerns that the individual may have. Take them seriously; refer them to the right people and always update records.

6Cs

Care, committment

Qualification mapping

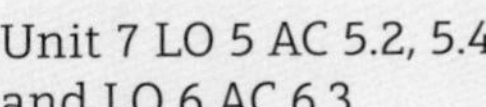

Unit 7 LO 5 AC 5.2, 5.4 and LO 6 AC 6.3

Summary

An individual's situation and needs can change, so the care plan must be regularly monitored and reviewed in order to reflect their current needs. The lead adult care worker may have the responsibility to check the care plan regularly. A formal review will take place at which the individual and those involved in their care will assess the plan and make changes as necessary.

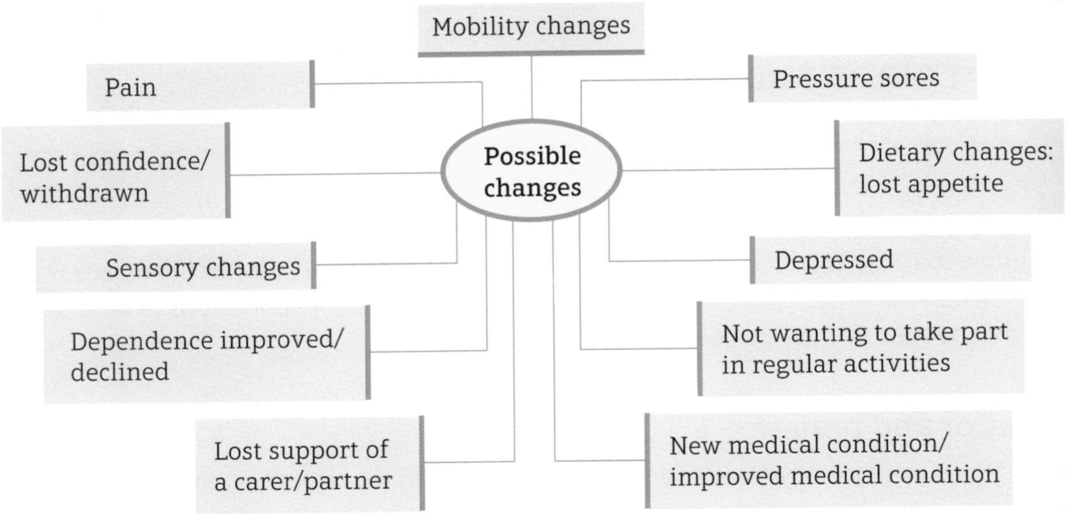

Possible changes:

- Mobility changes
- Pain
- Pressure sores
- Lost confidence/ withdrawn
- Dietary changes: lost appetite
- Sensory changes
- Depressed
- Dependence improved/ declined
- Not wanting to take part in regular activities
- Lost support of a carer/partner
- New medical condition/ improved medical condition

Figure 18: Examples of changes in the individual that you might notice

The review meeting

Encourage the individual to be actively involved and try to ensure that the environment encourages active participation. It can feel overwhelming for the individual, even if you have done your best to ensure a relaxed atmosphere. Nevertheless, the individual should feel comfortable with you and tell you if they are not happy about any decisions that are made, even if this happens after the review.

Tips for a successful review meeting

You can help to ensure a successful review meeting by observing the following points:

- Ensure that everyone has been informed about the meeting.
- Arrange a suitable venue that will encourage active participation. The individual might prefer a relaxed, informal and comfortable arrangement.
- Prepare all the information that you need beforehand; this is especially important if a key individual cannot attend.
- Gain consent from the individual for those present to contribute and to be able to share information.
- Support the user of the service to feel comfortable in making a direct contribution to the meeting.
- Accurately record the activity of the meeting and the outcomes.
- Share information with those involved after the review meeting has taken place.

Keep records up to date

The care plan will be adjusted after the review meeting, so that it reflects the current needs of the individual, as well as any further goals or actions. Care-planning documents will differ between services so become familiar with those that are used in your organisation. Some may be electronic.

Remember that all goals must be SMART: Specific, Measurable, Achievable, Relevant and Timely.

Offering information and respecting choice

An important part of your role as a lead adult care worker is to provide individuals with information and to respect their choices. If users of service are offered information on the support and care available, it means they can make choices about how they are supported.

Qualification mapping

Unit 3 LO 2 AC 2.2, Unit 7 LO 1 AC 1.2, LO 2 AC 2.2, LO 4 AC 4.1, 4.3, LO 5 AC 5.1, LO 6 AC 6.3

Activities

Care plan assessment

How accurate are the care plans that you are responsible for? And how closely do they reflect what the individual wants?

If you work for a large organisation, try 'peer assessing' each other's care plans. This involves two professionals looking at each other's care plans and noting how well they reflect the needs of the individual and what could be more detailed or made clearer. However, you must get permission beforehand.

Peer assessing is a good way for you both to build your care-planning skills. You can learn a lot when looking at how other people do things.

If you do not have the opportunity to peer assess, ask your supervisor to give you feedback on how clear and detailed your care plans are. You could use the feedback that you receive to help with your self-assessment for your appraisal and personal development plan.

Checking for choice in how individuals are supported

You are the lead adult care worker for Tess, who has learning difficulties and lives at home with her mum. Tess would like to do a vocational course at college but is not sure what she should do. She has asked you to help her because she feels that you know her well.

Create a mind map on the information Tess will need to help her decide what course to apply for.

Explain how you will be able to support her, for example:

- to investigate what courses she can apply for
- to check on the college website and direct her to book an appointment with the careers advisor.

How could you ensure that Tess has sufficient information so that she can make the right choices for herself?

How would you support Tess to be actively involved at each stage?

What is her mother's role in all this?

Think about the different support Tess might need; for example, what about transport to college?

How about the other people in her life who might need to be involved for practical reasons?

▶ Supporting individuals in their choices

Darius has a terminal illness and is giving some thought to his plans for when he reaches the end of his life. Darius was a keen biker and still has his motorcycle clothing, leather jacket, gloves etc. He has expressed to you that when he dies he does not want to stay in the funeral home but wants to be returned home dressed in his motorcycle clothing prior to his funeral. Darius wants his friends and family to see him in his home where he has had a happy life. You are his lead adult care worker.

- What information do you think Darius should have so that he can make choices about the funeral he would like?
- Is there any information you will need so that you can effectively support Darius?
- How could you help Darius to actively participate in planning his own funeral?

▶ Finding information for decision making

You are the lead adult care worker and provide support to Devika. She is 82 and lives independently but has no close family. Devika has decided that sheltered housing would be better for her now. There are a few options in the city where she lives as well as some in rural locations. There is a lot for her to think about.

Devika has asked you to help her move forward as she doesn't know where to start.

- What information do you think that Devika needs to help her make the right choice?
- Is there any information that you could provide or direct Devika to that would help with her decision?
- Moving home is a big decision. How will you make sure that Devika is involved every step of the way?

▶ Enabling and respecting choices

Individuals who have issues with addiction can sometimes believe that they will never be able to live a normal life again. Their family and friends are often desperate to free them of their addiction and may make well- meaning comments such as the following:

However, such attitudes can make the individual feel overwhelmed and angry. Their response might be, 'This is my life and I will live it how I choose'. A skilled lead adult care worker will have a different approach. They will give information to enable choice and to support the individual to be actively involved in how they wish to be supported to live with or recover from their addiction.

Imagine you are a lead adult care worker and work in a service that supports individuals with addictions. You want users of the service to know they will be given accurate and helpful information so that they can make choices about how they want to be supported and how they can take an active role in their care.

You have decided to create a poster that will be helpful to individuals who use the service and also to new and junior members of staff.

You could include the following on your poster:

- a range of information to help users of the service make choices about how they want to be supported
- guidance on how information would be given; for example, face to face and useful phone applications
- reasons why your organisation believes that individual choice is important
- examples of how users of the service are actively involved in their own support plans.

You could adapt your poster to a subject area closer to the sector or organisation that you work in.

Practice for professional discussion

Prepare for a 10-minute professional discussion on how you promote choice to users of your service.

You could consider the following points:

- Why you must respect individual's choices on their care and support.
- Discuss examples (without using names) from your own workplace practice on information that you have given to individuals so that they can make informed choices about how they wish to be supported.
- Assess the effectiveness of your organisation in respecting the choices of all users of the service.
- Evaluate your own practice in relation to respecting choices that individuals make.

Situational judgement questions

1. You are key worker to an individual and must contribute to the assessment of an individual's spiritual needs. Which areas will you consider?
   a. What the individual likes to do socially
   b. What makes the person feel at peace with themselves
   c. Their mood and behaviour
   d. If they are they depressed
2. You have been asked to organise an activity for users of the service. It is outside your normal duties and something that you have not done before but it is within your job role. What do you do?
   a. Tell your manager that, as you haven't done this before, you don't feel that you can do it
   b. Use the skills that you already have to help you to carry out the activity
   c. Ask someone who has done the activity to do it and complete a task for them
   d. Suggest that it would be a good learning opportunity for a junior member of staff to do
3. You work in a domiciliary setting and an individual says she is starting to struggle with walking because she has an arthritic knee. She thinks that a walking aid would help. There is a walking stick in her garage. It was her father's stick and she says he was a similar height to her. Do you:
   a. Check the walking stick is in good order, clean it and give it to her?
   b. Suggest that you both look online for a new walking aid?
   c. Advise that you refer her to a specialist to assess her for a mobility aid?
   d. Signpost her to an osteopath who might be able to help?
4. You have organised a formal review of an individual's care plan; it is in a week's time. Today, the individual's health needs have changed. What should you do?
   a. Make a note in your diary to invite the GP to the review meeting
   b. Wait to discuss the health needs in depth next week at the meeting
   c. Re-assess their current needs and update the care plan
   d. Ask your manager to speak to the GP
5. A junior care worker is having difficulty establishing consent to enable her to help an individual with their personal hygiene. They simply refuse. What initial advice would you give?
   a. Suggest they ask in a different way and if the individual still won't consent, leave them for a little while and return later to ask again
   b. Ask the manager to have a word with the user of the service
   c. Contact the next of kin
   d. Accept that they do not want to have their personal hygiene attended to and leave them alone
6. A junior colleague is raising money for a local charity. She tells users of the service about the charity and her social media page, where they can donate electronically if they wish. What do you do?
   a. Congratulate her on her efforts and donate yourself
   b. Help users of the service to access her social media page to donate if they wish
   c. Arrange for local media to be involved to raise awareness of the good cause
   d. Congratulate her on her efforts but explain that she cannot allow users of the service to access her personal social media site
7. A new procedure has been agreed following a complex change in the law. Individuals in your workplace need to know how the changes will affect their work. You have been asked to ensure that all staff understand the new procedure. Do you:
   a. Print a copy of the law and related amendments and give each person a copy of the new procedure?
   b. Arrange a training session and summarise the key points, linked to situations they may face at work; create training materials that are concise and clear on the procedure?
   c. Arrange for an expert in the law to come in and deliver training?
   d. Add a target on each individual's personal development plan to research information about the law and the changes?

B

Values and behaviours

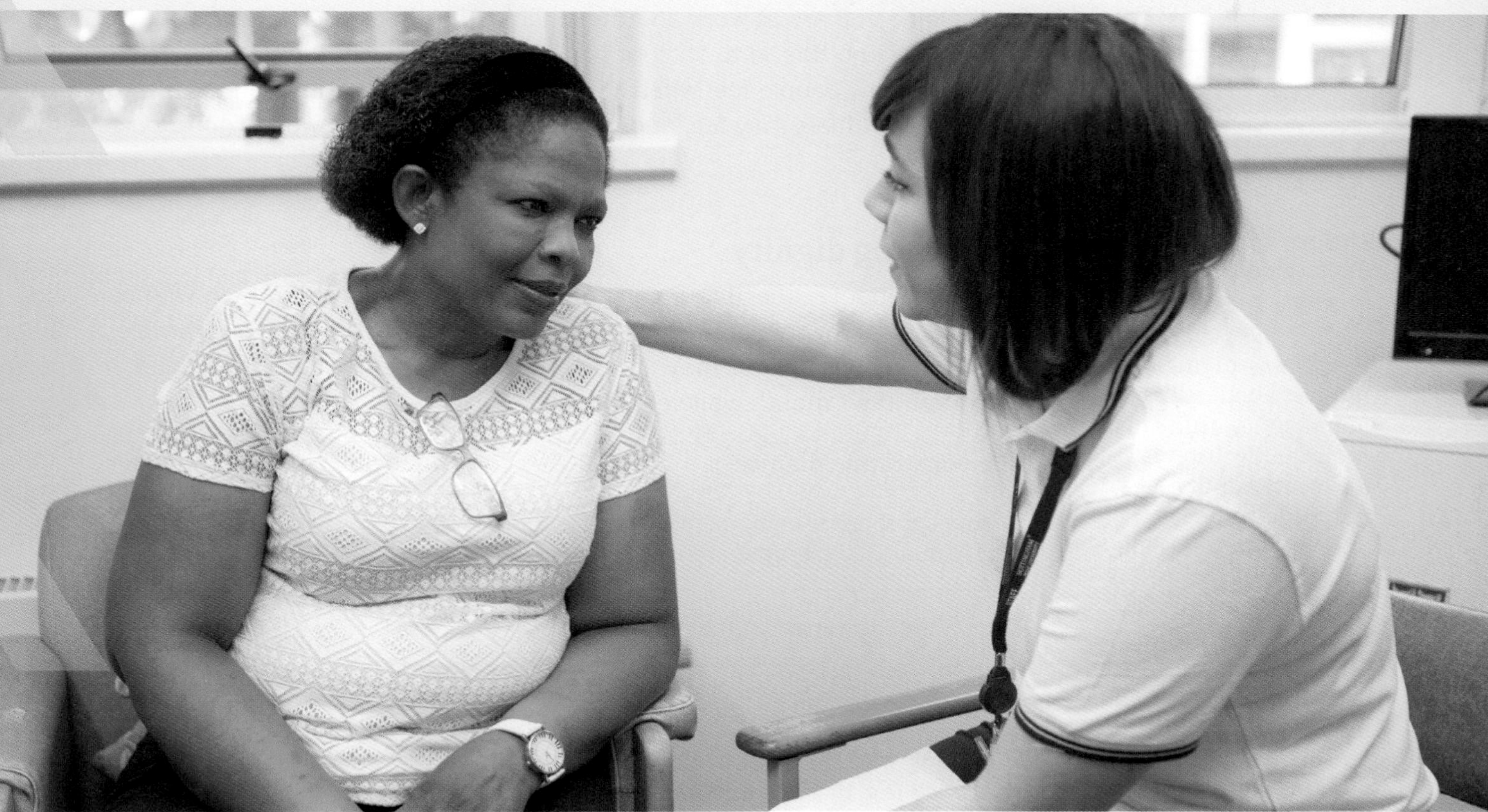

How would you feel?

In your role as a lead adult care worker you will be working with individuals who are likely to be some of the most vulnerable in society. They will be experiencing sensitive, difficult and embarrassing situations, often on a daily basis. Putting yourself in their shoes and thinking about how you would feel in their situation will help you to support individuals and guide other adult care workers to be caring and compassionate in their work.

This topic will cover the following areas:

- the importance of dignity
- respecting diversity, the principles of inclusion and treating people fairly
- how to be empathetic in your practice
- how you can demonstrate courage and challenge your own cultural and belief systems.

You will also learn about the skills you will need so that you can apply this knowledge in the care setting where you work.

What is dignity?

Imagine you are at work and the stitching has become loose on your trousers; you have no thread to stitch it back together and you have a long shift to work. This is how people feel when they lose their dignity. You need to be aware of how individuals may feel and support others who you work with to be sensitive as well.

Professional working

Respecting dignity is not just about users of your service: think about their family, friends, **advocates** and others, not forgetting visitors to your setting. You should extend your sensitivity and care to everyone, including colleagues you work with. As a lead adult care worker, you should model good practice and challenge any poor practice that you see.

Key term

Advocate – someone who will act in the best interest of the individual

Respect your colleagues and value their work

Respecting dignity

Dignity is about respecting a person's self-worth and treating them with care and respect. Some people are unable to protect their own dignity. For example, a person with physical disabilities may not be able to take themselves to the toilet or wipe spil food from their mouth while eating.

Demonstrating dignity	Not demonstrating dignity
Using appropriate equipment for the individual - for example, adult feeding utensils	Using, for example, children's feeder cups and bibs instead of age-appropriate equipment that has been adapted
Involving the person in their own care	Not discussing with a person what their care will be
Helping the person go to a toilet/bathroom	Telling the person they should use a bed pan or incontinence pad
Checking with the person what they like to be called (e.g. by their first name, by their last name or any other name they suggest)	Calling a person 'love', 'darling' or 'dear'; or assuming it is fine to use their first name without their permission
Giving the person the time they need	Rushing a person
Making the person feel valued	Making the person feel they are being a nuisance

Table 1: Demonstrating dignity versus not demonstrating dignity

There are other ways to demonstrate dignity and respect towards people:

- Don't talk in a childlike way to adults.
- Use professional language and speak quietly when discussing personal things so that others cannot overhear.
- Keep information about individuals secure and do not gossip; always maintain confidentiality.
- Involve the person in decision making as well as any others that the individual wants to be involved.
- Include the individual in conversations; do not ignore them.
- Respect your colleagues: be a good role model, value their work and opinions.

Case study: Respecting Ana's dignity

Ana is in a hospice and receiving palliative care. Recently she has had chemotherapy treatment which resulted in loss of hair. Ana has worn a wig since her hair loss. She had always been particular about her appearance.

Ana is now nearing the last days of her life. She is very sleepy and unable to communicate. Justine, a lead adult care worker, is with a junior colleague who is supporting Ana with her personal care. Justine washes Ana with care and respect, keeping her body covered as much as possible. She cleans Ana's teeth, dresses her in clean clothes, fits her wig and gives her a hand massage; she also paints her finger nails. Before they leave the room, Justine puts on a piece of Ana's favourite music. Justine makes a point of explaining to her junior colleague about why it is so important to respect a person's dignity. Justine is a good role model and guides others who she works with to support individuals in a dignified way.

- How does Justine respect Ana's dignity?
- How could you respect an individual's dignity and support others to do so as well?

Figure 1: Adult care workers must show respect to all individuals – here they are not modelling good practice or showing respect because they are talking over the individual and not including her.

Think about how you would feel

No matter what the person's circumstances, for example, if a person cannot go to the toilet or feed themselves independently, it is a key task to protect their dignity and to be sensitive to their needs. Always support the individual in a caring and kind way, and remember that others who you work with and support might need some guidance in how to work in a way that respects dignity. If you notice that others are not respecting a person's dignity, such as the situation shown in Figure 1, it is up to you to challenge the situation; remember, users of your service may not be able to speak up for themselves.

Case study: Jazmin

Jazmin is a lead adult care worker and is a mentor to Julia. Julia mentions that she noticed some colleagues telling individuals to use their pads to urinate in instead of offering to take them to the toilet. Julia is new to care work and was not sure if this was OK or not. Jazmin explained to Julia that it's not OK because it is important to help individuals to use toilet facilities where possible as it is more dignified. Jazmin used the opportunity at the staff meeting the next day to raise awareness of dignity and will keep an eye on practice.

- How would you feel if you were the user of the service?
- How do you think you would have reacted in this situation?
- Why was it wrong to tell users of the service to use their pads instead of helping them to the toilet?
- How else could Julia have raised awareness around the importance of dignity to other members of the team?

6Cs

Care, compassion

Summary

Dignity is about supporting people with respect. Think about how you would like to be treated if you were in a sensitive or embarrassing situation. Remember that as a lead adult care worker you should be a good role model to your colleagues.

Demonstrate dignity

Respecting dignity involves not just users of your service but also their family, friends and visitors to your setting. You should demonstrate dignity and sensitivity to everyone, including your colleagues. As a lead adult care worker, you should model good practice to junior staff.

Activities

Qualification mapping

Unit 2 LO 2 AC 2.2, Unit 3 LO 2 AC 2.2

Respecting the dignity of different individuals

Respecting dignity is not just about how you support the user of the service. Lead adult care workers should model good practice and respect the dignity of individuals of all ages, backgrounds and abilities.

Complete the table below by giving two examples of how you would treat each person with dignity.

User of service	How would you demonstrate dignity to each individual?
Jake is 19 years old and suffers from anxiety and depression. At times, he gets very angry.	
Martine is 25; she is homeless and injects heroin.	
Cliff is 85 and has had a stroke; he can't communicate or look after his own personal hygiene. His daughter is his advocate.	
Cally is 30; she has bipolar disorder and her moods are unpredictable.	
A junior colleague comes to work with worn shoes and greasy hair. Other members staff avoid her and say that she smells.	

Table 2: How would you demonstrate dignity?

Ensuring dignity for Rafa

Rafa is a new user of your service. His family are worried about him accessing social care services because of some things they have read in the media about individuals not being treated with dignity and respect.

One of Rafa's relatives asks you how you treat users of your service in a dignified and respectful way, and how you would ensure other workers did too.

Make notes about what you would say.

Respecting dignity – reflection

Sometimes it is difficult to demonstrate dignity; for example, if a person who has dementia tries to get undressed in public, or an individual chooses to wear soiled clothing and not wash or bathe despite being encouraged to do so. It can be challenging to manage these situations. You need to have good communication skills and demonstrate empathy and compassion.

Think about a time when you found it difficult to preserve a person's dignity and use Kolb's reflective cycle (see page v) to reflect on the situation. Reflection can help you to think about how and why you do things; it can also help you to be more professional in your approach to situations at work.

Link 

Topic C: The importance of communication and Topic F: Professional working and professional development

Identifying strengths and areas to develop

Lead adult care workers regularly reflect on how they respond to situations. Reflection helps you to learn from experiences and improve how you work. It is important to be really honest with yourself and remember that no one is perfect.

Use the information from the activities in this section and the Kolb reflective cycle to identify your strengths and areas that you need to work on when treating people with dignity. Remember to include the following: users of the service, their family, friends and your colleagues.

Strengths	Areas that I need to develop
What can I do to help to develop my skills in supporting people with dignity?	

6Cs 

Competence, care, compassion

Practice for professional discussion

As a lead adult care worker you must actively demonstrate dignity and respect to users of your service and the colleagues who you work with. Having a good understanding of the 6Cs can help.

Prepare notes for a 10-minute professional discussion on respecting dignity and the 6Cs.

- What do you understand about the 6Cs?
- Give examples of how you have applied the 6Cs in your role as a lead adult care worker. (You could refer to witness testimonies that you have or self-reflective accounts.)
- Think about a time when you believe that a person was not treated with respect.
- Reflect on how you as a lead adult care worker dealt with the situation and justify your actions.
- Assess and evaluate your performance.

Empathy and dignity

6Cs

Care, compassion

Empathy is about putting yourself in other people's situations and will help you to support individuals with dignity. Putting yourself in this mind set will help you to demonstrate and feel empathy for them.

Key term

Empathy – ability to understand and share the feelings and emotions of someone else

Empathy

When supporting an individual you should think about how you would feel in the same situation. **Empathy** is shown not just in words, but through your body language. The way you present yourself reveals more about you than what you say or do. About 90 per cent of a person's emotions are shown non-verbally so you need to have a good self-awareness of how you come across.

Look at the examples below and try to imagine how the individuals feel.

Kira	Josie
Kira has complex needs. You have just helped her with hygiene. Kira has an upset stomach. You have just helped her to settle into a chair to rest when she is incontinent of faeces. This is the second time this morning that Kira has not made it to the toilet.	Josie is an adult care worker in your organisation. You have changed over from written records to computer-based ones. You have shown Josie several times how to use the technology but she is finding it difficult. Josie tells you that when she was using the system something happened and the whole system has shut down. You think it's something that Josie has done.

As a lead adult care worker you will be able to support Kira and Josie. But it is not just your actions that are important but how you come across as a person. You need to be kind and compassionate to show that you are sincere and really care. It can be difficult when you are under pressure, especially when you are really busy at work, but it is one of the most important skills to develop. You can have a kind, caring manner and still be efficient at your job. If you show impatience and annoyance, you will break down the valuable relationships that you have built with service users and colleagues.

What would happen if you didn't show empathy towards Kira and Josie?

Kira would probably feel embarrassed and anxious in case it happened again; if it did, she might not tell anyone and she could develop painful sores on her skin. Kira may become scared of you and your potential future reactions. It is likely that she would prefer someone else to support her in future.

Josie may feel useless and concerned that she cannot do her job properly. She may feel worried about carrying out new tasks in case she made a mistake; this could then lead to anxiety and stress for fear of getting things wrong. She may prefer to not work with you. Josie may cover up any future mistakes which could put users of the service and the organisation at risk.

Tragic life events

At some point in life everyone is likely to be faced with tragic events; for example, bereavement, serious illness, relationship breakdown, job loss or financial problems. For the individual feeling such emotional pain, it can sometimes seem impossible to bear and they cannot believe that anyone else could understand how they feel. They are probably right; you will not fully understand how the person feels but you can do your best to imagine how difficult it is for them and support them in a way that shows you really care. This is being empathetic and compassionate.

Can you learn to have empathy?

Everyone has a different personality; some people seem to be naturally more patient and understanding than others. Life experiences can sometimes make you more understanding and empathetic because you know how you felt in that situation. However, you do not need to have experienced what individuals are going through in order to have empathy; you can work on developing empathetic skills. You can do this by:

- understanding why empathy is so important
- observing other people who have effective empathetic skills
- reflecting on your own practice
- practising your skills.

6Cs

Communication, care, compassion

Compassionate care

The Francis Report in 2013 exposed poor practice in a hospital that needed to change because the caring focus had been lost. A plan was put together for all health and social care staff to work in a kind and caring way; this is known as compassionate care.

How to show that you really care

- Be patient
- Show sensitivity
- Be understanding
- Actively listen
- Have a positive outlook
- Be encouraging
- Have genuine concern for other people

You should actively seek feedback from users of the service (see Figure 2), as well as feedback from staff, for example, during appraisals or if they leave employment.

Figure 2: These individuals have given feedback about their experiences with compassion and empathy

The feedback in Figure 3 is about the kindness that has been shown to the person rather than the physical activities. It cannot be underestimated how important these kind and caring behaviours are. What might people say about you?

Summary 

Everyone sometimes has to face difficult situations and circumstances in their lives – as will users of your service. Try to think how you would feel in their situation and be understanding. Being empathetic will maintain the trusting and caring relationship that you have both taken time to build.

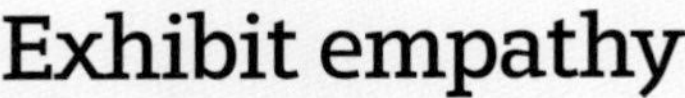

Exhibit empathy

You must be able to feel and demonstrate empathy for the individuals you support, displaying your understanding and compassion.

Activities

How empathetic are you?

How empathetic are you? Look at the questions below and choose answer A or B to best describe how you feel in different situations.

A	B
It bothers me when other people feel upset about something.	I never let other people's misfortunes bother me. I prefer to keep a distance.
I hate to see people being treated unfairly.	It's a fact of life that we all experience times where we are treated unfairly.
I like to try to help people feel better about themselves.	It's the responsibility of each individual to take control of their own happiness.
When someone is upset, I give time to let them talk.	If a person is upset I change the subject to something else. I don't like to get too involved with emotions.
I am good at picking up on other people's moods, for example, if they are sad.	I try not to look too deeply at people's moods; they can bring on conversations that I would rather not have.
I feel concern for people even if their actions have led to their situations, for example, if a heavy smoker develops lung cancer.	I have little time for people who bring on their own illnesses, for example, those who smoke or abuse alcohol.
When a colleague is absent from work because of personal difficulties, I hope that they are OK.	I become quite irritated when colleagues are absent because of personal difficulties; they need to develop more resilience.
When a colleague gets upset and cries, I try to comfort them.	If a colleague is upset and cries, I try to direct them to someone else.
I have concern about how other people feel.	I prefer not to get involved with other people and their emotions.
I can understand when a person cries at a happy event.	Crying when you are happy is not natural.

How did you do?

If you chose mostly A, you are very empathetic. You are in tune with other people's emotions and want to help and support them.

If you chose mostly B, you have lower levels of empathy. Try to take time to think about how you would feel if you were faced with situations that others are experiencing and see things from their perspective.

Receiving care

Imagine you have just been given some bad news. How would you like the people around you to show that they empathise and care for you in your trouble? Complete the mind map below to show how you would like others to show that they empathise and care for you.

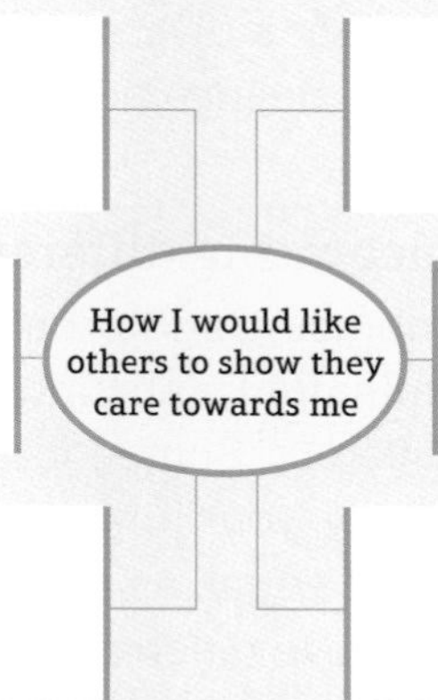

Showing understanding and compassion

Elda is a user of your service. Her partner died some years ago and she has no family other than her two sons, who she adores. Elda developed a condition recently that meant she needs support with physical needs. As her lead adult care worker you have developed a good working relationship with Elda.

However, Elda's son Jake struggled with his mental health for some years. Despite good care from his doctor and psychiatrist, Jake's mental state became unstable and last week he took his own life. When you visit Elda, she is completely distraught.

- Explain how you could show empathy towards Elda. (You should refer to the 6Cs.)
- If you did not demonstrate empathy towards Elda, explain what effect it could have on your relationship and why.

Witness statement

In your work, you will support individuals who are experiencing all sorts of different challenges in their life. You may supervise work colleagues who are going through difficulties such as a relationship breakdown or bereavement. If you have a caring and empathetic nature, it can make all the difference to the person who is going through a tough time.

Ask a colleague to write a witness statement that shows how you have exhibited empathy towards an individual while they have been going through a difficult time.

Reflection on being empathetic

Think of a time when you have been empathetic towards an individual at work; for example, an individual's much-loved cat or dog has died and they are very upset. Alternatively, perhaps a colleague's relationship has broken down and they are unhappy (even though you might think it is positive because the relationship was an abusive one) or a user of your service was incontinent in front of several people.

Using the Kolb reflective cycle (see page v) complete a self-reflective account and discuss what you have reflected upon with your mentor or assessor.

Respecting diversity

Qualification mapping 

Unit 3 LO1 AC 1.1

Everyone is different and the people you support will all be different too. Diversity makes society more interesting. A lead adult care worker will value and embrace the opportunities that a diverse society brings and actively promote the right for everyone to be included and treated fairly.

Key terms 

Diversity – recognising differences and that each individual is unique

Equality – providing everyone with equal opportunities and chances, for example, access to services

Inclusion – placing individuals at the centre of planning and support, regardless of their circumstances or background

Discrimination – treating an individual unfairly or less well because they are different

Treating people fairly and celebrating differences

Treating people fairly is about embracing and promoting **diversity**, **equality**, **inclusion** and challenging **discrimination** – ensuring that no one is treated unfavourably because they are different. Some individuals may not be able to speak up for themselves. Additionally, your junior colleagues may not understand how to work in a way that is fair and equal. As a lead adult care worker, you must model good practice and make positive differences to people's lives. You should set a good example to others and always challenge negative behaviours. Equality and inclusion means treating people fairly regardless of any differences in background or circumstances, and providing everyone with equal opportunities and chances; for example, enabling equal access to services and facilities.

Diversity is about differences, as shown in Figure 3. We are fortunate to live in a society that is very diverse, where each person has their own valued identity. Take an interest in people: recognise the value of differences in society and encourage others to do so as well. Respect and embrace difference; as a lead adult care worker you should never pre-judge an individual's capability based on their gender, age, race or ability or disability.

I like to socialise and have a glass of wine with friends sometimes

I don't like alcohol, because I think that it's harmful to my body

I would never go out without my make-up applied

I don't care for make up, I prefer to look more natural and let my skin breathe

My best holiday would be an all-inclusive resort abroad

I like to go camping in the UK

I follow my religion and worship regularly

I don't believe in any religion

I value my health and will do what I can to be healthy

I live for today and don't worry too much about the future

Figure 3: See how different we all are

These adult care workers are supporting this individual with his future goals and dreams and demonstrating inclusive practice

Our diverse society

To work in a way that includes everyone, you do not need to be an expert and know everything about different beliefs and cultures, but it is respectful to show an interest and try to find out more. In our society we promote the value of diversity and welcome the richness that it brings. You should do your best to make sure that everyone feels valued and included, and help to remove any barriers or difficulties that individuals might face; for example, by respecting specific dietary and hygiene requirements. Some individuals have specific worship and care preferences too. Ask the person what their preferences are. Do not presume that if a person says they have a particular belief they will follow all aspects of it at all times: it is always important to check first with the individual.

Put the person at the centre of all that you do

For each person that you support, treat them as a unique and valued individual, no matter what their abilities or circumstances are. They are an equal member of society; your care and support should reflect this. If your role involves supervising others, ensure that they too help individuals in a way that promotes inclusion for everyone. By doing so yourself, you will be a good role model to others.

Professional working

Sometimes the small things can make a positive difference; for example, making sure that notices are at a level that everyone can see – remember that wheelchair users could miss out on events if notices are too high. Also, think about the language that is used; can everyone understand what is written? Being inclusive in all aspects of your practice, and supporting others to do so, will show that you value individuals and promote and welcome diversity.

Help everyone to join in

Inclusion is about enabling everyone to join in and not feel left out; for example, there are so many cultural celebrations, you could try to include some activities to raise awareness in your organisation. You could offer different national foods on the menu: a cooking activity is often popular. You could create displays and invite visiting speakers to share their knowledge and experience. If you have a community magazine, share what you do with the local residents.

Some local schools have connections with older people who have dementia and write to the children; adult care workers will help those who cannot write so that everyone can join in and share experiences. Activities like this are great for joining the community together.

As a lead adult care worker, you should always support individuals to participate in activities and enjoy the same privileges and experiences, regardless of their circumstances or background. You may face barriers but these can often be easily overcome with a little thought and forward planning.

Remember also to consider the needs of visitors to your organisation – the family and friends of users of your service. They must be included and might have their own specific needs as well.

6Cs

Care, compassion, commitment, communication

Summary

Everyone is different; it is what makes our society so interesting. Always respect differences and support others to do so as well. Treat people equally and work in a way that is inclusive to all. Sometimes simple actions and forward planning can easily reduce barriers.

Support others to understand inclusion

It is part of your role as a lead adult care worker to support others to understand the importance of inclusion in adult care work and to model good practice in all aspects of equality and diversity.

Activities

Qualification mapping

Unit 2 LO 2 AC 2.2, Unit 3 LO 1 AC 1.1, LO 2 AC 2.2, LO 3 AC 3.1 and 3.2

Promoting diversity in your setting

Imagine that you have had an enquiry from an individual who is looking for a service similar to yours for a close friend or relative. There has been some recent local media coverage about social care providers not respecting differences or being inclusive. You feel confident that your organisation fully embraces diversity and is inclusive to all users of the service.

Write an account that could be sent to the person who has made the enquiry about how you personally promote diversity and inclusiveness.

Finding positive qualities

When you work closely with individuals you can get to know each of them well. A useful skill is being able to identify the positive qualities that individuals have; for example, their different strengths. This is the start to valuing diversity.

Copy and complete the table below to give examples of positive qualities that you have identified in users of your service and staff that you supervise.

	Positive qualities
Individual 1 [user of the service]	
Individual 2 [user of the service]	
Individual 3 [staff member]	
Individual 4 [staff member]	

Table 3: Finding positive qualities in individuals and colleagues

Respecting differences

The individuals you support, their family members and those who you work with are all unique.

Copy and complete the table below with examples to show how you have worked in a way that respects differences; for example, in relation to their *beliefs, culture, values, abilities and preferences*.

Individual	How I have supported their beliefs, culture, values, abilities and preferences
User of the service	
Their family members or friends	
Colleagues	

Table 4: Respecting differences

Reflection and witness testimony

As a lead adult care worker, you will help to maintain the highest standards of work in your organisation. This includes promoting diversity, equality and inclusion. Colleagues, especially new and junior ones, will look up to you and observe how you work; you need to be a positive role model to others.

Discuss with your supervisor or mentor a recent event when you have modelled good practice by working in an inclusive way. Ask them to complete a witness testimony for you.

Before they give you the testimony, complete a self-reflective account using Kolb's model of reflection on page v.

Remember to maintain confidentiality and do not include names.

- What similarities are there between your testimony and the self-reflective account?
- Are there any differences?
- Are there any ways that you could improve how inclusively you work?

You will learn more about reflection in Topic F (Professional working and professional development).

6Cs 6Cs

Competence, care, communication

Supporting others at work with diversity and inclusion

When a new member of staff begins working in the adult care environment there can be a lot to learn. Respecting diversity and being inclusive is an important part of adult care work.

Create a resource pack with information that relates to your area of work to be used by a new member of staff to show how diversity, equality and inclusion are promoted in everyday work. You could include information and examples around personal hygiene, food and drink, dress, access to services, communication and choices.

Include web links where possible.

Include a section that asks the new staff member to give an example on how they have respected diversity and demonstrated inclusive practice, then prompt them to show it to their mentor or supervisor at their next meeting.

Discrimination and being treated fairly

Qualification mapping

Unit 3 LO 1 AC 1.1, and 1.2

Key terms

Prejudice – forming a negative opinion about someone before you even know them (for example, where the person lives, age, sexuality or job they do); there is no firm evidence around the prejudiced judgement

Stereotyping – negatively judging groups of people (for example, because of their race, culture, sexuality); all individuals of that group will then be viewed unfavourably and often offensively

Imagine how you would feel if you were not treated equally or fairly because you were different in some way. This is discrimination and it is wrong. The effects can be emotionally and physically damaging. You must never ignore or tolerate discrimination.

How discrimination can start

Discrimination can often start with individuals being **prejudiced** against others or **stereotyping** groups of people. An individual who is prejudiced and stereotypes often does so because of ignorance, it was how they were brought up, or the result of being influenced by those around them. But it can lead to people not being treated fairly.

Discrimination can begin with jokes about minority groups. Few people will challenge negative comments because they believe that the comment will do no harm and that more damage would be done by challenging it. Serious cases of discrimination usually start with small actions and what could be described as 'just a bit of fun'. There are many types of discrimination.

Case study: The Tuesday group

Mike is a lead adult care worker and supports individuals who have learning disabilities. Each Tuesday evening six of the residents like to visit the local pub and take part in a karaoke event. It is great fun for everyone involved and the owner of the pub provides snacks for them. A couple of the group make loud noises; they do not realise they are doing this. On the last visit, Mike and a junior care worker overheard a customer at the pub saying that he didn't think that it was right to have this group 'take over' and using very disrespectful language about the group.

Mike approached them and introduced himself politely. He explained why the six individuals liked visiting the pub and that they had a right to be there as well. Mike also said how taking part in the karaoke was a real highlight of their week. He explained that disrespectful comments and language is wrong. He then explained that one of the group had recently raised money for a local charity by organising his own karaoke event. The other customer was very apologetic, he simply did not see that the individuals had the right to the same opportunities as himself. Towards the end of the evening, he joined in with the Tuesday group and they had a great night.

- How was Mike a good role model to the junior care worker?
- What could have happened if Mike had not spoken up for the Tuesday group?
- Why do you think that the customer decided to join in the karaoke with the group?

Direct discrimination

Direct discrimination is deliberate. The person intends to treat an individual less favourably; for example, because they belong to minority group owing to their age, gender, sexuality or disability. An example of direct discrimination would be if a person was denied access to a service because of a disability they have or because of their sexuality. As a lead adult care worker you should be mindful not only of your own practice but that of others as well.

Institutional discrimination

Institutional discrimination is where an organisation mistreats or denies a person or groups of individuals access to their services. The discrimination is usually due to the organisation's policies and procedures.

Case study: Abbey Hall Nursing Home

Mrs Craig is finding it hard living at home. It has been suggested that a nursing home would be a good option to consider. Mrs Craig and her daughter make an appointment with the manager at Abbey Hall to discuss the possibility of moving into an available room. Towards the end of the meeting, the manager says that she cannot offer Mrs Craig a room despite them advertising that they provide for individuals with needs such as Mrs Craig's and even though they have available rooms.

Abbey Hall tends to offer their services to individuals who are fit and self-caring, rather than those such as Mrs Craig who need more support and resources.

- What kind of discrimination is Mrs Craig being subject to?
- Explain how the manager of Abbey Hall is being discriminatory to Mrs Craig.
- Imagine if you were Mrs Craig's lead adult care worker and accompanied her on the visit to Abbey Hall. How would you have responded to the manager's comments?

Indirect discrimination

Discrimination can also be indirect, which means that it is not intentional or obvious. It is often not recognised. It can happen when a working practice is applied equally but creates a disadvantage to those in a minority group.

Users of your service may experience indirect discrimination; for example, you may encourage an individual to be independent when shopping but they do not yet feel confident with technology and there are no cashier checkouts, only self-service electronic ones. As an adult lead care worker you need to be mindful and vigilant of others who you work with; are they discriminating? For example, do they fully include everyone in activities and events or choose not to involve those who are more challenging to support? You may need to remind them about their responsibilities around inclusiveness and tell them not to discriminate.

Figure 4: Gender-neutral facilities are less discriminating

Professional working

Materials in your workplace, such as your service user handbooks, should show minority groups in a positive way and represent the different cross-sections of society; otherwise your service may appear discriminating to some people and create a barrier to access.

Professional working

The Code of Conduct for healthcare support workers and adult social care workers in England states that you must not discriminate or condone discrimination against people who use health and care services, their carers and your colleagues, and any concerns must be reported as soon as possible.

Discrimination is damaging to everyone

The effects of discrimination are usually very damaging, both physically and mentally, and can be long lasting. Discrimination not only affects the victim; it can affect others as well, such as their family and friends. When discrimination occurs in the workplace it can affect those who work there, the mood of the team, the reputation of the organisation and work efficiency.

Look at these examples of the damaging effects of discrimination on different individuals.

Qualification mapping

Unit 3 LO 1 AC 1.3

Sabil: belongs to a minority faith group and is resident in a care home; Sabil is hearing impaired. There has been media coverage lately about fatal violent attacks by extreme members who claim they belong to the same religious group as Sabil. Some residents and staff now view Sabil in a negative way and avoid him. Sabil feels isolated and lonely; he cannot sleep and has lost his appetite. He is feeling very stressed and anxious, and now his skin condition, psoriasis, has flared up due to the stress he is under. No one appears to care about how Sabil feels.

Helen: lives in a supported living complex; she has learning disabilities. She finds socialising difficult and sometimes shouts at other residents and staff. They have stopped including Helen in activities and this has resulted in her becoming more upset and angry. Helen often phones her mum in tears because she is so unhappy. Helen's mum, Sarah, is worried about her daughter and the worry is making her ill. Sarah has raised her concerns but is unable to sleep or eat properly. She has had to take time off work. Sarah is becoming depressed and the worry is causing problems between her and her partner.

Raymon: is an experienced lead adult care worker, aged 61. Recently a vacancy arose for a deputy manager's post. Raymon has the qualifications and experience as well as a good attendance and track record. He was not shortlisted for the job. A younger applicant with less experience was appointed. It appears that Raymon was discriminated against because of his age. Raymon's opportunities for progression have been taken away. He feels useless and angry about the situation. He decides not to be so reliable and committed to the job anymore as he does not feel valued.

Professional working

Social media is great for sharing information and keeping up to date with events but it can be damaging to some people when negative stereotyped comments and attitudes arise towards minority groups and are spread quickly across the internet. As a lead adult care worker and positive role model, you should not tolerate this. Support and protect users of the service and assist colleagues to do the same.

Summary

Discrimination often starts with what you may think of as harmless jokes and comments. Discrimination takes many forms and is damaging both mentally and physically.

Understanding the importance of inclusion

'Have you heard the one about ...?' Jokes are fun and laughter is good, but too many jokes often stereotype minority groups. Is it ok to laugh along with others? How does this fit with the importance of inclusion?

Activities

Identifying stereotypes

Look at the following statements and tick the box if you agree with the statement.

Older people are no good with technology	
People from Yorkshire are mean	
Blondes are not clever	
All black people are good at basketball	
Asians are really clever	
Women take a long time to get ready before going out	
Men are stronger than women	
Men are better at sports than women	
The Irish drink too much alcohol	
All Christians are homophobic	

All of the above statements are stereotypes. If you have ticked any, give some thought to why you have done so. It's important especially in social care not to stereotype individuals.

Qualification mapping

Unit 3 LO 1 AC 1.1

Pre-judging and prejudice

Do you pre-judge individuals? Take a moment to reflect on this and be honest with yourself.

Most of us would like to think that we don't but imagine you are in a supermarket and the person in front of you is very overweight. Their clothes are very tight and do not fit properly. You notice that their trolley is full of unhealthy food.

For a split second, do you make a judgement that the reason they are overweight is because of the food in their trolley? There is no evidence to suggest that the shopping is for them, it could be for an elderly relative who is disabled and cannot shop or cook for themselves. The individual shopping might have a valid medical reason for their size.

- Make a list of potential prejudices that individuals in your workplace might experience – think about both users of the service and your colleagues.
- Use your workplace policies and procedures, as well as advice from your mentor, and explain what you would do if you heard an individual making negative judgements about an individual you support.

Social media and discrimination

Social media can be a good tool for interaction and sharing information but it can also be used to spread views and attitudes that discriminate against others.

Note down four examples of how social media can be discriminating and harmful to individuals.

Check to see what your workplace policies say about social media and write a summary of the key points.

Social media is widely used but it can be discriminating and harmful to staff as well as to users of your service.

At your next staff meeting remind the team about your social media policy.

Qualification mapping

Unit 3 LO 1 AC 1.2, LO 3 AC 3.3

Discrimination at work

Lin has worked in your organisation for a few years as an adult care worker.

Lin is transgender and recently another member of staff discovered this by accident and has now told other workers as a piece of gossip.

- How could Lin be discriminated against?
- What could be the effects of discrimination on Lin?
- How do you think Lin might feel about this?
- How would you support her?

Professional working

Get into the habit of challenging your own personal prejudices and look for the evidence behind your thoughts before you make a judgement. An important part of your role is to support others to challenge their own prejudices too.

Promoting the rights of individuals

You do not need to be an expert in law but you should have a working knowledge of your code of conduct and relevant laws to make sure that you are doing your job properly and helping others to do so as well. This will give you the confidence to promote the right of individuals who need your support.

Qualification mapping

Unit 3 LO 2 AC 2.1

Code of Conduct for Healthcare Support Workers and Adult Care Workers

Your code of conduct says that you must respect individuality and diversity, not discriminate against anyone and promote equality. You must also promote the right to confidentiality and comply with your employer's agreed ways of working. You should always follow policies and procedures. You are accountable for your actions and omissions (what you fail to do). If you have any concerns, you must not ignore them; you may need to pass them on to someone more senior. If you are supervising others, make sure that they know about the code and how to work to it.

Laws that protect the rights of individuals

Laws are in place to protect people. You work with vulnerable individuals; many cannot speak up for themselves. Users of your service and junior colleagues may need your help to ensure that they are treated fairly and equally.

The laws that you will need to know about to promote equality, diversity and inclusion are outlined below; information has been summarised. You can access the full documents via www.legislation.gov.uk. Documents are often complicated but you can search for easy read versions for most legislation and these can be particularly useful to share with users of your service.

The Human Rights Act 1998

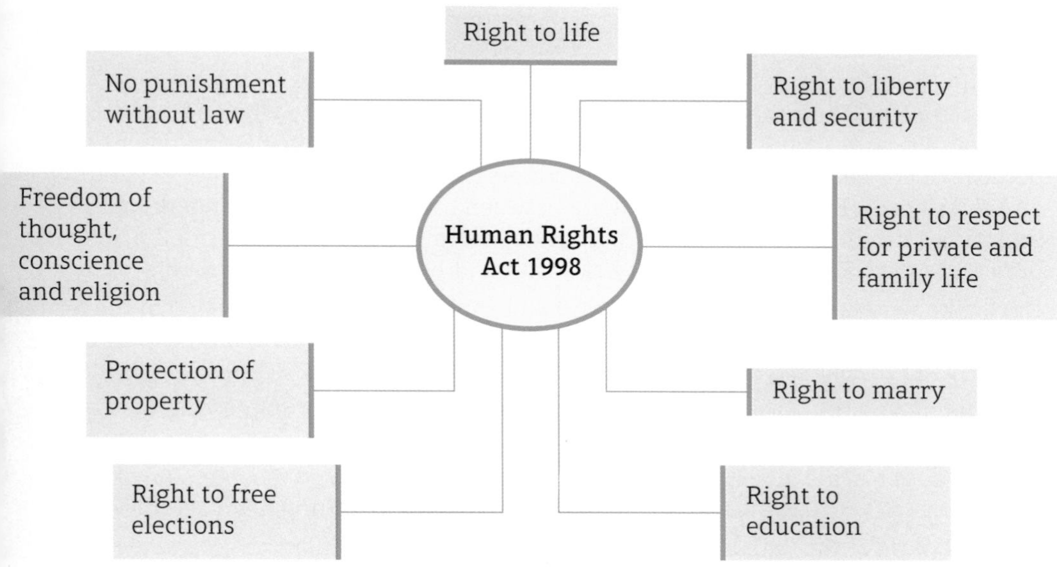

Figure 5: In the United Kingdom our basic human rights are protected by law

The Human Rights Act Article 2: Right to Life

Human life must be protected at all times. For example, an individual who is in an abusive and violent relationship is at risk of harm to their life and they must be protected. If you are a lead adult care worker supporting individuals who are at risk, you must take steps to follow procedures in order to protect them.

The Equality Act 2010

The Equality Act 2010 makes sure that everyone is treated fairly. The following groups are protected in law; they are known as protected characteristics:

- Age
- Disability
- Gender reassignment
- Race
- Religion or belief
- Sex and sexual orientation
- Marriage and civil partnership
- Pregnancy and maternity

Qualification mapping

Unit 3 LO 2 AC 2.1

Prohibited behaviours

The above groups are protected and certain behaviours towards individuals are not allowed. Being aware of prohibited behaviours can go a long way towards protecting individuals from discrimination. As a lead adult care worker, if you witness such behaviours you must not tolerate them and you must act. Some examples of prohibited behaviour are listed here:

- not considering a pregnant woman for a job
- treating a person less favourably because they are linked to a person with a disability; for example, if they have a child with a disability
- refusing access to a service because the person is transsexual
- putting the person at a disadvantage because of their disability; for example, not making provisions for a person who has dyslexia, no ramp access for a wheelchair user
- harassment, unwanted offensive behaviour
- victimisation, where the person is singled out and treated cruelly, maybe because they have complained.

Case study: Marnie and Erica

Marnie is a lead adult care worker and personal assistant to Erica who has multiple sclerosis. Erica was a full-time teacher for a business course but has reduced her hours because of her health difficulties. Marnie adapts the support that she gives depending on Erica's needs. Erica's abilities fluctuate between being mostly independent and sometimes needing support. Erica's sight is deteriorating and she finds small print very difficult to read. Erica worries about her position at her place of employment.

Marnie knows about the Equality Act 2010 and shares the easy read version of the Act with Erica because her eyesight is impaired. Erica is able to read and understand the Equality Act so that she fully understands her rights.

- What do you think that Marnie's manager might be saying or suggesting in relation to Erica's abilities and disabilities?
- Why does Marnie give Erica a copy of the larger print, easy to read version of the Equality Act 2010 rather than just telling her about it or giving her a standard copy?
- What parts of the Equality Act 2010 are related to Erica's situation? Explain why.

Race Relations (Amendment) Act 2000

This protects individuals from racial, national and ethnic discrimination.

The Care Act 2014

This act empowers individuals and their carers to be involved in their care. Local authorities must ensure that individuals are assessed (and their carers if they want an assessment). The local authority must make sure that there are appropriate services for those that need them.

European Convention on Human Rights

This is an agreement that protects human rights. Member European states have signed a contract to confirm their promise.

Use laws to support individual's rights

These examples show how laws can promote the rights of equality, diversity and inclusion for different individuals:

Jon has a learning disability; his support worker helped him to apply for a course at the local college. When he completed the course, with help he applied for a job as a car park attendant. His employer did not discriminate against him and offered him a job. Jon had training and he is a valued and committed employee.

Jazz had reduced her hours at work because she is the main carer for her mum who has dementia. Jazz spent many hours during the day and night caring for her mum. The local authority carried out an assessment of her needs and Jazz now has extra support to help care for her mum.

Jayne works in a woman's refuge. Many of the women she supports have suffered domestic violence and sexual abuse. The refuge provides a place of safety for the women and their children so they cannot be hurt by their abusive partners.

Summary

Laws protect the rights of individuals and promote equality, diversity and inclusion. You can make a real difference to people's lives by supporting them to access their rights.

Professional working

Parliament makes laws that must be obeyed by everyone. Organisations use laws to create policies, explaining how the law will be followed. The policies are used to write instructional procedures, outlining how to work within the policies.

Professional working

Laws can be amended (updated) and there may be changes that affect how you work, so keep yourself and other people updated. You may need to support your manager in reviewing policies and procedures in view of changes.

Support others to follow laws and procedures

As a lead adult care worker, you need to support others to understand the importance of equality, diversity and inclusion in adult care. This involves working within the law and following your workplace policies and procedures.

Activities

Qualification mapping

Unit 3 LO 2 AC 2.1, 2.2, LO 3 AC 3.2

Your colleagues' knowledge of the law

Find out what your colleagues know about the law.

Ask three colleagues to tell you what they know about laws that relate to equality, diversity and discrimination.

Make notes of their answers.

What do you know about the law?

As a lead adult care worker, you need to know about an individual's rights and responsibilities and work in a way that promotes this. Part of your role might involve contributing to policies and procedures in order to make sure that others also work within the law.

Read and match the statements below to the three laws.

Support individuals in a dignified and respectful way; not be treated in an inhumane way, for example, being left in soiled clothing; have sufficient access to food and drink; not be refused lifesaving treatment	The Equality Act 2010
People must not be discriminated against and should have equal opportunities; individuals cannot be treated unfavourably, for example, because of their disability, sexual orientation, beliefs or pregnancy	Care Act 2014
Individuals and their carers have a right to assessment of their needs and they should be fully involved in their care; the local authority should make sure that there is suitable provision for those that need support	Human Rights Act 1998

Laws are amended from time to time. You need to keep informed of any changes so that you and those in your team continue to work within the law.

Access a UK government website, for example, www.gov.uk, and make notes of key points that relate to your work area.

Carry out an audit of three of your workplace policies and procedures.

You could choose those that relate to the areas listed below or decide on others of your own choice:

- Staff recruitment
- Admission for users of your service
- Holiday and staff hours working arrangements

Do the policies and procedures fully comply with the current law?

Supporting others to work within the law

Copy and complete the table below to show how you have helped others to be aware of and work within the law.

Laws that relate to your work	How have you supported others to work within the law?
Human Rights Act 1998	
Race Relations (Amendment) Act 2000	
The Equality Act 2010	
Care Act 2014	

Qualification mapping 

Unit 3 LO 3 AC 3.2

Promoting equality, diversity and inclusion

New members of staff need to know what equality, diversity and inclusion mean in relation to your area of work.

You have been asked to help with an induction programme for new staff.

Create a short presentation that explains the following areas to new staff members:

- what equality, diversity and inclusion mean
- laws that are in place to protect and promote equality, diversity and inclusion
- how your workplace policies and procedures support equality, diversity and inclusion.

Practice for professional discussion

Prepare for a 10-minute professional discussion on equality, diversity, inclusion and the related laws, policies and procedures.

You could include the following points:

- laws, policies and procedures that support equality, diversity and inclusion
- how you promote equality, diversity and inclusion
- how you have supported others to understand the importance of equality, diversity and inclusion in your work setting.

Qualification mapping 

Unit 3 LO 1 AC 1.3, LO 2 AC 2.1 and 2.2, LO 3 AC 3.1 and 3.2

Challenging discrimination

Have you ever witnessed someone being discriminated against? Were you able to support them? It can often seem easier to walk away and not get involved because it can feel uncomfortable or you may not be sure what to do. Each workplace will have policies to help you promote equality.

Would you feel confident to challenge discrimination?

When you see or hear someone discriminating against an individual, it can be easier to walk away and not get involved; you might pretend that you were not aware that it happened. It can be especially difficult when the person who is acting in a discriminatory way is someone that you work with; they could possibly be your manager or supervisor. The person themselves may not even realise that they are being discriminatory. For example, they might suggest that a person who is incontinent does not join in on a trip because toileting situations may be difficult or awkward; or always roster a member of staff to work on a Christian celebration day because they do not follow this belief.

Equal opportunities for all

By law, all social care organisations will have an equality policy and this must be followed. It will outline how the organisation will meet the requirements of the law. The equality policy will protect the users of the service, staff and visitors; it will promote equality and inclusion, and prevent discrimination. You need to know about and work in a way that supports equality policies and ensure that others that you supervise do so as well.

Equality policies

Policies that support equality may include the following points:

- All users of the service will be treated as a unique individual.
- No one will be refused access to the service if they meet the assessment criteria, as long as there is a space for them.
- The service will be reviewed regularly to make sure that it meets the diverse needs of individuals who use it.
- Staff will have equal access to training.
- The organisation will not tolerate bullying or harassment.
- Users of the service must not discriminate against other service users, staff or visitors.
- All individuals will have equal access to the services and facilities that are provided.
- The organisation welcomes applications from all areas of society to work for and access services.
- The organisation will discipline any individual who breaches equality, diversity and inclusion procedures.

Qualification mapping

Unit 3 LO 2 AC 2.1, LO 3 AC 1.3 and 3.3

Professional working

Policies will be reviewed regularly, often yearly, but if you find that the policy and procedures are difficult to follow or do not work, tell your manager and they may be reviewed sooner. Your code of conduct also requires you to treat individuals equally and promote inclusion.

Reporting concerns

You will have policies and procedures at work to help if you think that someone is being treated unfairly. These will explain what you should do. It can feel uncomfortable to report concerns but you must remember that it is your duty to protect and speak up for individuals.

If you have reported a concern, do not gossip or discuss it with others: keep it private. It is also a good idea to keep your own private notes about the incident otherwise you may forget important information that you later need. Access and become familiar with your own workplace procedure. Figure 6 shows an example from Holly View.

Do you have concerns about discrimination?

1. Discuss it first with your supervisor. Many issues start as minor breaches of policy because of accident or forgetfulness. These issues are best dealt with by talking them through.
2. If the issue is with your supervisor and you feel you cannot discuss it with them, speak to their supervisor or line manager.
3. More serious concerns should be put in writing. Written concerns should detail how these issues breach your policies and procedures, and have clear dates and times.
4. Detail any steps you have already taken (e.g. reporting to a member of staff).
5. In serious cases, you should gain the support of your trade union to advise you further. If cases need to be taken to your local inspectorate body you will be protected by the Public Interest Disclosure Act 1998.

Figure 6: Holly View's procedure for reporting concerns on discrimination towards staff

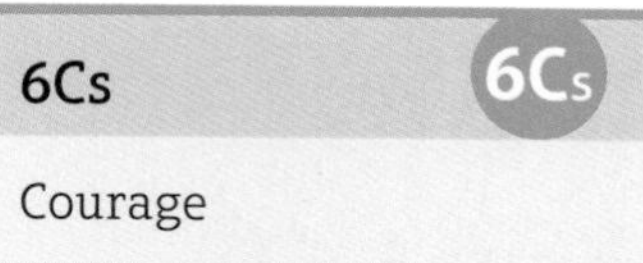

6Cs

Courage

An inclusive environment is good for everyone

An inclusive environment, in which everyone is encouraged to join in and their contributions are valued, benefits everyone.

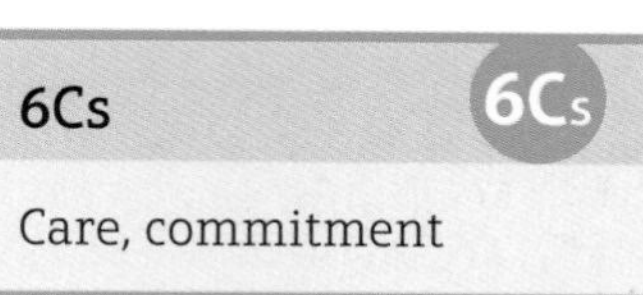

6Cs

Care, commitment

It creates a positive environment in which individuals are more likely to feel happy and fulfilled; this in turn usually leads not only to better quality care but improved mental and physical health for users of service and for the people who work there. It is important to be a positive role model for other members of staff and especially those working in your team.

Some of the benefits of inclusion are listed here:

- everyone is given the opportunity to join in and contribute to society
- sharing of knowledge and talent
- shows respect to others and supports a safer environment for all
- helps individuals to reach their full potential and builds confidence
- encourages a more understanding and kind society
- has a positive impact on mental and physical wellbeing
- better living and working environment.

Can you think of more?

Summary

Never ignore discrimination or unfair practice and make yourself aware of equality policies at work. An inclusive environment is a positive one, where both users of the service and staff feel valued and fulfilled.

Support others to challenge discrimination

An important part of your role as an adult lead care worker is to support others to challenge discrimination and to be a good role model to junior care workers. All adult care workers must understand the importance of respecting diversity, the principles of inclusion and treating everyone fairly.

Activities

Qualification mapping

Unit 3 LO 3 AC 3.1, 3.2 and 3.3

Support others to work in an inclusive way

Your code of conduct is an important document that helps you to understand what is expected of you and the required standards of work. Knowing your own responsibilities in relation to your code of conduct will help you to guide others to work in an equal and inclusive way.

Access the Code of Conduct for Healthcare Support Workers and Adult Social Care Workers in England and make a note of what is expected of you in relation to the following:

- equality, diversity and inclusion
- what to do if you witness discrimination or other omissions.

Copy and complete the following table and keep your notes safe for future reference.

Part of the code of conduct	What does it say?

Qualification mapping

Unit 3 LO 2 AC 2.1

Policies and procedures

Find the following documents and highlight the important points:

- your workplace equality policy
- your workplace procedure that explains what to do if you have concerns for an individual who you think is being discriminated against or being treated unfairly.

How inclusive is your organisation?

Carry out an audit of your organisation to assess how inclusive it is to individuals (both users of the service and staff who work there).

Consider the following and compile a list of positive points that you have found:

- Age: are there any young people employed (aged under 18) or those post retirement age? Compile a bar chart to show your findings.
- Disability: how are people with disabilities appropriately supported? Could additional measures be put in place to improve things for them?

Do not restrict your audit to the caring roles but include other areas such as the kitchen and housekeeping roles as well.

Demonstrating good practice

Share your findings from the previous activity with your supervisor.

Ask for feedback to help generate an article to illustrate elements of good practice. This could be shared across the organisation or even outside the organisation via a community publication.

Prepare an electronic presentation to share with your colleagues that illustrates your organisation's good practice on inclusion.

Qualification mapping 

Unit 3 LO 3 AC 3.3

Managing inclusion in practice

Ali is a junior care worker and is transgender. Ali is going through the difficult process of transitioning. For a long time her feelings have been kept inside for fear of what others would think or say but she now feels that it is the right time to be more open. Ali's name has been legally changed from Alexander to Alexandra. One day, at the end of the shift, Ali changed from the uniform of tunic and trousers into a dress.

When Ali returned to work the next day, there were problems. Some users of the service refused to be supported by Ali and the staff were not happy to use the same toilet and changing facilities. You are leading the shift.

- What difficulties do you think Ali has faced and is experiencing now?
- Why do you think that users of the service and staff are reacting in this way?
- How would you manage the situation?

Qualification mapping 

Unit 3 LO 1 AC 1.2, LO 2 AC 2.2, LO 3 AC 3.3

Having the courage to accept differences

Qualification mapping

Unit 3 LO 2 AC 2.2, LO 3 AC 3.1 and 3.2

6Cs

Courage

Professional working

Use supervision for yourself for support and, if you are supervising others, to create an environment in which the individual feels comfortable and valued; this will enhance the outcome of the meeting.

How do you support someone who has done something terrible in society, for example murder or child abuse? Situations such as this will test your courage and strength to cope at work.

Most people in society are honest, caring, law-abiding individuals, and usually you will choose to spend time with individuals with similar values to your own. However, in care work you have no control over who you will need to support and you must do so in a caring and compassionate way – regardless of the individual's past history.

There can be many reasons why some individuals take a negative path but it is not for anyone to judge. It can be a challenge to support individuals who have different cultural and belief systems, but in adult care work you must put your own feelings to one side. This takes courage and real strength of character. It does not mean that you have to agree with the person, but you do need to give them an equal standard of care in a supportive way.

You may also need to help others to work with individuals who have different beliefs to themselves and it is important that you always aim to model good practice and are supportive of all concerned.

Case study: Leila

'My name is Leila. I work with individuals who have been released from prison. They are on a sex offender's rehabilitation programme. This is the hardest job I have ever done because it goes against my own values and beliefs. I have a child myself; I really feel for the victims and their families.

At first, I struggled to work with J – knowing what he had done. The job is emotionally draining but I remind myself that J is a human being and try to put his past to one side. J was scared to leave prison as he felt safer there. But outside he knows that people do not want to be near him; he will be judged and he is a target for hate crime. Building up trust with him has taken time and I am now helping him with life and social skills. I have been non-judgemental, and supportive but not overly empathetic because that might send a message that I think it was ok what he did. It's a fine balance.

J knows that what he has done and his feelings are wrong and wants the rehabilitation programme to work. It is early days; I feel hopeful that it will be a success.'

- How do you think working with J challenges Leila's values and belief system?
- Explain how Leila is exhibiting courage in the way that she works.

Get the most out of your supervision meetings by being prepared

How to prepare yourself

Leila, in the case study above, has chosen to work in a challenging environment. She will have thought about it a lot beforehand, knowing that her own values and belief system is likely to be challenged – probably on a daily basis – because of the area in which she is working. You may work in an area where this is less likely and you may not have the daily challenges to your own belief system that Leila faces each day. However, there will be times when you need to support others who have different

values and beliefs from your own and, if you are not prepared for this to happen, it can be difficult. You have a responsibility to be caring and compassionate towards all individuals, but it can sometimes be challenging.

Look at the case study below and think about how Sudipta's values and beliefs are challenged.

Link 

Topic C: The importance of communication

6Cs 

Courage

Case study: Mary and Sudipta

Mary and Sudipta work closely together as adult care workers. Mary has just discovered that she is pregnant and plans to have an abortion. This will be her second termination of pregnancy. Sudipta has been trying to become pregnant for some years and she is actively anti-abortion. Sudipta's last chance of IVF was unsuccessful and she cannot afford to have more treatment.

Sudipta has been asked to cover Mary's shifts while she has the procedure. When Mary returns to work she is still feeling unwell and has abdominal pain and cramps.

It will be difficult for Sudipta because Mary's actions challenge her own values and belief system but she must have the courage to put to one side her own thoughts and views. She should also be sensitive to Mary's needs. She does not have to agree with what Mary has done but she does need to work with her in a way that respects her choices. It is part of her responsibility to do so.

- Explain how you think Sudipta might be feeling about Mary's pregnancy and her decision to have an abortion.
- How do you think that Sudipta should respond to Mary while she is feeling unwell? Explain why.
- Can you think of any examples of when your own culture and belief systems were challenged? How did you respond?

As a lead adult care worker, you do not have to agree with what others have done or are doing but you must show sensitivity. Remember that this is not just about saying the right thing: your body language and actions must support the words that you speak. Refer to the 6Cs to remind you how to support individuals in a caring, compassionate and empathetic way.

Supporting others

Some adult care workers might only infrequently have to support someone with a different value, and belief system but for others it is a daily occurrence. It is important that you recognise your feelings and manage them otherwise you could go on to develop stress-related mental and physical health problems. As a lead adult care worker you will also need to support others in this situation.

- Use supervision (it helps to talk situations through with your supervisor).
- Exercise is good for mental and physical health.
- Eat a healthy diet and do not drink alcohol too often.
- Make time for your interests and hobbies.
- Get enough sleep (exercise and good diet will help).
- Access support systems when you need help.

Summary 

It is important that you have the courage to speak up if you feel that someone is being treated unfairly; they may not be able to do so themselves.

Show courage in challenging your own values and beliefs

There will sometimes be situations in which you have to support an individual with values and beliefs that are very different from your own. This can be challenging and not always comfortable. You have to show courage and be a good role for other members of staff.

Activities

Qualification mapping

Unit 2 LO 2 AC 2.3; Unit 3 LO 2 AC 2.2, LO 3 AC 3.1

Reflecting on values and beliefs

Reflect on your own values and beliefs and consider potential opposing ones that you may come across.

Complete two mind maps considering the areas below:

- my values and beliefs: what I feel strongly about
- other values and beliefs that may be very different from mine.

Using the 6Cs

Use the 6Cs as a guide and make notes on how you could apply them if you needed to support someone with opposing values and beliefs to yourself.

Getting support

Supporting someone with contrasting values and beliefs can put a strain on your own physical and mental health, so it is important that you look after yourself and get support when you need it. Copy and complete the mind map below with ideas for how you can maintain your own physical and mental health.

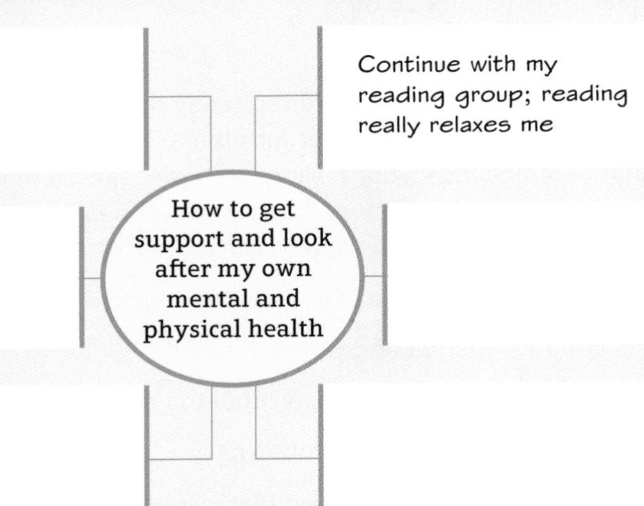

Figure 7: Look after your own physical and mental health

Finding out about differences

Ella works in a setting that provides care for individuals who have been discharged from hospital and are waiting to return home. Wang-Wei is recovering well from an operation and just needs some support with personal care. Adjustments are being made at home so that he can live independently with minimal assistance. Ella is supporting Wang-Wei with mobility. He wishes to have a short walk outside. Ella begins sneezing because she has hay fever and her nose is running. Ella gets a clean tissue, blows her nose and puts the tissue in her pocket until she can find a bin to dispose of it. Wang-Wei looks very disapprovingly at her. Wang-Wei later clears his throat and spits on the pavement. Ella offers him a tissue; he declines and continues to spit. Ella says that it is not appropriate to spit on the ground.

Both Ella and Wang-Wei have different beliefs and could be seen to be offensive to each other.

- Find out why Wang-Wei and other Chinese individuals choose to spit.
- Why do individuals from the Western culture find spitting offensive?
- What difficulties could Chinese individuals face if they were given care by someone who does not understand their culture?
- How could you support others to be sensitive towards those with different beliefs to theirs?

Reflective account

Writing things down can be a good way of getting issues in perspective. It can also be a good support to share thoughts with others. Complete a self-reflective account, using the Kolb cycle on page v, on a situation in which you supported someone with opposing values and beliefs to yourself.

Discuss the reflective account with your supervisor or assessor.

Qualification mapping 

Unit 2 LO 3 AC 3.2

Practice for professional discussion

Prepare notes for a 10-minute professional discussion on courage and how you have supported an individual with values and beliefs that are very different from your own.

You could include the following:

- your values and beliefs
- potential differences in values and beliefs that others may have
- why it is important to have the courage to support individuals with care and compassion when their values and beliefs are different from yours
- how you have exhibited courage in supporting individuals when your own values and beliefs have been challenged (give specific examples where possible).

Qualification mapping 

Unit 2 LO 2 AC 2.2 and 2.3

Situational judgement questions

1. A user of the service, who is deaf and does not use a hearing aid, is sitting in a wheelchair in the communal lounge area, waiting to go out. You notice that they have been incontinent. Do you:
   a. Discreetly and quickly wheel them into the nearest bathroom?
   b. Write on a piece of paper to ask if you can take them to the bathroom?
   c. Get down to their level, speak loudly and clearly and say that you need to help change them?
   d. Use gestures and clear speech to explain what you need to do?
2. A colleague is very upset because of serious relationship problems; their partner has recently left them. You are this worker's supervisor. Do you:
   a. Keep them busy; give them lots of work so they have less time to think about it?
   b. Explain that they must keep their home and work life very separate; they must not let one affect the other?
   c. Be careful not to draw attention to the issue as it might upset her more?
   d. Explain that you think you understand how she feels and ask if you can make any temporary adjustments at work that could help?
3. You are working with an individual who is an ex-prisoner; their crime was serious and involved innocent and vulnerable people. They do not appear to have any remorse. You are finding it difficult to support them. Do you:
   a. Try to put out of your mind what they have done and support them professionally; mention it at a one-to-one session with your supervisor?
   b. Allocate the support to another member of staff who is always patient, caring and understanding?
   c. Divide the allocation so that you all have a turn in supporting this person?
   d. Support their physical needs and make conversation with them; tell them to ask if they need anything but don't go out of your way to do any more?
4. A recent CQC inspection indicated that not all users of your service were treated equally. A training need was identified and your manager asked you for suggestions. A couple of the staff have dyslexia. What do you suggest?
   a. Bring in an expert lawyer who can give detailed information about equality, rights and the law
   b. Arrange a meeting for all staff to remind them about their responsibilities and draw their attention to the disciplinary procedure
   c. Arrange a series of online training sessions around equality and the law; staff could complete this either at work or at home
   d. Arrange a training session at work at which staff can learn about relevant laws and policies and how they can be applied in your workplace setting
5. You support an individual with a physical disability; she has good cognitive ability. Part of your role is to do her weekly shop. Her neighbour mentioned the individual's preference for organic and free-range foods. You usually shop for the best deal to save her money now that she is not working. Do you:
   a. Continue shopping as before, getting the best deals and more for her money?
   b. Think that it's not in the plan of care so she must have changed her views?
   c. Ask the family?
   d. Ask the individual if they want you to buy specific organic and free-range foods but explain that they are likely to be more expensive?
6. You are finding it difficult at work because you support people who have different values from your own. Do you:
   a. Look for a job somewhere else in the care sector where you will only work with and support like-minded people?
   b. Make time for hobbies outside work, reflect on difficulties and discuss the situation with your supervisor?
   c. Organise a night out with your colleagues so you can all share difficulties and frustrations over a meal and a few drinks?
   d. Harden up and remember that it's a job, think about your days off and a holiday you could book?

C
The importance of communication

Communication in care settings

Communication is one of the 6Cs, the fundamental values and behaviours underpinning *Compassion in Practice* – the national strategy for nurses, midwives and care staff. The 6Cs have also been adopted and implemented by Skills for Care, which identifies them as values that underpin quality social care provision. Your ability to communicate effectively in different care settings will help to ensure that you can meet the needs, preferences and wishes of individuals. You will also be able to support other adult care workers by promoting excellent communication skills.

This topic will cover the following areas:

- barriers to communication
- identifying and determining solutions to barriers when communicating with users of services
- verbal and non-verbal communication
- advocacy
- ensuring the safety of confidential information
- communicating clearly and responsibly.

You will also learn about the skills you will need so that you can apply this knowledge in the care setting where you work.

Why communicate?

Qualification mapping

Unit 1 LO 3 AC 3.1 and 3.2

Being able to communicate effectively is an essential part of your job as a lead adult care worker, as well as being an important life skill. Successful communication means identifying barriers and finding ways to overcome them.

As well as talking to users of care, their family members and your colleagues, you use touch, gestures and facial expressions to communicate, in addition to written and electronic communication. Effective communication with staff and users of service can make people feel valued, but there may be reasons why communication might be less effective than expected.

Key terms

Barrier – a circumstance or obstacle that keeps people or things apart or prevents communication or progress

Dialect – a form of language that is specific to a particular geographical area or group of people

Barriers to communication

There are different reasons why communication may not be as effective as you would like, and these are known as barriers. For example, a **barrier** might be that an individual cannot see, hear or receive the message – this may be due to:

- visual and/or hearing impairment
- environmental problems, such as poor lighting or noisy spaces.

Alternatively, someone may not be able to make sense of the message due to:

- the use of different languages – including sign language
- the use of slang, jargon or **dialect**
- physical and/or intellectual disabilities.

Another reason is that an individual misunderstands the message because of:

- cultural influences – people from different cultures interpret verbal and non-verbal messages in different ways
- assumptions they have made about people
- labelling or stereotyping
- the social context – friends and family may understand behaviour and statements differently from strangers or work colleagues
- emotional barriers – someone's emotional needs may prevent them from engaging with others
- time pressures
- emotional differences – someone's emotional state may create misunderstandings.

You should never assume that you can be heard and understood when you are working with a user of your service. Holistic care requires all care workers to consider the abilities and situation of each individual and to ensure that the communication is appropriate.

An individual's emotional state may prevent them from engaging with other people

Case study: Communicating with Mrs Evans

You and your team provide domiciliary care for Mrs Evans who is 94 years old and lives alone. She is still very independent but has significant hearing loss. Although she has a hearing aid, she does not often use it and frequently loses it. One of the adult care workers reports to you that Mrs Evans mislaid her hearing aid several days ago and it has not been found. He had considerable difficulty communicating with Mrs Evans this morning and phones you to ask what can be done to help her.

- What suggestions can you give your colleague about how he can communicate with Mrs Evans?
- What do you need to do to help Mrs Evans? List the tasks that you would have to complete to ensure that Mrs Evans regains her ability to communicate with your staff and others she comes into contact with.

Could your colleague write down any questions or information so that Mrs Evans can read them and respond, or use gestures to get his messages across to her? You could contact the supplier of her hearing aids and organise for a replacement to be provided. You would need to arrange an appointment and transport for Mrs Evans, and ensure all the information is recorded in her care plan.

Sensory problems

If you are working with someone who has a visual or hearing impairment, you will need to find out the level of impairment they have and how they normally communicate. You will then be able to establish what (if any) assistance is needed. Some people with hearing impairment are experts at lip reading so do not need any extra assistance. However, you may need to organise the services of a sign language interpreter in some cases. People who are visually impaired will not be able to respond to facial expressions, so it may be more appropriate to use words and touch. You may be able to source large print books, Braille and audio tapes if required. You must allow enough time for someone to respond to you. Remember, you may also work with colleagues who have sensory impairment, so you must ensure they have the support to do their job effectively.

Confusion caused by dementia or mental health conditions

If possible, remove all distractions, such as background noise, and try to find a quiet location where you can focus more easily. Ask the individual's family or friends about the best ways of communicating with the individual you are caring for.

Non-English speaker

Many simple needs can be established by imitating different activities. More complex conversations may require the help of a relative, friend or translator.

Lack of privacy

Health and social care environments are often busy and noisy, and this can create problems, especially if you want to discuss a sensitive or complex issue with an individual and his or her family. There can be distractions in domiciliary settings too, so you might need to encourage the person you are working with to turn down the volume of a television or radio, or turn it off altogether, or close windows to reduce the noise of passing traffic or roadworks.

Professional working

The environment can also cause barriers to communication. Noise, space, climate, time and place are generally thought of as being the main environmental barriers to communication.

6Cs

Communication, care

Key term

Sensory – relating to the five senses – sight, hearing, touch, smell, taste

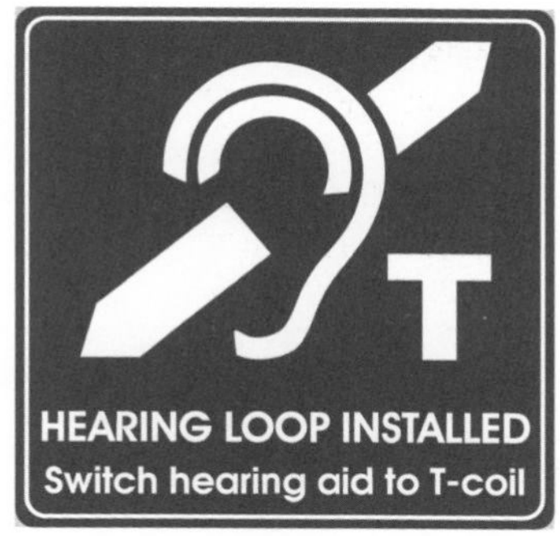

Figure 1: A hearing loop is a sound system used by people who have hearing aids to reduce noise and improve sound quality

Summary

Ensuring that you and the staff you supervise and support understand the possible barriers to communication and how to overcome them will contribute to the provision of excellent care for your users of service.

Demonstrate and promote excellent communication skills

Qualification mapping

Unit 1 LO 1 AC 1.2, LO 3 AC 3.1

As a lead adult care worker, you will set an example to junior members of staff, demonstrating that you are able to promote excellent communication skills.

Activity

Communication skills at work

Reflect on a group discussion or meeting that you have recently been part of at work to discuss changes or developments in the management of your service. Consider the following questions.

- Did you know what the meeting was about and were you able to prepare for it?
- How did it feel to be in the group?
- Would you say that the discussion/meeting was successful? Why?

Most of the communication you take part in at work is formal, and you will probably be aware that you adjust your speech at work depending on who you are speaking with. Your role includes communicating with colleagues, other professionals, users of the service you provide and their family and friends.

Case study: Interpersonal skills

Beth works as an adult care worker in your team. The individuals she cares for have given feedback to the company about her:

'I love the days when Beth cares for me. She is always so cheerful and optimistic.'

'Beth is so professional when she cares for me. I would trust her absolutely to do the best she can for me.'

'Beth always has time to stop for a little chat before she leaves me. It makes me feel like someone really cares about my health and welfare.'

'Beth cares for my father and he tells me how much he values seeing her. He says he gets a real lift from her positive and caring approach to caring for him.'

'I really appreciate how Beth explains everything, and if she doesn't know something she goes and finds out and then comes back to me with an answer.'

- Identify the qualities Beth has and consider why her interpersonal skills are so good.
- Ask your team to reflect on their own interpersonal skills.
- What do they think they are good at and what would they like to improve? They may wish to include this as part of their next appraisal.
- What do you need to do to help Mrs Evans? List the tasks that you would have to complete to ensure that Mrs Evans regains her ability to communicate with your staff and others she comes into contact with.

Professional working

Remember that it is not enough simply to provide information or instructions to individuals, their family and friends, and staff. You need to ensure that they understand the information you have given them. Similarly, you must ensure that you receive and understand information given to you.

Activity

Different types of communication

Once you have given staff time to reflect, organise a training session to discuss the importance of different types of communication. You might wish to provide some scenarios that could be discussed.

Ask them to discuss how they would recognise the emotions of different individuals and what appropriate support they could offer.

People feel valued when their individuality and the impact their experiences have on their lives are acknowledged. Use the examples below to discuss with your staff how they can ensure that they practise excellent communication skills with users of your service:

1. James is a 31-year-old wheel chair user and has hearing and sight impairment. He requires help to get up and go to bed every day. You are concerned because he has become very dependent on Marek, one of your staff who is the same age as him. He has asked Marek to go on holiday with him and two friends to Tenerife, all expenses paid. Marek is very short of money and wasn't expecting to have a holiday abroad this year. He is keen to accept. What advice should you give James and Marek, and why?
2. Bilal (aged 67) has been told that his cancer has progressed and he is now in need of end-of-life care. His medical team have informed him that he has between three and six months to live. He doesn't want his family to know and all the staff have been informed of this. One of your carers, who has been visiting Bilal at home, has told you that his two daughters are at his house every time she visits asking for information about Bilal's care. Although she has told them that she can't speak to them about this, they continue to press her for information. What advice should you give her?
3. Miss Underwood lives in sheltered accommodation where she has been very independent. However, she is becoming confused and her sister has contacted you to ask for support with personal care. She has type two diabetes, which is managed with Metformin tablets that she has to take twice a day. You visit to make an assessment and notice that she has fewer tablets left than she should. When you ask Miss Underwood about the tablets, she seems unsure about when and how many she should take. You suspect that she does not remember when she has taken them and takes more than she should. Who do you inform and why? What steps can be taken to ensure Miss Underwood takes the right number of tablets at the right time? What instructions should you give your staff?
4. You are a lead adult care worker in a nursing home. Mr Francis, an elderly resident, has collapsed suddenly while his wife and daughter are visiting. Dr Smithson, the GP, is in the home and is called to see Mr Francis. He determines that Mr Francis has suffered a major stroke and an ambulance is called. As he is being taken out to the ambulance, Mrs Francis says to the GP 'He is going to be alright isn't he Doctor?'. Dr Smithson is in a hurry and says to her 'Frankly, I can't see him making it' and rushes off. Mrs Francis and her daughter are distraught. What action should be taken, and by whom?

Professional working

Make sure when you are giving information to individuals, their family and friends and staff, that they understand what you have told them. You may have to repeat the information in different ways to be absolutely sure that they do understand. Similarly, you must ensure that you receive and understand information given to you, and then act on it when necessary.

Identify and determine the best solutions to achieve success when communicating

Qualification mapping

Unit 1 LO 2 AC 2.2, LO 3 AC 3.3

At work, you will listen to obtain information, to understand and to learn. As a lead adult care worker you will be delegating responsibility to the staff you supervise, and expecting them to listen and act on information or instructions you give them.

One of the most important skills that adult care workers can develop is that of listening. Research suggests that most people will remember no more than 50 per cent of what they hear. This can have quite an impact on how effective you might be if you are only taking in half of what you have been told. The individuals you care for might understandably feel aggrieved if they feel that you have not listened to them. You must develop the skills to communicate successfully and support staff to do the same.

Active listening

Key term

Active listening – the 'active' part is using skills to gain information that someone might otherwise choose not to share

Being a good listener is a very skilful quality and is more than simply hearing words. It includes encouraging someone to talk to you and letting them know that you are interested and concerned about what they have to say. How you listen will make a big difference to how easy someone finds it to talk to you. Nodding and saying 'mmm' can be enough to prompt an individual to disclose information to you. It indicates that you are interested in what they are telling you.

Active listening techniques include:

- building trust and establishing rapport
- demonstrating concern
- paraphrasing to show understanding
- non-verbal clues that show understanding, such as nodding, eye contact and leaning forward
- brief verbal affirmations like 'I see', 'I know', 'Thank you'
- asking open-ended questions
- asking specific questions to seek clarification
- waiting to disclose your opinion
- disclosing similar experiences to show understanding.

(Source: https://www.thebalancecareers.com/active-listening-skills-with-examples-2059684)

Professional working

The next time that you have a conversation with a user of your service, or a relative who is distressed, reflect on how you acted and reacted to him or her. Did you know when to let the individual speak and when you needed to interrupt? How did you end the conversation?

Asking questions

You can ask both open and closed questions when you are having a conversation, but you must ensure that your questions will get you the information you need.

Closed questions allow people to answer yes or no. This may not allow you to get the information you need and you may end up asking a lot of questions, causing the individual to feel as if they are being interrogated. For example, you might ask someone, 'Do you like spicy foods?'. If the answer is yes, you can be fairly confident you could serve them a curry or chilli for lunch. If they say no, you have established that they do not like spicy food but you have not found out what they do like.

Open questions require someone to give more than a yes/no answer. For example, you could ask 'What foods do you enjoy eating?'. You will gain much more information and will allow the person you are talking to to express their feelings. They may well feel more valued because you showed a greater interest in their needs and wishes.

What you say and the way in which you say it can have an impact on the responses you get. Make sure that you are not the one doing all the talking. For example, telling someone what you would do if you were them is not good practice or good communication. You also need to be aware of the speed and volume of your speech. If you speak too quickly or too quietly, people may not catch what you say.

User of services	Response	Outcome
User of services 'Oh no, not you lot again! I've told you I don't need any help from you. I can manage on my own. I don't need babysitting!'	**Aggressive response** 'Well if that's all the thanks we get then you can just get on with looking after yourself. Goodbye.'	The aggressive response meets the needs of the care worker but not the service user. The service user is made to feel vulnerable: 'I win, you lose.'
	Assertive response 'I'm sorry that you are angry but please let me come in and find out why you don't want our help.'	The assertive response is aimed at meeting the needs of both the care worker and user of service. 'We both win.'
	Submissive response 'I'm terribly sorry. I'll tell my manager that you no longer want care from us.'	The submissive response meets the needs of the service user and not the care worker. The service user may dominate the care worker: 'You win, I lose.'

Figure 2: Different approaches to responding to a complaint lead to different reactions

An emotionally safe atmosphere

Whether you are working with individuals in your care or supporting care staff, you need to create a supportive atmosphere. People who feel that they can communicate their emotional needs without being concerned that their dignity or self-esteem are threatened will feel more comfortable talking about sensitive issues. You will need to use active listening skills and provide a private and secure environment for a private conversation.

Assertiveness

A way of showing respect for people is to be assertive. Although many people believe that this is 'sticking up for yourself', it requires you to stay calm and show respect for the people you are communicating with. This is particularly important in challenging situations where emotions are running high, and will help to prevent aggression in others.

How assertiveness can be positive

The diagram in Figure 2 shows how the different approaches you could take when responding to a complaint will result in different reactions. Aggression may lead to the breakdown in a relationship between care worker and user of service, and as a senior carer you may be called upon to resolve the issue so that you can staff your provision adequately. If you have a care worker who comes across as submissive, you might need to discuss assertiveness with them and suggest how a situation like this could be approached differently in the future.

Summary 

As a lead adult care worker you may be required to support staff and service users in resolving communication issues, so you should reflect on how effective your skills are. How confident are you in your communication with others and about resolving conflict?

Communicate clearly verbally and non-verbally and maximise the quality of interaction

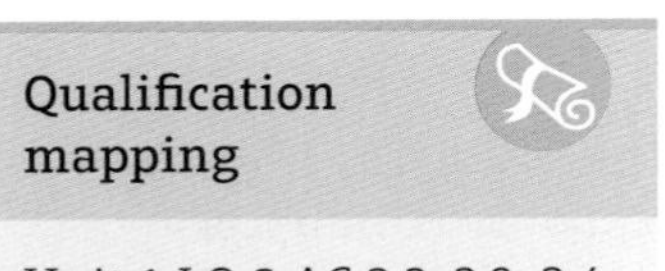

Qualification mapping

Unit 1 LO 2 AC 2.2, 2.3, 2.4

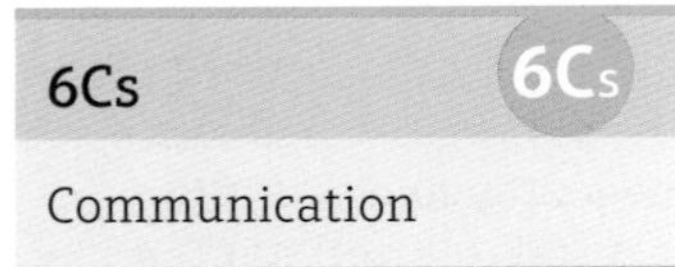

6Cs

Communication

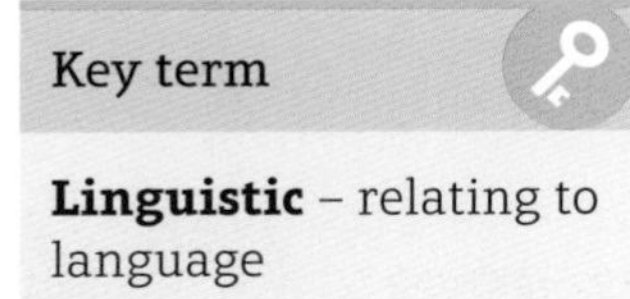

Key term

Linguistic – relating to language

As a lead adult care worker you have a responsibility to ensure that you can communicate effectively with both the individuals you care for and your staff.

Understanding different methods and styles of communication, both verbal and non-verbal, will help you and your team to ensure that you practise good quality interaction and achieve your intended outcomes.

Verbal communication

Being able to communicate clearly using speech can depend on a number of factors When you are communicating verbally with others, you must consider the skills, background and ability of the person you are with. You need to ensure people can make sense of what you are saying.

Linguistic tone, pitch and vocabulary

Your tone of voice can indicate that you are rushed, distracted or cross about something, and the quality of the interaction may be reduced because of this. People might feel that you are unapproachable, and this may also be shown in non-verbal signs you display.

The way in which you and your staff speak to users of your service should take into account the individual's age, culture and level of understanding. Older people may not understand slang or jargon, and young people may use language that you are not familiar with. Varying degrees of formality will be used between different people or groups of people in professional settings as shown in Table 1.

Context	Communication issues
Between professionals and users of service	May be formal or informal depending on the context. Language, tone and speed of speech should be adapted to ensure understanding and enable time for response. Professionals may sometimes need to communicate more formally in certain circumstances.
Between colleagues	Usually informal, but all parties need to ensure that they show respect for each other.
Working with multi-agency or multi-professional professionals	Likely to be more formal. May need to consider use of technical language and make sure that they understand and are understood.

Table 1: Communication in different contexts

Language skills

You should take into consideration whether English is the individual's first language. If not, they may need time to translate what you have said into their first language – perhaps using a translation service – and then to translate their response back from their first language into English in order to reply. You may find that communicating effectively takes longer than you expect, so it is important that a user of the service or a member of your team is given the time to express their thoughts, needs and wishes clearly.

Non-verbal communication

This is communication without words, but using gestures and body language; even the way in which we dress or our personal scent can be expressive. You may find that you can read how someone is feeling quite quickly and easily by considering cues such as posture, facial expression and gestures.

Touch and **proximity** are other methods of non-verbal communication, but people are not always comfortable with being touched or having another person standing too close to them. There are cultural issues with touching, so you need to be aware of how your user of service or colleagues might respond. Even though touching someone can demonstrate caring, it can be misinterpreted. You might want to encourage your team members to ask permission before touching users of the service. In the same way, standing or sitting too close to someone can make them feel very uncomfortable.

Active listening

Active listening helps people optimise the quality of their communication. It involves listening to what someone says, thinking about what has been said and then considering your response. It is also called reflective listening because you can reflect back or **paraphrase** the information you have been given to confirm that you have understood what has been said.

Your non-verbal communication skills will also help you; for example, you could show that you are interested by leaning forward or by sitting at a slight angle. Successful active listening requires concentration and practice.

Case study: Team meeting

Moti has joined a new team as lead adult care worker in a residential home. She learns that the team meetings happen infrequently and always at the end of the day – people are tired, make their excuses and it is usually rushed so the meetings are not effective. She looks at the rota and the daily workload and finds a quieter time in the afternoon. She books the meeting room and asks for input on the agenda from all of the team, buys some muffins and grapes, and sets a realistic time. It is a success.

- How has Moti maximised communication in her team?
- What might be the positive longer-term outcome for the team of meeting in this way?

Summary

Maximising the quality of interaction by recognising verbal and non-verbal means of communication will help you to develop good relationships with colleagues and users of your service.

Professional working

Reflect on a situation in which you had difficulty communicating with someone at work – either a user of service or colleague. What different methods did you try using? Did you ask anyone for advice or help? How successful do you think you were? What different things would you try if you found yourself in a similar situation in the future?

Key terms

Proximity – closeness

Paraphrase – express the meaning of something using different words

Use and facilitate preferred methods of communication

As an experienced adult care worker, you know that establishing an individual's preferred method of communication should take place at the initial assessment.

You should establish with the individual or a member of their family what their first or preferred language is, their preferred method of communication and if they have any additional learning needs, physical illness or disability, dementia or confusion, or sensory impairment. Once you have this information, you and your team can find ways to use the individual's preferred method of communication.

Activities

Qualification mapping

Unit 1 LO 2 AC 2.1

▶ Overcoming communication difficulties

One of your 18-year-old newly appointed care workers has asked you why she is finding it so difficult to communicate with Mr Samuels, one of your users of service who is blind. She tells you she is not sure how to establish a relationship with him. You are concerned that the staff may not be as confident in communicating as they should be.

Carry out some research into the reasons why there may be communication barriers between your staff and users of your service.

Prepare and lead a training session for staff on the different types of barriers that might exist between them and the users of your service, or between them and other colleagues. Create some case studies for discussion and ask them to work in groups and agree how to overcome the barriers. You could also ask them to discuss the implications of not being able to overcome barriers. What would be the consequences for the individuals and the team caring for them?

Professional working

You may find that you work with senior care workers and care workers who have communication difficulties. You may need to support them by helping them to develop strategies to overcome these difficulties.

▶ Sensory impairment

Find out what support there is for users of your service or staff members who have a sensory impairment, and how they can access it.

What reasonable adjustment might need to be made for a staff member with a hearing impairment?

Both the Alzheimer's Association in the United Kingdom and the Alzheimer's Association in the United States of America produce information on communication for people living with dementia and their families. This can be found at:

https://www.alzheimers.org.uk/categories/support/communication

https://www.alz.org/media/Documents/alzheimers-dementia-communication-all-stages-b.pdf

▶ Reflecting on communication issues

Identify a situation in which an adult care worker came to you for advice about the difficulty he or she was having when communicating with a user of your service.

Using the Kolb reflective cycle, explain the situation and what you advised the care worker to try. Evaluate how successful your advice was, and what you might do differently if a similar situation arose in the future.

Figure 3: Some gestures are universally acceptable
(Source: Pease, Allan and Barbara, 2004, *The definitive book of body language*, Orion Publishing Co, ISBN 9780752861180)

It can be useful to develop some knowledge of how touch and gestures can vary in different cultures. In our multi-cultural society, having the ability to understand and use such gestures can help you to communicate with people who do not have English as a first language. In the UK, people who work in health and social care regularly use touch as a means of communication with users of different services. However, research suggests that in some cultures touching is not acceptable in social situations (see Table 2 below). Of course, if you are providing physical care for individuals, you will need to touch them, but you must gain consent before you do.

Touching not acceptable	Touching acceptable
Germany	Middle East
Japan	Parts of Asia
England	India
USA & Canada	Turkey
Australia & New Zealand	France
Portugal	Italy
Northern Europe	Greece
Scandinavia	Spain

Table 2: A guide to touching in different parts of the world

Activity

Practice for professional discussion

Organise a professional discussion with one or more members of your team. Ask them how they feel if someone stands too close to them. Do they feel threatened?

How would they feel if a user of the service stood too close to them? How would they feel if a colleague stood too close to them? How would they feel if a senior member of staff stood too close to them? Would they feel able to speak up if they felt uncomfortable?

The role of advocates and when they might be involved

Key term

Advocacy – taking action to help people say what they want, secure their rights, represent their interests and obtain services they need

Advocacy involves ensuring that the individual can have their opinions heard, their rights defended and safeguarded, and their views and wishes considered when decisions need to be made about their life.

There may be occasions when you have supported a user of your service to identify their rights and provided them with information. But there may be reasons why an individual is not able to exercise their rights. For example, this might include if:

- their rights are being infringed by someone else
- there are physical barriers
- there are emotional barriers.

6Cs

Communication, competence, commitment

Advocates are independent and their role is to represent an individual's views and wishes without judging them or imposing their own opinions. This can be helpful if an individual's wishes conflict with those of friends, family or health and care workers.

Advocacy does not just occur formally, however. You will probably advocate informally for the users of your service on a regular basis. You might have to act if someone's rights are being infringed, but you will have to balance the rights of one person against those of another and decide whose rights have been infringed.

In order to be entitled to advocacy under the Care Act 2014, an individual would experience substantial difficulty in doing one or more of the following:

a. understanding relevant information

b. retaining that information

c. using or weighing that information as part of the process of being involved

d. communicating the individual's views, wishes or feelings (whether by talking, using sign language or any other means), and there is no one appropriate and available to support and represent their wishes.

(Source: http://www.legislation.gov.uk/ukpga/2014/23/part/1/crossheading/independent-advocacy-support/enacted)

An advocate must represent an individual's views and wishes

Even if an individual has someone appropriate to support them, there are three instances when an advocate must be involved. These are:

- if an individual is in hospital for longer than four weeks
- if an individual is in a care home for longer than eight weeks
- if there is a disagreement between the local authority and the appropriate individual and all agree that the involvement of an advocate would benefit the person.

When might advocates be involved?

An individual may need the involvement of an advocate in the following situations:

- a needs assessment
- a carer's assessment
- a transition assessment
- care and support or support plan preparation
- care and support or support plan review
- a safeguarding enquiry
- a safeguarding adult review
- an appeal or complaint about a local authority decision.

If advocates are supporting people with assessments, care planning, reviews or safeguarding issues, they have the right to access their health or social care records. Advocates must:

- have the appropriate experience
- have appropriate training and have gained the National Advocacy Qualification within one year
- have regular supervision
- have integrity and be of good character
- be independent.

Case study: Advocacy to support Julia and Sam

Julia is a single mother who is profoundly deaf and has spent most of her adult life caring for her son, Sam, who is 25 years old. She and Sam sign to each other, and Julia can lip read. Sam has learning disabilities and does not cope well with changes from his usual routine. He can become violent and has hit Julia twice in recent months when his routine was disrupted at short notice. He attends a day centre every weekday and works in a garden centre on a Saturday. Sam has just received a letter informing him that his day centre visits are being cut from five to two days a week. He became very angry about this and hit out at Julia, knocking her to the floor. Julia was shaken by this and is very concerned about the cuts as she works and cannot afford to drop her working days from five to two. There is no one who can care for Sam while she is at work, and he cannot be left alone. She tells Gus, the manager of the day centre, that she doesn't know who to turn to for help. She wants to appeal the decision to reduce Sam's day centre visits. Gus listens sympathetically but tells her that he is leaving the service so will not be able to help her.

- What are the issues for Sam and Julia?
- What potential problems could arise and how can they be resolved?
- What role could an advocate play in supporting Sam and Julia?

Summary

Remember that when advocating for someone, you must ensure that you are listening to what they want and communicating their wishes clearly so that their needs can be met.

Professional working

Advocates and advocacy providers work in partnership with the people they support and take their side. Advocacy promotes social inclusion, equality and social justice. Advocates have to adhere to their code of practice.

(Source: Advocacy QPM Code of Practice Revised 2014)

Professional working

Have you ever been asked to advocate for an individual you have cared for? How did you ensure that you listened to him or her and communicated his or her wishes (and not those of a family member or friend)? Did you feel that the relative or friend was trying to pressurise you into doing what they wanted? If so, how did you deal with this? Did you feel that you had successfully supported your user of service?

Taking the initiative and reducing environmental barriers to communication

As a lead adult care worker, you will be expected to exercise judgement and to take appropriate action to support individuals in maintaining independence, dignity and control. This includes being able to take the initiative to influence and effect change.

Activities

Qualification mapping

Unit 1 LO 2 AC 2.4, LO 3 AC 3.5

Adapting the environment

Noise, space, climate (or temperature), time and place are generally thought of as being the main environmental barriers to communication. How could you take the initiative to reduce the following environmental barriers to communication in your workplace if they became an issue? Think why this might be and the benefits to people working and living in the workplace.

Barrier	Why is it a barrier?	What are the benefits of reducing the barrier?
Place		
Noise		
Space		
Time		
Climate		

Qualification mapping

Unit 1 LO 3 AC 3.2 and 3.3

Taking the initiative

You work for an organisation that provides independent living for young adults with learning disabilities. Recently, Jade has moved into one of the houses. The house has always been very happy and the four original residents are close and spend a lot of time together in the sitting room watching television or listening to music.

Jade loves music and turns the volume up very loud and dances round the room. The other residents and staff have asked Jade not to have the music so loud, but each time it is turned down she turns it up again. This has resulted in the other residents going to their bedrooms after supper to avoid Jade and the noise.

The staff are concerned that the atmosphere is deteriorating and the residents are becoming isolated. They are struggling to resolve the situation and have asked you for advice. What actions can you take to support the staff and restore the atmosphere in the house?

Case study: Overcoming environmental barriers to communication

Gerry is 48, morbidly obese and has Type two diabetes. He lives alone in a bedsit. He has a hearing impairment and can lip read, but he refuses to wear his hearing aid. His television is always on and the volume is very high. Although there are lights in the bedsit, only one bulb works and it is nowhere near Gerry's chair. You and your team visit him to dress his leg ulcers once a week, but this is becoming increasingly difficult due to the state of the bedsit. Gerry has a dog that is not house trained and he can't take it for walks; it yaps loudly and is sometimes aggressive. The smell is intense but Gerry does not seem to notice it or the general dirt and dog mess on the floor.

Your staff have said that they cannot visit Gerry while the bedsit is in such a poor state as they cannot provide good quality care in such an environment. Two weeks later, Gerry is admitted to hospital with pneumonia. You have told him that he cannot return to his bedsit in its current state as he is at risk of further infection. Gerry is desperate to go home to the dog (being cared for by a neighbour), saying he'll be fine and that there is nothing wrong with his bedsit. You want the council to do a deep clean before Gerry goes home but he refuses to allow access and will no longer talk to you or your team. When anyone tries to talk to him, he turns away and will not speak.

- What environmental barriers to communication can you identify and how will they affect Gerry in the long term?
- What effect will working in such an environment have on Gerry's relationship with you and your team?
- Can you identify any solutions to reducing the barriers?
- What benefit would there be for Gerry and your team from reducing the barriers?

6Cs

Care, communication, commitment, courage, competence

Qualification mapping

Unit 1 LO 1 AC 1.3, LO 2 AC 2.4, LO 3 AC 3.2, 3.3 and 3.5

Your role as lead adult care worker means that as well as establishing good communication with the users of your service, you also have to do this with your staff.

Activity

Taking the initiative in communication issues

You work alongside another lead adult care worker, but you do not spend much time together. However, you have heard comments from other staff that she is difficult to work with. Two of the care workers have come to ask for advice as they are having difficulty working with her as their team lead. They say she is constantly barking orders at them and when they do what she has asked, she tells them that they have done it wrong. When they ask her to explain exactly what she wants them to do, she says 'Look, I've told you once, I haven't got time to tell you again. Just get on with it!'. The care workers feel that their relationship with her is deteriorating and have asked to be assigned to your team. You say you will see what you can do to help, but can't make any promises.

- What do you think would be the best way to approach this situation?
- Could you manage this situation on your own, or would you seek advice and support from someone else? If so, who?

Professional working

It is your responsibility to support individuals to communicate. To do this, you may have to plan ahead and think about what you will need to take into account. Remember that you will also be supporting colleagues with developing appropriate communication skills.

Your own and others' responsibility for ensuring confidential information is kept safe

As a lead adult care worker, you should have a knowledge of all the policies in your organisation and ensure that your staff also know that policies exist and where to find them. It is particularly important that you and your workers are familiar with the policy on confidentiality.

Qualification mapping

Unit 1 LO 4 AC 4.1, 4.2 and 4.3

Key term

Confidentiality – the state of keeping or being kept secret or private

Principle – an accepted or professed rule of action or conduct

Activity

Keeping information confidential

Discuss the following scenarios. What are the possible consequences in each case?

- A health worker tells a friend about a person who lives on their street that has a mental health problem and the treatment they are receiving.
- A social worker tells someone that a person with a criminal record related to children's issues is moving into the local community.
- An adult care worker tells a colleague a piece of personal information and asks her to keep it secret. You later hear another colleague talking about it.

Confidentiality is one of the most important aspects of communication. A lead adult care worker has a responsibility to ensure that they know and understand the principles of maintaining confidentiality. This applies to both users of the service they work for and colleagues. All care workers are in a position of trust and people need to be confident that information they disclose is managed sensitively.

The main legislation relating to confidentiality is the Data Protection Act 1998, and the General Data Protection Regulation, which came into effect in May 2018. The Data Protection Act has eight **principles**, as shown in Table 3.

First principle	Personal data shall be processed fairly and lawfully.
Second principle	Personal data shall be obtained only for one or more specified and lawful purposes, and shall not be further processed in any manner incompatible with that purpose or those purposes.
Third principle	Personal data shall be adequate, relevant and not excessive in relation to the purpose or purposes for which they are processed.
Fourth principle	Personal data shall be accurate and, where necessary, kept up to date.
Fifth principle	Personal data processed for any purpose or purposes shall not be kept for longer than is necessary for that purpose or those purposes.
Sixth principle	Personal data shall be processed in accordance with the rights of data subjects under this Act.
Seventh principle	Appropriate technical and organisational measures shall be taken against unauthorised or unlawful processing of personal data and against accidental loss or destruction of, or damage to, personal data.
Eighth principle	Personal data shall not be transferred to a country or territory outside the European Economic Area, unless that country or territory ensures an adequate level of protection for the rights and freedoms of data subjects in relation to the processing of personal data.

Table 3: The eight principles of the Data Protection Act

Information is confidential and should not be accessible to unauthorised people. In addition to the principles in Table 3, users of services have a right to know what information is held about them and to have access to it. They also have the right to refuse to provide information. The Data Protection Act covers both paper and electronic records.

6Cs

Competence

General Data Protection Regulation 2018

The General Data Protection Regulation (GDPR) was agreed by European Union countries and aims to strengthen the laws regarding the storage and use of individuals' personal information. It was written in response to the increasing use of technology and the difficulties of keeping information securely. There are new rules on how organisations can handle and use information they hold on their clients or customers, and GDPR gives individuals more control over what happens to the information held about them.

An individual can also ask for access to the information held about them and this must be supplied within one month of an organisation receiving such a request. There are eight rights for individuals under GDPR, as shown in Figure 4.

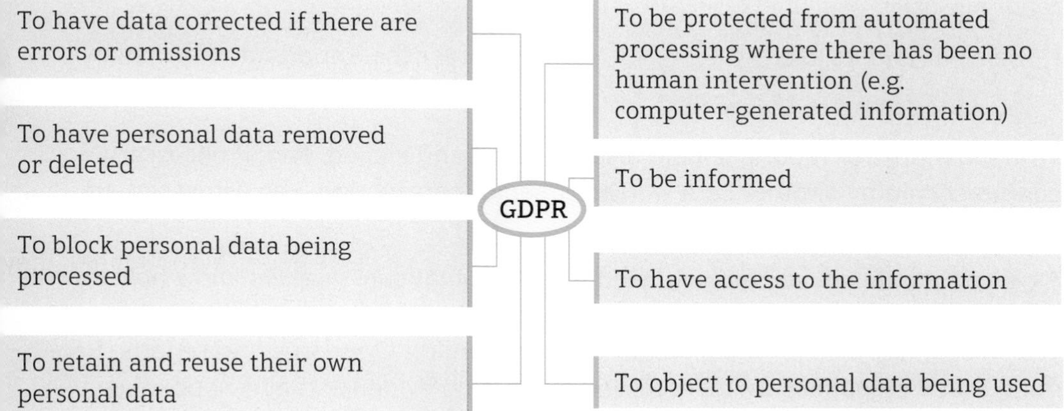

Figure 4: Individuals' rights under GDPR

Professional working

As a lead adult care worker, you may not be required to discuss what happens to a user of service's information, but you should make sure that you know and understand this information in case you are asked about it.

You should also ensure that your colleagues refer any questions to you or another senior member of the team if they do not know how to respond. Users of your service have the right to refuse to provide information if they choose to.

Summary

As a lead adult care worker you are responsible for knowing about and understanding the principles of maintaining confidentiality. This applies to both users of your service and your colleagues.

Demonstrate and ensure that records and reports are written clearly and concisely

Written records, reports and other documentation are examples of non-verbal communication and are as important as verbal communication in health and social care settings.

It is important to ensure that records and reports are accurate as this can help to prevent communication barriers. As a lead adult care worker, you may need to support your staff in developing the skills to write reports or records. You may have to provide guidance in how to record information electronically as well as on paper and how to save and/or send it.

Care and support plans and notes are legal documents that might need to be referred to in a court of law if legal action is taken. Therefore written records and reports must:

- be clear and legible
- be concise and to the point
- cover the important information clearly and logically.

Written records or reports should also be dated and signed, and, if necessary, countersigned by another care worker or senior care worker who witnessed an incident, to confirm accuracy.

As a lead adult care worker, you need to ensure that care workers know how to write records and reports following the bullet points above. You should also be sure of your responsibilities for the clear and concise writing of records and reports. Bear in mind that if something is not recorded there is no evidence that it happened.

Activity

Kevin has been bad this week. On Monday he wouldn't go to colledge. He said he felt ill but he didn't have a temprature or nothing. I think he just wanted to stay here and see his new girlfriend next door.

Tuesday 2pm. After I had just gave him his dinner he was sick all over me. I know he can't help throwing up, but he could of given me some warning so I didn't have 2 change all my clothes. I sorted him out afterwards. Thursday we had archery in the lounge. Kev wanted to go in his wheelchair but hes sposed 2 use his stix, so I told him he had 2 try with them. He got really stroppy and refused 2 go in the end. I think we should arrange some other activities for him that he can do in his own house. Then we won't have these fights about him moving about.

What dyou reckon? Shelly

Figure 5: Can you see scope for improvement here?

Importance of record keeping

Arrange a professional discussion with one or more of your adult care workers on your organisation's policy for record keeping. Make sure that you have some examples of written reports and records that you can discuss. You could also use the example shown in Figure 5.

- What is your opinion of this report? Consider the factual detail, the attitude shown by Shelly (Kevin's key worker) and the suggestions made.
- What problems could be caused by poor report writing like this?
- If you were Shelly's manager, how would you respond when receiving a report like this?

Rewrite the report using the guidance above.

You could also use this report as an example of poor record writing for your care workers. Ask them to consider the same questions and rewrite the report more formally.

Professional working 

You should ensure that the adult care workers you work with know how to write legible and clear documents. You and they:

- must always write in pen
- must not erase, use correcting fluid or scribble out errors
- should cross through errors with one straight line
- should initial any crossings out so that you/they can be identified
- must re-write clearly what you/they want to record.

If you work with staff who have poor language skills, or who may be dyslexic, you might want to provide extra support. You could ask them to write a rough draft on a piece of paper before they write it on official documentation, or you might want to ask the education lead in your organisation what other support is available. It is sometimes difficult for people to ask for help, but it is one of your responsibilities to ensure that records are clear and accurate.

Activity

Recording incidents accurately

Poopak is an adult care worker in a residential home. Polly, the activities coordinator, has organised a painting session for some of the residents in the dining room and Poopak is helping with this. Martha, one of the residents, drops her jar of water and it smashes, sending broken glass and water all over the floor. Polly starts to pick up the broken glass and cuts herself. Her hand is bleeding badly. Henry, another resident, tells Poopak that he feels sick and would like to go and lie down in his room. Meanwhile, Ned, the new kitchen assistant, gives tea and cake to Arthur who has diabetes. His care plan says that he should not have cake as his blood glucose levels are difficult to control.

Poopak has to complete the relevant records before she goes off duty.

- How could Poopak make sure that she remembers all of the information accurately?
- What records would Poopak need to complete for each of the incidents?
- How could you support Poopak to ensure that everything is recorded accurately?
- Think about your workplace and its policies – if this sort of event happened while you were on duty, what records would you need to complete?
- If you were responsible for managing the reporting of an event like this and it happened when you were off duty, what information and evidence would you expect to find on your return?

6Cs 

Communication, competence

Professional working 

The importance of accurate recording and reporting cannot be overestimated. Part of your role as a lead adult care worker is to ensure that you and your staff develop the skills to record and report clearly and accurately.

Ensuring confidential information is kept safe

You have looked at information on the law surrounding confidentiality. But you also need to know and be able to advise your adult care workers on how data should be handled so that it remains safe and secure at all times.

Qualification mapping

Unit 1 LO 4 AC 4.1, 4.2 and 4.3

Activity

Confidentiality issues

Discuss the following scenarios with your team.

What action do you think should be taken in each case?

- A user of your service confides in you that she thinks one of the care workers has been taking money from her purse. She doesn't want to get anyone into trouble so asks you not to say anything to anyone. You know that her daughter has power of attorney for her health and finance, and that she rarely has cash in her flat. You also know that she lives with dementia.
- A junior care worker has been taking selfies of users of your service and posting them on social media. Some of the users of service also post photos of themselves and the care worker on the same site.
- A relative has come to you asking what the red star on his father's folder means. This is your organisation's system for identifying quickly if a user of the service is not for resuscitation. You are new to the organisation but realise that the son has not been told that his father is not to be resuscitated.
- An adult care worker posts the following on a social media site: 'Another **really bad** day – short staffed, no breaks to speak of and had to deal with a really difficult user of the service who had to be admitted to X hospital. I went with him and when we got to A & E the dozy male staff nurse was hopeless – I really don't know why he bothers to work there, completely unprofessional! I hope I never have to be a patient there. I'm off to down a bottle of wine or two!!' (You know who the staff nurse is as he is the only male nurse working there.)

When you or your staff are handling data it is essential to do the following:

- date and sign any entry made (get someone to counter sign if needed)
- enter all information correctly
- make sure the information is secure
- return files after use
- log out of electronic systems securely after use
- only provide and receive information on a 'need to know' basis
- inform users of your service when entries are made into their files.

Guidance on what *not* to do when handling data is shown in Figure 6.

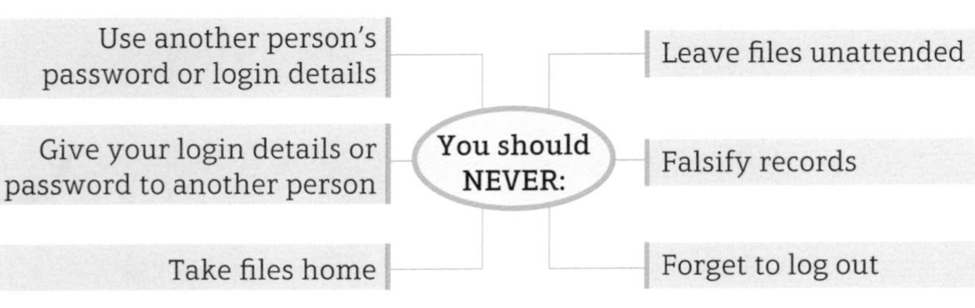

Figure 6: What not to do when handling data

It is not only written information that needs to be handled in a secure way. Telephone conversations can be overheard so it is important that you and your staff are aware of your surroundings when making calls that require you to disclose sensitive information.

Importance of supporting others to handle information securely

Everyone who works with sensitive information should understand the need for secure handling of data and record keeping, and should attend relevant training about data handling. You may need to support others in your work setting to handle information securely, as they will need to understand:

- the law concerning data
- confidentiality
- the need for accuracy
- how to contribute to manual and electronic records
- what information is shared on a 'need to know' basis only
- the setting's policy on record keeping, and the length of time of storage
- the impact of losing or mislaying records
- the impact of records ending up in the wrong hands.

The 'need to know' principle

As a lead adult care worker you will need to know when to keep information shared between you and the users of your service confidential and when to pass the information on to other people who need to know. This is an important principle that all care workers need to know and understand. You should ensure that the care workers you supervise pass information to you or your superiors so that disclosure can be managed appropriately.

There are times when confidential information may need to be disclosed, and in some cases it is a legal requirement.

Information may need to be passed on to a doctor or the police if an individual's health or safety is considered to be at risk, for example:

- someone has committed or may be about to commit a crime
- other people may be at risk due to an individual's actions
- there has been suspicion or disclosure of abuse
- there is a court order for disclosure of information
- an individual is at risk of harm, such as displaying suicidal behaviour.

Summary 

How you and your staff record and report information can have a profound effect on how trusted you are by the users of your service, their relatives or friends and the people you work with. You should ensure that both you and your staff understand the legal issues surrounding confidentiality.

Professional working 

Make sure that you and your staff are aware of what to do when you need to make confidential phone calls, and where you and they are when making them. If you and your team work in an office or a health or social care setting such as a residential home, do you always remember to close doors? If you work in the community, how do you and the team ensure that you maintain confidentiality if you have to make a phone call?

6Cs 

Competence

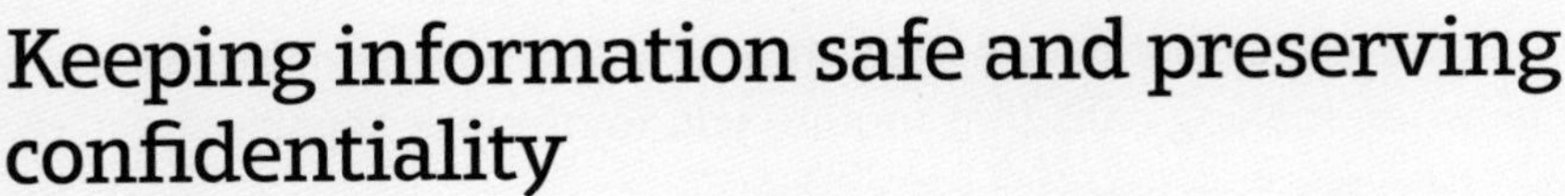

Keeping information safe and preserving confidentiality

Qualification mapping

Unit 1 LO 4

Your role as a lead care worker means that you not only have to ensure that you maintain confidentiality, but that your care workers are trained in how to keep information about users of the service safe and how to work according to data protection principles and the policies and procedures of your workplace.

6Cs

Care, courage, competence

Case study: Breach of confidentiality

The Glebe Care Home is a private 20-bedded residential unit for older people with moderate care needs. Mr Kowalski has had a troubling cough for several weeks. One day Mr Kowalski's daughter, Kasia, was travelling to visit her father on the bus. Two of the adult care workers got on the bus and sat in front of her. They were the only passengers. They were both new care workers at The Glebe and didn't recognise her. Neither of them had worked in care before. One said to the other 'Oh by the way, did you know that Mr Kowalski has been referred to the hospital for tests for lung cancer?'. Kasia was shocked to hear this as she had not been informed. She arrived at the home and demanded to see a senior member of staff. She asked to know if her father had been informed of the referral and wanted to make a formal complaint.

The manager was out assessing a possible new resident and you were in charge.

- What are the confidentiality issues in this case?
- How could you deal with Kasia's immediate distress?
- How would you deal with the two staff members?

It is extremely important to keep written records confidential. They should not be left where they can be accessed by people who do not have the right to see them.

Activity

6Cs

Communication, competence

Dealing with information at work

Using current legislation, and the relevant policies, copy and complete the table below about the dos and don'ts of dealing with information in your organisation.

Information	Do	Don't
Incoming phone calls		
Outgoing phone calls		
Texts		
Written information		
Correcting an error in handwritten information		
Sending emails		
Receiving emails		

Reflective account

Identify an occasion when you had difficulty accessing or finding vital information that you needed about a user of your service.

Write a reflective account of what happened and what you did to solve the problem.

How could you ensure that an incident like this would not happen again?

6Cs

Care, courage, communication, competence

Practice for professional discussion

Read the following scenario about Betty:

Betty is a 58-year-old woman from West Africa. She has three grown-up children who all live and work abroad. She escaped from her abusive husband a year ago and is now in sheltered accommodation. She has leg ulcers that are being dressed twice a week by adult care workers and is also receiving support from a social worker. Her husband, Chima, often told her that he would find and kill her if she ever left him. He used to beat her every day and she was forbidden from leaving the house on her own. She is terrified that he will find her.

Betty told the social worker that she did not want any information about her to be disclosed to anyone as she knew Chima would use any means to find her. But one day he did turn up at her door and tried to get into her flat, shouting and making threats.

The adult care workers arrived while he was pounding on the door and the police were called. Chima was arrested. It was later established that Chima had phoned the care agency pretending to be Betty's son calling from abroad. The adult care worker who answered the phone in the office told him where Betty lived, thinking she had done the right thing. She said she thought he was genuine.

Have a professional discussion with one or more members of your team. You should cover the following questions:

- What confidentiality issues can be identified in this scenario?
- What would the adult care workers do in a situation like this?
- What could have been done by the care agency to prevent this breach of confidentiality?

Professional working

Many of the users of your service are vulnerable, and you may discover that some of the adult care workers you work with are also vulnerable due to their personal circumstances. You have a duty to safeguard everyone so keep in mind the principles of confidentiality and apply them appropriately.

Situational judgement questions

1. Which of the following is an example of positive communication?
   a. Treating all users of service exactly the same
   b. Asking a user of service to repeat your instructions
   c. Interrupting a user of service who doesn't understand what you are asking him or her
   d. Telling a user of service that you are too busy to spend time with them
2. Which of the following is an example of an environmental barrier to communication?
   a. Hearing loss
   b. Poor lighting
   c. Not speaking English
   d. Using slang
3. Which of the following is an example of an open question?
   a. 'Hello Joan, would you like to go out today?'
   b. 'Hey Peter, do you want breakfast?'
   c. 'Hello Zoe, what would you like for breakfast this morning?'
   d. 'Hello Mrs Khan, would you like an apple for dessert?'
4. Active listening involves:
   a. Asking someone to clarify what they are saying
   b. Maintaining eye contact
   c. Nodding to confirm you have heard
   d. All of the above
5. You hear one of your adult care workers saying to a user of the service 'You don't look very comfortable. What can I do to help you?' This is an example of:
   a. Blocking communication
   b. Aggression
   c. False reassurance
   d. Assertiveness
6. In which of these situations would you share information without the individual's consent?
   a. When informing staff of a change to an individual's care plan
   b. When giving information about a user of service to the next of kin who has power of attorney
   c. When you are concerned that someone is displaying suicidal behaviour
   d. When you ask a doctor about a change to a user of service's medication
7. A man phones and tells you that he is the husband of A, one of the users of your service. He asks you how she is. What do you do?
   a. Ask for his number and tell him you'll call him back when you have spoken to A
   b. Tell him how she is and say you'll let her know that he phoned
   c. Confirm that A is a user of the service but provide no other detail
   d. Tell him that you cannot give out any information over the phone about any person who may or may not be a user of the service
8. A relative is angry about their father's care and is shouting at you in the corridor where everyone can hear. What do you do?
   a. Shout back
   b. Say 'I am sorry to hear that you are angry. Please come into the office so that we can discuss this.'
   c. Burst into tears and run off into the staff room
   d. Walk off without acknowledging the relative or what she is saying

D
Safeguarding

This topic will cover some of the most difficult issues you may face as a lead adult care worker. Part of your role is to support people who have been subjected to abuse by the people who care for them. It is vital that you are aware of what to look for and how to respond so you can support and protect users of service from harm, and support colleagues in your team and in the wider setting. Understanding risk factors and knowing how to intervene in potential abusive situations is the best way to support and protect the people in your care.

This topic will cover the following areas:

- what abuse is and what to do if you have concerns someone is being abused
- the national and local strategies for safeguarding and protection from abuse
- what to do when receiving comments and complaints
- recognising and preventing unsafe practices in the workplace
- the importance and process of whistleblowing
- dilemmas between a person's rights and their safety.

You will also learn about the skills you will need so that you can apply this knowledge in the care setting where you work.

What abuse is

Qualification mapping

Unit 5 LO 1 AC 1.3 and 1.4

Abuse of vulnerable adults can happen anywhere. It can involve one person or a group of people. It can be perpetrated by a family member, health care professional, volunteer or friend.

Signs and symptoms of abuse

An important factor is that if abuse has happened once there is a strong likelihood it will happen again. Some of these instances of abuse can be criminal offences, such as fraud, rape or theft, but not all can be prosecuted in this way.

The signs and symptoms of abuse are often accompanied by negative emotional responses or behaviour that can signal potential abuse (see Table 1). You need to be aware, however, that this is not proof of abuse in itself, although it can indicate the possibility. In this case, you must work with colleagues and other appropriate professionals to observe and communicate, in order to build a more detailed picture.

Type of abuse	Signs to look for
Physical abuse: hitting; burning; pushing or kicking someone; rough handling; unreasonable restraint (including misuse of medication); locking someone in a room	Injuries that are unexplained or have not been treated
Domestic abuse: controlling and coercive behaviour; forced marriage; female genital mutilation or honour-based violence	Signs of domestic violence can be any of those relating to the different types of **harm**, abuse or neglect that can occur in any incident
Sexual abuse: rape; inappropriate touching; forcing or grooming someone to take part in or witness any sexual act against their will	Pain, sores, bruising Pain and discomfort when walking or sitting Psychological signs can be: depression, anger, self-harm, unexplained fear, isolation
Emotional/psychological abuse: intimidation; bullying; shouting; swearing; taunting; threatening or humiliating someone	Anxiety, lack of confidence, low **self-esteem**, disturbed sleep
Financial/material abuse: theft; fraud coercion over wills; misuse of someone's money, property or other belongings without their agreement	Misuse or theft of money Fraud, exploitation or pressure in connection with wills, property or inheritance

Key term

(Adult at risk of) harm – an adult at risk of harm is someone who needs care and support, and is experiencing, or is at risk of, abuse or neglect and unable to protect themselves

Self-esteem – confidence in yourself as an individual person

Modern slavery: human trafficking; forced labour and domestic slavery	Unclean, not allowed to travel alone, under influence of others, few personal belongings or documents, avoids eye contact, appears frightened to talk to strangers and police
Discriminatory abuse: ill-treatment based on a persons' age, sex, sexuality, disability, religious beliefs or ethnic group	Verbal abuse and disrespect
Institutional/organisational abuse: poor care/organisational culture; lack of resources; no choice; lack of dignity and respect	Lacking personal clothing and possessions No flexibility on bedtimes, eating times or visiting hours Dirty bed linen or clothing
Self-neglect: not looking after yourself or where you live	Indicators of neglect by others and self-neglect are similar
Neglect by others: neglect/acts of omission by people responsible for giving care	Malnutrition, dehydration, dirty clothing and bedding

'able 1: Types of abuse – signs and symptoms
Source: https://www.bsab.org/what-is-abuse/definitions-of-abuse/)

Factors that may contribute to individuals taking risks

'here are many factors that can lead to individuals taking risks and it will not always be possible for you to protect against this; nor should you. When we consider the isks people take, there are situations that may be dangerous, but individuals have he right to take risks in order to take control of their lives.

'his needs to be managed and balanced against the importance of dignity, empowerment and an individual's right to choose. Although it may be difficult to emain objective at times, it is easy to get too involved, putting you in danger of osing perspective. As a lead adult care worker you will also need to be supportive of unior colleagues. Supportive working relationships are essential; although they can be interpreted in many different ways, depending on the context and the support. Part of your role as lead adult care worker will be noticing when a colleague is having difficulties at work, if they are nervous or unsure of a task or perhaps require further raining. If your team is working efficiently then this will be better for everyone, ncluding the people you are supporting.

Factors that may contribute to an individual being more vulnerable to abuse

The risk of abuse and harm can also be an issue with carers who are family nembers or friends. Some of the factors known to be associated with the risk of harm or abuse of adults by family and friend carers include those shown in Table 2.

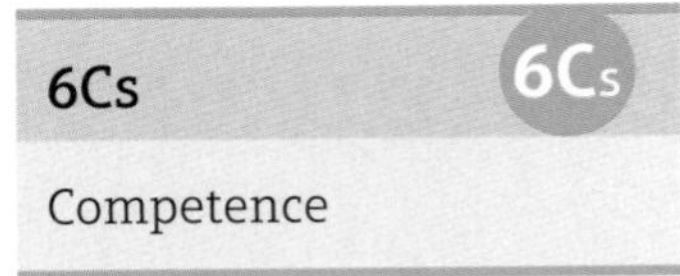

6Cs

Competence

Abuse by family member or friend	
Poor communication	Between the user of service and the person responsible for their care; this could be because of medication, a medical condition or a breakdown in their relationship
Challenging behaviour	The user of service might demonstrate behaviour that the carer or family member is not qualified to cope with
Age or experience	The carer or family member does not have the emotional intelligence to look after the cared-for person
Alcohol or drug dependency	Being dependant on drugs or alcohol can seriously affect the capability of the carer, leading to potential abuse
Violent behaviour	If the person being cared for is violent to the carer, this could lead to an abusive response
Carer being stressed	If the carer has other caring responsibilities, young children or an older relative, for example, they may experience feelings of stress
Social isolation	Can lead to abusive relationships, particularly financial abuse
Abuse by professionals	
Poor supervision	Lack of support in the work place can lead to abusive situations, particularly if the staff member does not have regular supervision
Unprofessional culture	This has been an issue in recent years leading to serious breaches in conduct and abusive situations
Poor training	The lack of appropriate training can lead to behaviour that causes abusive situations to occur
Lack of knowledge/ professional development	Unprofessional conduct, which can lead to abusive situations, can arise from a lack of knowledge or professional development

Table 2: Risk of harm or abuse from family and friend carers, and professionals

How to respond to suspected abuse

The overriding principle when considering a **disclosure** of abuse is to believe what the individual says. Many individuals who report abuse have a very real concern that they will not be believed; it is important that you do not compound this fear by acting in any way that could be considered disbelief.

This might sound obvious but it can be difficult if you have not been in or experienced an abusive situation before. The thought that someone could abuse another person can be difficult to understand.

If a user of service makes an allegation of abuse, try not to get into too much detailed information. Your first obligation is to reassure the individual that you believe them. Then, report the allegation immediately to a senior colleague and hand over the responsibility.

There may be occasions when this is not possible. This might be because of the location or because the individual feels that they need to disclose everything to you at that time.

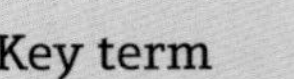

Key term

Disclosure – revelation of information that was previously kept secret

Leading question – question expressed in such a way that it suggests what the answer should be

Mental capacity – the ability to make decisions for yourself

If this is the case, and you are being given a lot of detailed information, try avoiding **leading questions,** for example, 'Was it then that he punched you?'. Instead, progress the conversation with phrases like 'and then what happened?'.

In a situation like this you would use your core communication skills to keep the person reassured that you are listening and they can trust you. Stay focused on what the person is saying to you; ask them to repeat something if you are unsure what is being said. This will help you record the information more accurately.

6Cs 6Cs

Courage

Confidentiality

Confidentiality is an important issue. You need to reassure the user of service that their disclosure will remain confidential but that there will be certain people to whom you must disclose what they have told you.

Confidentiality is a key principle in supporting people and is the right of every person. However, allegations of abuse are one of the few situations in which you may not be able to promise this. It is very important that you do not make such promises. You can state, however, that you promise not to tell anyone *except* those who will help.

You may find yourself in a situation whereby a user of service flatly refuses to allow you to share anything they have said. Situations like this are very difficult to deal with. You would, of course, have to share any such reports with your manager, and would then need to continue to work with the user of service, monitoring the situation and encouraging them to share the information with the appropriate people.

There can be circumstances where it might be necessary to breach confidentiality; for example, if the user of service was in imminent danger or being systematically stolen from by a member of staff. Situations like this must only be dealt with in discussion with your manager and recorded fully.

The only other exception to this rule would be if the user of service did not have **mental capacity** (see page 143).

Institutional abuse

Institutional abuse is generally seen through the prism of large-scale physical or sexual abuses that have been widely publicised in the media, however, this type of abuse has also occurred on a much smaller scale within organisations where individuals should expect to be protected, cared for and supported. Abuse in this context may not be as direct or obvious, as indicated in the signs and symptoms in Table 1, but rather the effect of institutional behaviour that prioritises the convenience of staff above a respect for the needs, rights and dignity of the users of service.

This type of situation can lead to extreme cases of abuse of vulnerable adults. An example of this was the case of Winterbourne View, a residential hospital for adults with learning disabilities. The residents of this hospital were routinely subjected to verbal, physical and emotional abuse. Six people who worked at the privately-run hospital near Bradley Stoke were jailed after cruel and degrading treatment was exposed by an undercover reporter.

A factor in recognising institutional abuse is that these kinds of practices are routinely accepted and/or ignored by the organisation or management and that the systems and processes that are in place do not identify the needs of the people using the service.

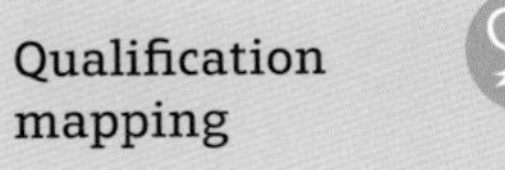

Qualification mapping

Unit 5 LO 1 AC 1.3, LO 2 AC 2.1 and 2.2

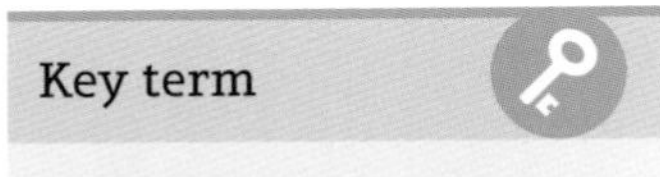

Key term

Advocacy – taking action to help people say what they want, secure their rights, represent their interests and obtain services they need

6Cs

Care

Examples of these types of practice include the following:

- People in residential settings are not given any choice regarding basic decisions, such as meal times or when to go to sleep.
- Freedom to leave the premises is limited by the organisation.
- Personal correspondence is opened by the staff.
- The convenience of the staff is prioritised over the support of the users of the service.
- There is overuse of sedatives and inappropriate medications.
- There is limited or no access to **advocacy** or advice.
- Complaints procedures are not made known or are unavailable.

Safeguarding

When safeguarding vulnerable adults there are four key priorities you should observe when responding to allegations of abuse, as shown in Figure 1.

Priority 1: Protect

The first priority is arguably one of the most important. You must ensure that the person making the allegation of abuse is protected from further abuse. You might also have to make sure that any potential medical support is arranged, while all the time reassuring and comforting the individual. It is important to point out that this remains a priority even if the allegation of abuse was a long time ago or has been systematic over a period of time. You do have a responsibility to support and take action if you suspect someone is being abused or neglected. It may mean removing someone to a safe place, or moving the alleged perpetrator; it could even involve medical assistance.

Figure 1: Key priorities when responding to allegations of abuse

Priority 2: Report

If you are aware of an abusive situation you must report it. This would normally be to your manager or a nominated person, according to the workplace policies and procedures concerning protection of vulnerable adults. An exception would be if the allegation of abuse or neglect was made against the manager or nominated person. It may be that there is an established procedure for reporting incidents of abuse or neglect of vulnerable adults in your workplace. Whatever system is in place, you should provide a full detailed written report as soon as possible after the event.

The Data Protection Act 1998 requires that you ensure that all confidential information is kept securely. This is particularly important with regard to information concerning allegations of abuse and neglect. Information must be stored securely and password protected if it is being kept electronically, with hard copies stored in a locked cabinet. It is also important that you keep only essential and relevant information regarding the allegation.

Priority 3: Preserve

Preserving any evidence is also an important priority, especially if it is a potential crime scene. You must be very careful not to destroy or contaminate any potential evidence. If the alleged incident is of a physical or sexual nature, then there is likely to be forensic evidence. It is essential that this is carefully preserved until the police arrive.

For example, **do not:**

- clear up
- wash or clean any part of the location or room in which the incident took place
- remove bedding or clothes the abused person is wearing.

Priority 4: Record and refer

You are required to record any information you might have regarding the situation regardless of whether it is hard evidence or an allegation. You must also record your evidence, using an electronic recorder if you are unable to write it down. This can then be **transcribed** later.

Key term

Transcribed – written down

You must not verbally pass on information without backing it up with a written report; verbal reports are at risk of details being forgotten or changed in the telling. You may find that your workplace has a specific report form that needs to be completed regarding concerns about abuse or neglect.

It is important to include:

- everything that you have observed
- anything that you have been told, making sure that it is clear that it is not something you have seen for yourself
- any previous concerns you may have had
- what raised your concerns regarding the situation.

Recording what you have been told or witnessed is very important. You may be required to make a formal statement at a later date to the police or an investigation team. You will also have to record the key details for your own workplace team.

This could result in a referral to another organisation, such as the police or social services. The type of information you should collect, for example, would be:

- what happened
- what you saw, if anything
- what you were told
- who said or did what.

It is important that you do not get confused with what is fact and what is opinion; state clearly only what you know. You may also include what you have heard from others, but be sure to identify it as third party evidence and not fact.

Summary

The process of responding to allegations of abuse or neglect can have a very negative effect on the vulnerable person at the centre of the claim. It is vital that those vulnerable people are protected from further abuse and that you can support and reassure them throughout the procedure. You also need to support others to recognise and respond to potential signs of abuse according to agreed ways of working.

Recognise and respond to potential signs of abuse

In your role as a lead adult care worker, you will need to support others to recognise and respond to potential signs of abuse.

Activities

Qualification mapping

Unit 5 LO 2 AC 2.1 and 2.2

Recognising abuse

You are the lead adult care worker in a residential care home and you witnessed a user of service, who has Parkinson's disease, drop a mug of tea that had just been handed to her by a support worker. The mug broke and hot tea went everywhere. The support worker shouted at the individual, telling her to be more careful. After this incident the individual would not talk to that particular support worker again and she seemed afraid.

- How should the support worker have acted?
- What action, if any, should you take?

Signs of abuse

Copy the table and draw a line to link the type of abuse to the explanation of what it may involve.

Physical		Carers fail to meet individual's needs for basic necessities such as food, shelter, clothing or medical care
Sexual		Individuals may be harmed by ignoring them, by belittling them or through name calling
Emotional		Individuals are hurt, leaving marks such as bruises in places where they would not occur in normal activities
Neglect		Harmful behaviour by other individuals that makes a person fearful
Bullying		Individuals experience inappropriate contact with others

Sharing information

Information sharing is an essential aspect of safeguarding vulnerable people. Explain why it is important to share information with relevant people and agencies.

How can this be seen as being supportive?

Reflection

For this reflection, use the Kolb reflective cycle on page v. Think about a time when you did not have enough sleep and record your answers to the following questions:

- How did you feel?
- Could you still make important decisions?
- How do you think such a situation could lead to an individual being abusive to others?

Signs and symptoms

Copy the table below and in each row write two possible signs or symptoms of abuse.

Type of abuse	Sign/symptom 1	Sign/symptom 2
Physical		
Psychological		
Neglect/acts of omission		
Financial/material		
Institutional		
Self-harm/abuse		
Sexual		

Policies and procedures

Do you know where to find the Safeguarding Adults at Risk policies and procedures in your workplace? Find out what these procedures and policies are, so you understand what actions to take if you suspect an individual is being abused or if an individual tells you they are being abused. Make notes for future reference.

Practice for professional discussion: Mental Capacity Act 2005

As the lead adult care worker you have been supporting a user of service who has an acquired brain injury and difficulties processing information with regard to decision making. You have an in-depth knowledge of their likes and dislikes and have been trying to support and promote their independence. It has been suggested that the user of the service would benefit from attending a day centre to decrease social isolation and to improve their social interactions, however, the individual is not able to make this choice.

- How could the processes of the Mental Health Act 2005 help you decide if the user of service has capacity or not?
- How would your knowledge of them support the user of service in this decision-making process?
- Discuss the different strategies that are used in your workplace to support decision making for users of service whose capacity to make decisions is either permanently or temporarily impaired?

Think about your own work context. Include evidence/experience from your own practice to support your answers, for example:

- expert witness testimonies
- reflective accounts
- observation records
- work products.

Giving and receiving support

Keep a diary of support you give and receive at work for two weeks; a month would be better if you have capacity. At the end of every working shift, note how many times you gave support and how many times you received support. The level to which we give and receive support is proportional to an effective and successful team. They should be similar in both cases. If you are receiving more support than you are giving, then you need to explore additional ways you can support your colleagues; if it is the other way around then that it something you should raise at a staff meeting.

National and local strategies for safeguarding

Qualification mapping

Unit 5 LO 4 AC 4.1, 4.2, 4.3 and 4.4

6Cs

Competence

The Safeguarding Adults agenda for the protection of vulnerable adults forms part of the national and local programme of support. There are a number of national policies and local systems that relate to safeguarding and protection from abuse.

The government has developed legislation that provides us with a basis for dealing with abuse of vulnerable adults. These laws regarding the abuse of vulnerable adults are not as comprehensive as those developed for the protection of children. There is no law in England dealing specifically with abuse, but the situation is different in Scotland. This section looks at legislation specifically in relation to your role as a lead adult care worker.

Table 3 identifies some of the laws, policies and guidelines that, as a lead adult care worker, you may refer to with regard to supporting adults in an abusive situation.

Act of Parliament/ regulation or guideline	Use	Type of abuse
Criminal Justice Act 1998	Criminal prosecution by police for assault	Physical
Civil action by the victim	For assault and battery or false imprisonment	Physical
Care Standards Act 2000	Regulation of residential and nursing homes, S10 - cancellation of registration, S11- emergency cancellation for breach of regulations. However, it is the driving up of quality as a result of this Act which offers the best protection against abuse	Institutional
Sexual Offences Act 2003	Police prosecution for rape, indecent assault and other sexual offences. This Act has greatly increased the protection for people with a learning disability or mental health problems as it has been able to define 'consent'	Sexual
Family Law Act 1996	Can provide injunctions and non-molestation orders	Physical, sexual, psychological
Offences against the Person Act 1861	Prosecution by the police for more serious offences of actual bodily harm or grievous bodily harm	Physical

Safeguarding Vulnerable Groups Act 2006	Sets up vetting and barring scheme for people who work with children and vulnerable adults in England and Wales	All
Criminal Injuries Compensation Scheme	Can provide payments for survivors of abuse that was the result of a criminal act	Physical, sexual, financial if criminally proven
Mental Capacity Act 2005	It is a criminal offence to ill treat or neglect a person who lacks capacity	Physical, sexual, neglect
Police and Criminal Evidence Act 1984	S37 regards the powers of a local authority, relative, or court to take out guardianship of a vulnerable adult S115 regards the powers of entry and inspection for approved social workers S117 regards providing aftercare for people with mental health problems S135 regards powers to remove people to a 'place of safety' S127 regards the ill treatment of patients with mental health problems	All
Protection from Harassment Act 1997	Regards protection from harassment and from fear of violence	Psychological
Theft Act 1968	Police prosecution for theft	Financial
National Assistance Act 1984 S47	Local authority has responsibility for matters to do with protection of property	Financial
Fraud Act 2006	Has made it an offence to abuse a position of trust	Financial
Care Act 2014	Improves people's independence and wellbeing. Places responsibility on local authorities to provide services that promote independence and wellbeing so as not to develop further need for care or support deteriorating to the point of needing ongoing care and support	All
Human Rights Act 1998	Supports the human rights of all without discrimination, regardless of nationality, place of residence, sex, national or ethnic origin, colour, religion, language, or any other status	All

Table 3: Legislation for supporting adults in an abusive situation

Roles of different agencies in safeguarding

The Care Act 2014 is the main legislation; it was updated in April 2015. It sets out the law relating to the provision of care and support to people over the age of 18. Skills for Care produced a briefing about the implications of the Care Act for safeguarding adults.

The Care Act 2014 puts adult safeguarding on a legal footing and, from April 2015, each local authority must do the following things.

- Make enquiries, or ensure that others do so, if it believes an adult is subject to, or at risk of, abuse or neglect. An enquiry should establish whether any action needs to be taken to stop or prevent abuse or neglect, and if so, by whom.
- Set up a Safeguarding Adults Board (SAB) with core membership from the local authority, the Police and the NHS (specifically the local Clinical Commissioning Group/s) and the power to include other relevant bodies.
- Arrange, where appropriate, for an independent advocate to represent and support an adult who is the subject of a safeguarding enquiry or Safeguarding Adult Review (SAR) where the adult has 'substantial difficulty' in being involved in the process and where there is no other appropriate adult to help them.
- Cooperate with each of its relevant partners in order to protect adults experiencing or at risk of abuse or neglect.

The Act also updates the scope of adult safeguarding where a local authority has reasonable cause to suspect that an adult in its area (whether or not ordinarily resident there):

- has needs for care and support (whether or not the authority is meeting any of those needs)
- is experiencing, or is at risk of, abuse or neglect, and, as a result of those needs is unable to protect himself or herself against the abuse or neglect or the risk of it.

The introduction of the Care Act 2014 means that councils must follow up any reports of concerns about any suspected or actual abuse of adults. Organisations are now subject to greater scrutiny than before, and all organisations that are involved in safeguarding adults must make sure that statutory guidance (including policies and procedures), good practice guidance and any other relevant materials are included in training and development programmes. This applies whether or not councils are providing services to the adults involved.

Safeguarding Adults Boards (SAB) ensure that local authorities deliver a multi-agency response to safeguarding adults. They also make certain that all related partner agencies are delivering a concerted response to safeguarding issues on both a strategic and individual level.

The SABs must ensure that there are local arrangements in place, defined by the Care Act 2014, so that they can safeguard adults who may have support and care needs. Their three core duties are:

- to develop and publish a strategic plan which identifies how they and partner agencies will work together to meet set objectives
- to publish an annual report detailing how effective they have been
- to commission any safeguarding adults reviews for cases identified as needing them.

The Care Act 2014 also states that the three core members of the SABs are the local authority, the clinical commissioning group (CCGs) and the police (specifically the chief officer), with other agencies also being involved.

While there is legislation that provides a foundation for dealing with abuse of vulnerable adults, this legislation is not as straightforward as it is for the protection of children. Also there is no law in England that would deal exclusively with abuse, although this is currently under review.

Factors featured in reports into serious case reviews

Safeguarding adult reviews (SARs), which were previously known as Serious Case Reviews, and Safeguarding Adults Boards (SABs) are set up following the death of an adult in an area as a result of abuse or neglect. This procedure takes place regardless of proof of neglect or abuse; it is also applicable if there is an allegation or suspicion that a partner agency has failed in some way resulting in the death. SABs must also arrange a SAR even if there has not been a death but there is reasonable concern or suspicion that the adult has experienced neglect or abuse. Also SABs are able to set up a SAR for any adult within its area who has a need for support and care.

Some of the factors that have featured in the instigation of a SAR are:

- poor or lack of communication between services, including not sharing important information
- ineffective partnership working between services
- those receiving care and support or their families and friends not being involved in decisions made about their care
- failure to identify signs of abuse
- lack of management support or presence
- limited learning and development opportunities for workers
- poor staff recruitment processes.

Sources of information and advice about your own role

It is important that you understand your role and responsibilities in relation to safeguarding and protecting those you care for from abuse. Vulnerable adults depend on you to keep them safe from harm, and you will be held accountable for your actions.

As a lead adult care worker, you should remember that a user of the service should be able to expect a certain level of confidentiality. If you are disclosing information, always make sure that you are the correct person to be doing this, and the person that you are informing has a right to have the information. If you are not sure whether you should be disclosing information, speak to your line manager for clarification.

You must also not disclose confidential information over the phone without the permission of your line manager.

You can get further information and advice regarding your role safeguarding vulnerable adults from sources such as those shown in Figure 2 on page 125.

Summary 

You must understand your role and responsibilities in relation to safeguarding. The nature of abuse and increasing understanding of how safeguarding can positively impact on the lives of vulnerable people, means that continued professional development is an integral aspect of that process.

Support individuals to remain safe from harm

Safeguarding means that you support individuals to keep them safe from harm. In your role as lead adult care worker you will also support your staff and challenge unacceptable practices and behaviour. You will need to be aware of legislation that applies directly to working with adults.

Activities

Qualification mapping

Unit 5 LO 4 AC 4.1, 4.2, LO 6 AC 6.1 and 6.2

Legislation to promote independent living

You have referred an individual with a mild learning disability to supported housing, where there is a live-in warden as well as yourself to support this person.

Describe what legislation you think would be relevant in reducing the risk to this individual from abuse and promoting independent living.

Challenging unacceptable behaviour

Challenging unacceptable behaviour can be difficult and may be handled in different ways, depending on the context. Interview four colleagues at work and ask them to describe a behaviour that they would find unacceptable in:

- a user of the service
- a staff member/colleague.

Make a record of the answers that you get and compare them. Do they have anything in common?

Discuss this with your manager/supervisor and find out what kind of behaviour is challenged and what is permitted.

Unsafe practices

In your role as a lead adult care worker you are concerned about the welfare of a user of service who a colleague is supporting. You suspect that they might be a victim of unsafe practices through inappropriate support. You are aware that their risk assessment has not been updated recently and that the individual is routinely seen in town unsupported when they are supposed to be supported by your colleague.

- What action should you take regarding this?
- What legislation/policies could you use to support your action?

Defining law and legislation

There can be some confusion regarding what is meant by law and legislation.

Carry out some research into these terms and describe in your own words what the difference is.

Then research a current law and piece of legislation that impacts on safeguarding vulnerable adults from abuse and informs a policy or procedure at your place of work.

Laws to protect vulnerable adults

Identify which of these pieces of legislation could be used to support the protection of vulnerable adults and make notes about when they would be used.

Children Act 2004	Public Interest and Disclosure Act	Police and Criminal Evidence Act 1984	Protection of Vulnerable Adults	The Control of Substances Hazardous to Health	Criminal Injuries Compensation Scheme
The Care Standards Act	Care Act 2014	The Transmissible Spongiform Encephalopathies (No.2) Regulations 2006	EEC Directives	Mental Capacity Act 2005	Human Rights Act
Criminal Justice Act 1998	The Data Protection Act 1998	Road Traffic (Vehicle Testing) Act 1999	Reporting of Injuries, Diseases and Dangerous Occurrences	Equal Opportunities Act	Local Policies and Procedures
Income Tax (Trading and Other Income) Act 2005	Sexual Offences Act 2003	Health and Safety at Work Act	Civil action by the victim	The Care Homes Regulations	Food Premises (Regulation) Regulations 1991

Researching a case of institutional abuse

Research the case of the Winterbourne View scandal.

You should look at how many risk factors and different examples of abuse you think took place. Consider how people should have seen these and what should have happened.

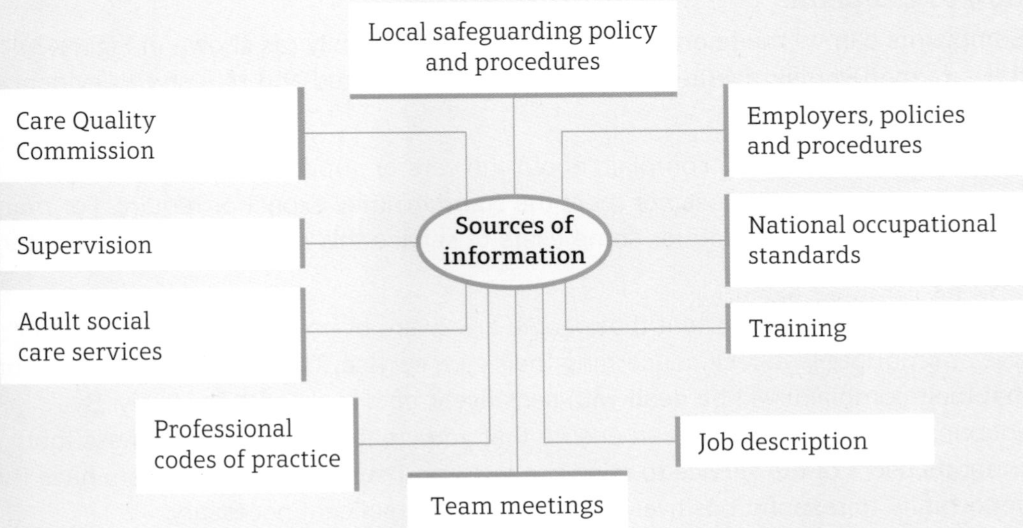

Figure 2: Sources of information about your role in safeguarding

Receiving comments and complaints

Qualification mapping

Unit 5 LO 5 AC 5.2

An important part of exercising rights is being able to complain if services are poor or do not meet expectations. It is part of your role to support this process.

Complaints process

The complaints process should not be seen as an opportunity to bemoan a situation but rather a way to improve services and the quality of lives of the people supported or working there. You will look at what needs to be done in a complaint situation and also how you can ensure that appropriate and timely actions take place. The complaints procedure is a good way to access information about people's experiences with the service you provide.

All public service organisations are required to have a complaints procedure and should ensure that it is available for people to use. Your role as lead adult care worker may involve supporting users of service to make a complaint, either directly by helping them to follow the procedure, or indirectly by making sure that they are aware that there is a procedure and are able to follow it. You also need to learn to respond openly and appropriately to any comments or complaints that you receive from people about their care. Most complaints procedures will include an informal stage, at which complaints can be discussed before they become more formal issues.

Complaints to an organisation are an important part of the monitoring process and should be considered as part of every review of service provision. If individuals tolerate the provision and do not complain, an organisation will not be aware of the problems and cannot make improvements. Also, if complaints are not responded to appropriately, the service will not improve.

6Cs 6Cs

Communication

How to complain

Complaints can be made orally, in writing or electronically (as shown in Figure 3). If they are made orally, a written transcript must be created and retained as evidence of the complaint.

Everyone has the right to complain about the care or support they are getting if, for any reason, they feel it does not meet the standard they expect or require. For many people this can be difficult; for some users of service this could be an even greater challenge.

For this reason, it is important that people are aware of how they can complain or give appropriate feedback concerning their care service. They should feel confident that their complaint will be dealt with sensitively, effectively and positively. By adopting this approach, you can ensure that you create a sense of openness that supports users of the service to raise concerns and ensures staff members have the opportunity to respond positively to improve the practice if necessary.

A straightforward and concise complaints procedure will support and protect the rights of the individuals using it. Each service provider will have their own complaints procedure, so it is important to be fully aware of all internal policies.

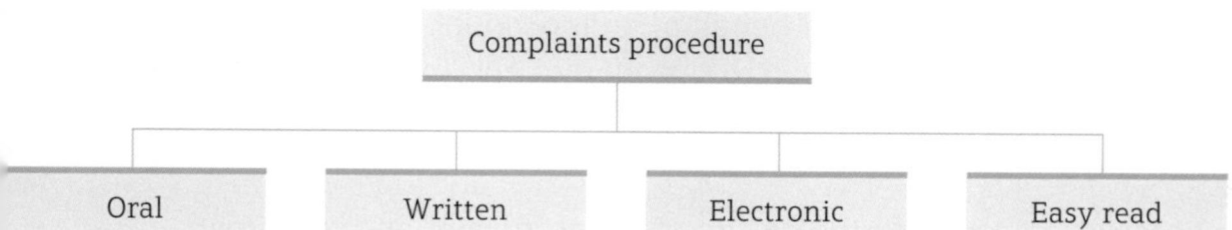

Figure 3: Complaints can be made in a variety of ways

Responding to complaints or comments

The following sequence is an appropriate way to initially respond to a comment or complaint:

- Listen to what the person is saying and do not interrupt them. They may be angry or upset, so you must not antagonise them. Demonstrate that you care and are interested in and understand their concerns.
- Try to restore confidence; assure them that you take their complaint seriously and will do something about it.
- Do not get offended: as a lead adult care worker it may be your duty to take complaints. If the complaint concerns you then somebody else must take the complaint.
- Never make excuses. Listen openly and without prejudice, and do not try to apportion blame.
- If necessary, provide the appropriate complaints information and procedure. This should be appropriate to the ability of the person making the complaint.
- Be clear about what you are going to do and then do it.
- Report the situation to your manager/supervisor.
- Learn from what has been complained about and reflect on ways to improve the practice.

Do not:

- try to resolve the complaint yourself
- talk to the person that the complaint is about
- do anything that would discourage people from making complaints
- make promises about the outcome
- discuss the situation with anyone else but your manager, if appropriate.

Supporting users of service to make complaints is part of your **duty of care**; it is your responsibility to exercise that duty of care to protect those individuals.

Key term 

Duty of care – providing care and support for individuals within the law and within the policies, procedures and agreed ways of working of your employer; avoiding abuse and injury to individuals

Agreed procedures for managing and handling complaints

All organisations will have an established complaints procedure and you should familiarise yourself with this. If you are working for an agency, then the agency should be informed of any concerns or issues concerning complaints – while you are working for them. Never dismiss or try to rationalise someone's complaint, they must be taken seriously. If it is a verbal complaint then it is good practice to deal with it immediately. If this is not possible, refer it to your manager or supervisor without delay. It is not always possible to resolve a complaint straight away. If this is the case then the complaint should be recorded in writing. Regardless of the outcome, a written record must be made.

You must support people if they have a complaint: it is their right

Sometimes a complaint is made on behalf of an individual. In this situation, you will need to seek consent from the person in question to ensure that they have agreed to this. It is usual for complaints to be acknowledged in a relatively short space of time – two or three days.

It will be necessary to establish the nature of the complaint and for a manager to conduct an investigation. An appropriate timescale will be written into the complaints procedure, by which time the person making the complaint can expect a response. There will be a meeting arranged with the investigating manager at an appropriate time to address the complaint, to attempt a local resolution.

However, when all local means of resolution have been explored, if the person making the complaint is not satisfied then they have the right to **escalate** the process by taking the issue to the Local Government and Social Care Ombudsman. This is an independent authority that investigates unresolved complaints and shares findings to improve practice. It can decide whether to investigate the case. Ombudsman services oversee how public bodies, such as local authorities, meet their legal duties and ensure accountability. For example, there is also a Parliamentary and Health Service Ombudsman.

Accessible for all

The complaints procedure should be accessible to every user of service; an easy-read version should be made available for users of service with a learning disability but many other people may also prefer such information to be delivered in this way.

The principle of the easy-read technique is similar to plain English; it just develops this idea further. Easy-read resources must:

- keep sentences short and ensure they contain just one idea
- use no jargon
- use simple images to support the text
- be direct and approachable, as if in conversation, like someone is talking to you
- leave space between paragraphs and use bullet points to break up information
- use simple and clear fonts with a larger text size.

For example, see Figure 4.

Key term 

Escalate – to bring any concerns to a more senior member of the team

Complaints procedure

What is a complaint?
A complaint is when you are worried or not happy about something. This can be about something that has happened to you. It can also be about something that has happened to someone you know.

What is a procedure?
A procedure is a way you can have your say. You can use this to tell the person who is in charge of the care service that you are not happy about the service. You can also tell us. If something has happened to you, or someone who you know, then this complaints procedure can be used to help sort out the problem.

Figure 4: An example of an easy-read version

Summary 

An important part of your role in protecting vulnerable adults is to have an effective complaints procedure in place. You must support and encourage people to use it. It is important that the complaints procedure is accessible to all, regardless of ability.

Making a complaint

Making a formal complaint can be a difficult and stressful decision; for vulnerable adults, this can be even more difficult.

It takes courage for individuals to feel able to make a complaint. They need to be sure that they will be taken seriously and not victimised for doing so. You must make sure that any complaint or concern is dealt with efficiently. Users of service must know they will be heard.

Activities

Complaints about staff

You have been receiving complaints from users of the service that the outreach team has not been working some of the evenings and weekends they are supposed to. You are aware that some of the team have raised concerns about having to work evenings and weekends because it has a negative impact on family and social life. You know this is part of their job description but also that a renegotiation of their contract might be possible in order to accommodate both the service and the staff.

You decide to hold a meeting with staff and users of the service to discuss the situation.

- What consequences do you think there may be for the users of service if their support would not be available at weekends and evenings?
- Can you think of ways that the service could be adapted to meet the needs of both users of service and staff alike?

Qualification mapping 

Unit 5 LO 5 AC 5.2

A clear complaints procedure

Obtain a copy of your organisational complaints procedure. Read it carefully and then rewrite the procedure in an easy-read version. You may use images as well.

Explain the importance of an accessible complaints procedure in reducing the likelihood of abuse.

Accessibility

Obtain a complaints procedure or policy from another organisation or agency, not necessarily a social setting – it can be from a restaurant or local GP surgery etc.

- Was it easy to obtain? Was it easy to understand?
- Did it give you enough information to be able to make the complaint?

Reflection

Imagine you are a user of service who lives in a small residential home. During the night there is only one member of staff on duty. This person touches you in a way you do not like but when you ask them to stop, they refuse. They tell you that no one will believe you.

Imagine being in this situation and feeling so vulnerable and helpless.

Use the Kolb cycle of reflection on page v to reflect on this situation.

Recognise and prevent unsafe practices

Qualification mapping

Unit 5 LO 6 AC 6.1 and 6.2

As a lead adult care worker, it is vital that you fully understand your responsibilities with regard to the principles and practice of safeguarding and preventing unsafe practices within the workplace.

An integral aspect for adult care workers who support adults with care and support needs is to help them achieve their personal goals and live as independently as possible. This section will look at those responsibilities, with regard to highlighting and preventing potential risks, unsafe practices and why you need to keep yourself and others safe and secure within the workplace. It will also consider relevant legislation with regard to the management of health and safety in the workplace.

It is very important that you implement and maintain effective safeguarding procedures within the workplace and that these procedures are reviewed on a regular basis to ensure the safety of the people who use the service as well as staff. This should be balanced with a culture in which needs and risks are observed within the context of a health and social care setting.

As a lead adult care worker, you and the people you work with have a duty of care to act in the best interests of both the individuals in your care and any other individuals who may be affected by your actions. You may, for example, witness unsafe practice which centres on the provision of personal care, the administration of medication or a misuse of authority, such as the inappropriate use of restraint. You may become aware of an inappropriate relationship or a failure to follow organisational procedures regarding requirements such as confidentiality, staff training on safeguarding issues or recruitment, such as completing DBS checks. Unsafe practice may also be caused by staff problems.

Unsafe practices, such as those shown in Figure 5, are not only examples of bad practice. They can also result in negative outcomes for the wellbeing of individuals and, in severe cases, can lead to accusations of or actual abuse.

Professional working

Recognising the signs and symptoms of abuse and neglect, and then acting appropriately, is the responsibility of all care workers.

Figure 5: Examples of unsafe practice

'Safeguarding adults' essentially involves reducing or preferably preventing the risk of significant harm or exploitation of vulnerable people, while at the same time enabling them to make **informed choices** regarding their own lives. As a lead adult care worker you have a particular part to play in securing this for those adults in your care. This outcome can be supported by adopting the six principles of safeguarding, as shown in Table 4.

Key term 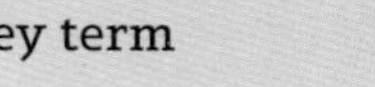 

Informed choice – the person is given information so they understand the benefits and the risks

Safeguarding principles	
Empowerment	People should be supported to make their own decisions based on the best possible information.
Prevention	It is better to take action before harm occurs.
Proportionality	What you do should be proportional to the risk: you don't want to be over-protective if the risk is low, as this in itself can disadvantage people and deprive of them of the opportunity to make their own decisions.
Protection	Those in greatest need require our support and protection.
Partnership	Safeguarding is about different people, professions, groups and communities working together to cover all the angles in preventing, detecting and reporting neglect and abuse.
Accountability	In all activities, you are accountable for safeguarding.

Table 4: The six principles of safeguarding

6Cs

Competence

In promoting safeguarding, you have a duty of care as an adult care worker to recognise the signs and symptoms of abuse and neglect, and to act appropriately. You must always act in the best interests of the individuals in your care and any others who may be affected by your actions. It is important that you are able to recognise the signs and symptoms of abuse, as this is sometimes directly linked to unsafe practices.

Look back at Table 1 on page 112, which details the different types of abuse and the signs and symptoms to be aware of.

Respond to suspected unsafe practices or alleged abuse

Reporting

If an individual has told you that they have been abused, or you suspect this, you must explain that you have to report it. This is your professional and moral duty. Reassure the individual that the information will only be provided to people who need to know.

What you must do

Listen to the victim: try to identify what sort of abuse they have experienced and who the suspected person is. Be careful not to judge the victim or influence them by asking leading questions. Listen carefully and show compassion. Reassure them that they were right to come to you for help and that the matter will be taken seriously.

6Cs 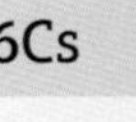

Communication, compassion

Report your suspicions and any allegations to a senior manager or staff member in a position of authority. If the allegation of abuse is about a senior manager, refer to your company policy.

Record details of the allegations clearly, using the individual's own words and any suspicions you may have had based on evidence you have seen.

Put a **plan of care** into place. Ensure the victim is reassured of their safety and kept informed. You must keep safe and store all evidence of abuse securely. You need to:

- write a report: state the facts, detail the type of suspected abuse, sign and date it
- take witness statements if necessary/possible – sign and date them
- take photographic evidence of any physical injuries if possible
- do not touch a potential crime scene or the victim, and restrict the area.

Ways to reduce likelihood of unsafe practices and potential abuse

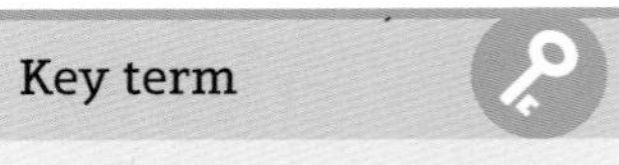

Key term

Person-centred support – ensuring the user of service is at the centre of everything you do

A crucial aspect of relationship building in your work is to ensure that people have choices and control over their lives. Many service providers are developing a person-centred approach to the way they work with and care for users of service to minimise unsafe practices. As a lead adult care worker, it is essential to be aware of the different ways in which **person-centred support** and focusing on prevention can effectively reduce the likelihood of unsafe practices and potential abuse. You can do this by:

- making sure that people have choices and control over their lives
- developing person-centred support
- encouraging participation from the person you support
- promoting rights and choices.

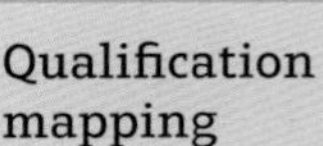

Qualification mapping

Unit 5 LO 5 AC 5.1

Person-centred support

This means that the person in question is placed at the centre of decision-making activities. Care must be focused on the specific needs and wishes of the user of service, ensuring that key values are observed, such as privacy and dignity. Individuals participate actively in planning their own lives and making their own choices, with help from family members, friends and professionals. This helps them to be empowered, independent and autonomous.

However, if individuals are not given the opportunity to make their own choices, whether about what they want to wear or eat, or the activities they want to take part in, they can quickly develop feelings of low self-esteem and lack of confidence. If they start to believe that they lack the ability to carry out tasks for themselves, they may become more dependent on others and less able to do things for themselves. This can make them more vulnerable to potential abuse by others.

Different ways of including individuals in the planning of their care have developed. These include advocacy, self-advocacy, facilitated decision-making, providing mentors and/or other support for family members, and providing training for staff and family members.

Table 5 describes what is meant by person-centred values.

Value	What it means
Individuality	Each person has their own identity, needs, wishes, choices, beliefs and values. 'One size fits all' does not work when it comes to providing care and support.
Independence	Promoting an individual's independence means looking at what they can do for themselves and empowering them to do as much as possible for themselves.
Privacy	Everyone has a right to private space and time when they need it.
Partnership	You work in partnership when you involve the individual and their family, and work alongside other workers.
Choice	Each individual should be supported to make choices about their care and support.
Dignity	Treating someone in a dignified way means treating an individual with respect, and valuing their individuality and their ethical and moral beliefs.
Rights	The Human Rights Act 1998 is the main legislation that sets out the rights of people in the UK. You have the right to speak your mind and to be kept safe from harm, as well as the right to respect, dignity and **equality**.

Table 5: The meaning of person-centred values

Key terms 

Equality – provide everyone with equal opportunities and chances, for example, access to services

Whistleblowing – the act of telling the authorities or the public that an organisation is doing something immoral or illegal

Guidelines to follow

What should you do if you suspect there are unsafe practices happening in your workplace, or that abuse or neglect has occurred? You need to know what you are looking for and how to act if you find evidence of it.

- You must report your concerns to your manager, verbally and in writing.
- Follow policies on **whistleblowing** (see page 136 for more detail).
- Never be tempted to take matters into your own hands or to act outside the policies and procedures that govern your workplace.
- Support the user of service.
- Remain professional at all times.
- Do not let your personal feelings affect your actions.

Professional working 

Whistleblowing is an important part of the disclosure process of misconduct in the workplace. It gives managers the opportunity to intervene early on and put things right before anything disastrous happens.

If nothing has been done

What happens if an allegation of abuse or suspected abuse has been reported but nothing has been done?

- Report your concerns directly to social services, the Care Quality Commission (CQC) or the police.
- Remember that anyone can report a suspicion or allegation of abuse.
- You have a duty of care to report abuse. You can be disciplined, suspended or dismissed for not reporting abuse or not following the correct procedure.

It is essential to report any *suspicions* of abuse or misconduct. You must follow the correct procedure by raising any genuine concerns and acting on them. Remember that you have protection from possible reprisals and victimisation following reporting.

When you are considering how to recognise and prevent unsafe practices in the workplace, it is very important that you evaluate the quality of the service being provided on a regular basis. There are various ways this can be measured.

Within the workplace setting or environment, it is essential that there is a practice of assessing potential risk, unsafe practices and security that is effective and efficient. While this remains the responsibility of all employees to observe, as a lead adult care worker you may have extra responsibilities in making sure a regular schedule of safety checks and risk assessment is carried out. This will not only ensure that these safety checks are observed but that there is a culture of working towards preventing unsafe practices in the workplace. All organisations will have appropriate policies and procedures in place to promote health and safety within the workplace and to guide on the reporting of unsafe practices; you should be familiar with these.

An organisation's complaints and compliments procedure can also be a good indicator of areas of the practice that are doing well or are in need of assessment due to bad or poor practice. Be aware, however, that if you are not receiving many complaints, this may not indicate that there are not any issues that need addressing. It could be that people are afraid to report an issue. If this is the case, it would also need investigating.

The Care Quality Commission (CQC)

The Care Quality Commission (CQC) is an independent regulator of all health and social care services in England. Its primary role is to ensure best practice and to improve social care standards throughout the sector. This requires that all adult social care services submit an Annual Quality Assurance Assessment (AQAA). This is a legal requirement. Care organisations must highlight what they are doing well, what could be improved and how they are going to improve. As a lead adult care worker, you will have a responsibility to provide information to the CQC about the standard and quality of your service. This process also has a section that allows you to highlight any potential issues that might prevent improvement to the service, called, 'barriers to improvement'. In this instance, you would be required to provide a description of evidence of any potential problems that might hinder improvement.

The Management of Health and Safety at Work Regulations 1999 describe your responsibility with regard to carrying out a risk assessment within the workplace.

Summary

It is very important that you implement and maintain effective safeguarding procedures, including person-centred support, within the workplace and that review procedures on a regular basis to ensure the safety of the people who use the service as well as staff.

Duty of care and complaints

As a lead adult care worker, it is part of your duty of care to uphold complaints and recognise and prevent unsafe practices in the workplace.

Activities

Dealing with a complaint

As a lead adult care worker, you receive a letter of complaint regarding one of your staff members from Jenny, a user of the service. The letter states that the staff member is generally late for Jenny's appointments and is quite often rude to her.

Explain your answers to the following questions in your own words:

- What course of action would you take?
- What would you do to ensure best practice was observed?

Duty of care and unsafe practices

Describe what is meant by 'duty of care' and how this can inform and prevent unsafe practices in the workplace. Be specific to your place of work and give examples where appropriate, highlighting any potential conflicts. Remember to maintain confidentiality and change any names as necessary.

Protecting vulnerable adults

Describe and explain the procedure if an allegation of harm or abuse was made in your own work setting.

- Does this prevent unsafe practice?
- Is this procedure accessible to users of the service?

Qualification mapping

Unit 5 LO 3 AC 3.1, LO 6 AC 6.1 and 6.2

Importance and process of whistleblowing

Qualification mapping

Unit 5 LO 4 AC 4.4

It can be very difficult to respond to an abusive situation within your own workplace. All staff, regardless of status, have a duty to report and 'whistleblow' any situation that they feel indicates malpractice or abuse.

This section describes the process of whistleblowing and the legislation that informs, protects and supports individuals who whistleblow, enabling them to report such incidents. The process of whistleblowing is essential within health and social care because it reflects on your professional practice and the positive development of the service you provide as an adult care worker. It should not be thought of as 'snitching', but it can cause anxiety and feelings of isolation in those staff members who speak up against possible misconduct. Remember that you are protected by law and cannot be treated unfairly or lose your job because you have highlighted problems or issues at your workplace.

You should follow your organisation's policy regarding the procedure of whistleblowing. For more information go to: www.gov.uk/whistleblowing

The importance of whistleblowing

It can be very difficult to report concerns of abuse or neglect within your own or another workplace, especially if they concern a senior staff member. There may be many reasons why you might feel that you should not raise a concern. However, recognising the signs and symptoms of abuse and neglect, and then acting appropriately, is the responsibility of all adult care workers. The Public Interest Disclosure Act 1998 offers legal protection for disclosures made in the public interest and ensures that you cannot be victimised by your employer for reporting unsafe or illegal practices, or cases of neglect and abuse. These are the qualifying disclosures protected by the Public Interest Disclosure Act 1998:

- a criminal offence
- failure to comply with legal obligations
- a miscarriage of justice
- danger to health or safety of any individual
- any damage to the environment
- an attempt to cover up information that would provide evidence that any of these five practices occurred.

It is important that you have a reasonable belief that a breach of safeguarding standards has taken place. The breaches and offences above are quite specific and it may be that you are incorrect in your assessment of the situation; however, this should not deter you from making the claim. If, after investigation the claim is unsubstantiated, you will be protected by law, as long as it was a sound assessment that appeared to violate one or more of the above offences.

If, for whatever reason, you believe your claim is not taken seriously or acted upon, you should escalate the matter to a more senior manager and keep moving through the management chain until you are satisfied. If this still does not alleviate your concerns, you should seek help outside the agency and contact your local authority and/or social services or professional body, if appropriate. If you believe that a potential criminal act has taken place, such as physical or sexual assault, theft or fraud, then you should refer the matter directly to the police and the CQC. (Note: this process should be clearly laid out within the organisational policies and procedure.)

Whistleblowing can reduce the risk of serious breaches or concerns being mishandled; this relates to both individual and organisational disclosures. As a lead adult care worker, it is important to be aware that employees must be able to raise concerns in confidence and without getting into trouble.

How are these claims investigated?

The local multi-agency Safeguarding Adults Board (SAB), which is responsible for the protection of vulnerable adults, is also responsible for setting out the policies and procedures that identify and protect those at risk. It must ensure that every agency has appropriate policies and procedures in place. Your organisation should have appropriate policies and procedures that identify abuse by a professional. They are likely to cover:

- immediate suspension of the person accused
- investigation by the police service if appropriate
- investigation led by an independent agency
- appropriate disciplinary procedures following the outcome of any police or protection investigation.

Claims regarding concerns over professional practice or the quality of service are not restricted to the actions of employees; organisational abuse is also covered within the terms of whistleblowing. It might be that you are working in an organisation where professional standards are not being met and the needs of vulnerable people are being abused. If this is the case, you should contact your local Safeguarding Adults Board. Public Concern at Work is a national organisation that provides legal advice to anyone who has concerns regarding malpractice at work. For more information, see www.pcaw.co.uk.

Getting it right

It is good practice for employers to offer open, transparent and safe working environments, in which staff members can freely raise concerns. This is especially important when working with vulnerable people. Currently there is no legislation to compel organisations to have a whistleblowing policy in place; however, such policies clearly demonstrate a commitment to the concerns of employees and the needs of the people being supported. In care settings this is especially important in facilitating timely interventions within client support. It also shows a willingness to have such concerns brought to the attention of management, and acknowledges that front-line staff are valuable assets when it comes to prompt intervention in matters that could lead to the organisation's reputation being damaged and the possible abuse or neglect of an individual.

Having a policy that supports whistleblowing is an important step with regard to promoting an open culture, which in turn supports prompt intervention. As part of your role as lead adult care worker, you should demonstrate clearly that you support and welcome disclosures from other workers. Further to this, organisations should offer appropriate training, support, mentoring and other support systems to ensure that **all** employees feel that they can easily approach a variety of people within the organisation with concerns regarding practice. It is in the best interest of all concerned if there is a practice of immediate intervention with regard to any allegation made through the whistleblowing procedure. This facilitates a prompt investigation and, where applicable, asks appropriate questions of an employee and provides feedback. Having an agreed policy that explains the benefits of this process is essential in promoting it. It can also be argued that organisations that embrace whistleblowing as a bona fide method of attaining information can make informed decisions and, most importantly, reduce the risk of abuse or neglect of vulnerable people as well as promoting staff confidence.

Changes in legislation to protect whistleblowers

The Public Interest Disclosure Act 1998 has been amended from the original legislation, following serious scrutiny and wide interpretation by employment tribunals. The definition of 'protected disclosure' has been narrowed to avoid 'misuse' by claimants using the Act to circumnavigate agreed employment contractual commitments and limitations set on unfair dismissal claims. It was also acknowledged that there was a lack of protection for whistleblowers, who were subsequently victimised or harassed by other employees. Amendments were introduced by the Enterprise and Regulatory Reform Act 2013 to reduce this abuse of the system and protect those making genuine interventions. This amendment was instigated by the government in order to close these 'loopholes'. Due to these amendments, any disclosure made will only qualify if it is 'made in the public interest' and fits into the categories laid out within the legislation, listed on page 136.

The amendments to the act is as follows.

Sections 17–20 of the Enterprise and Regulatory Reform Act 2013 have introduced a series of changes to the Public Interest Disclosure Act 1998.

Section 17 narrows the definition of 'protected disclosure' to those that are made in the 'public interest'.

Section 18 removes the requirement that a worker or employee must make a protected disclosure 'in good faith'. Instead, tribunals will have the power to reduce compensation by up to 25 per cent for detriment or dismissal relating to a protected disclosure that was not made in good faith.

Section 19 introduces protection for whistleblowers from bullying or harassment by co-workers.

Section 20 enables the Secretary of State to extend the meaning of 'worker' for the purpose of defining who comes within the remit of the whistleblowing provisions.

Summary

All staff are required to promptly respond to any concerns of malpractice and to be 'whistleblowers' if necessary.

You need to promote the view that raising concerns should be the norm and accepted as an important part of your day-to-day work as adult care workers who reflect on their professional practice and work to improve their services.

Responding to unsafe practices

As part of your role as a lead adult care worker, you must recognise, report, respond to and record unsafe practices at work and encourage others to do so.

Activities

Breach of professional practice

You find out that a work colleague has attempted to cover up a serious breach of professional practice. Who would be the first person you would inform regarding this situation?

- Your best friend
- The person in question
- Your manager/supervisor
- A senior person in human resources

Case study: Mr Morden

Mr Morden is an 85-year-old man who has lived alone since his wife died a year ago. He has poor eye sight and suffers with lumbago, which limits his mobility. Twice a week he is visited by a physiotherapist from the local GP surgery. You also visit Mr Morden on a regular basis to provide additional support. Today you arrived early at his house and can clearly hear someone shouting at Mr Morden, telling him to be quiet. As you walk in, the physiotherapist is surprised to see you and explains that he was just leaving. When he has left, you ask Mr Morden if he is all right. He says he is and that he does not want to cause any trouble.

- What action should you take?
- Would there be any barriers you might have to deal with?
- Would you describe this as abusive behaviour?
- In what way could you empower Mr Morden?

Protecting whistleblowers

The Public Interest Disclosure Act 1998 clearly describes and offers legal protection for whistleblowers. Check your own workplace policies and procedures.

- Is there a whistleblowing policy in place?
- Does it reflect this act with regard to protection?
- Does it clearly state what is expected of you in this situation?

Dilemmas between a person's rights and their safety

Potential conflicts can occur when addressing an individual's rights and your duty of care. Understanding how a person's rights and your responsibilities affect the people you support is a very important subject.

It is helpful to discuss this subject against the framework of the relevant laws and codes of practice, the national standards, guidelines, policies, and people's rights provided by law.

As a lead adult care worker your responsibilities to the users of the service may appear at times in conflict with the rights of those people. Protecting and improving an individual's rights while not **infringing** the **rights** of others is a fine balancing act; however, it is vital to understand that you cannot have one without the other.

Key term 

Infringing rights – when a person's entitlements are ignored through deliberate or accidental actions

A person's rights under the terms of the national standards, codes of practice or operational policies and procedures are not enforceable by law. However, there are standards that you are expected to work towards and which are enforceable within health and social care. These are designed to improve the quality of the service provided to the people who use those services.

National standards, codes of practice and policies

In England, the body responsible for inspecting all social care facilities to ensure that they adhere to the National Minimum Standards is the Care Quality Commission (CQC). It is the independent regulator of health and care services in the UK and inspects health and care services to make sure that they meet fundamental standards of quality and safety. These standards dictate the minimum requirement that any social care organisation has to meet and differ depending on the type of service providing them, for example:

- adults
- care homes
- younger adults
- fostering services
- children's homes.

Each individual service has a specialised set of standards that clearly define the minimum quality of care that users of that service can expect. These standards should also be available in a format that is user friendly and easy to understand so that the people who are using that service are aware of the level of support they can expect.

Codes of practice

In addition to this, the regulatory bodies in the UK have a code of practice that impacts on both people working in the field of social care and the social care work force. In England this is the Health and Care Professions Council (HCPC). This is an independent UK-wide regulatory body responsible for setting and maintaining standards of professional conduct within social care settings. The Code of Conduct for Healthcare Support Workers and Adult Care Workers in England 2013, which is published by Skills for Health and Skills for Care, provides guidance on the way you must act while at work. You can find further explanation of this code of conduct at www.skillsforhealth.org.uk (follow the links in Standards).

Figure 6: It is a fine balancing act between rights and responsibilities

Fundamental Standards

The provision of health and social care in the UK is governed by law laid down by Parliament. This is statutory legislation. The Health and Social Care Act 2008 (Regulated Activities) Regulations 2014 give guidance to service providers and managers on how to meet the Fundamental Standards.

The Fundamental Standards were introduced to improve the quality of care nationwide following the publication of the Report of the Mid Staffordshire NHS Foundation Trust Public Inquiry in February 2013. The report was about failings in care within the Trust and it made 290 recommendations for the improvement of care nationally. By following the codes of practice, you will ensure that you always support the rights of the users of service. These rights also involve responsibilities, one of which is not infringing the rights of other people, especially the people you are supporting or who use your services.

Rights covered by the codes of practice are shown in Figure 7.

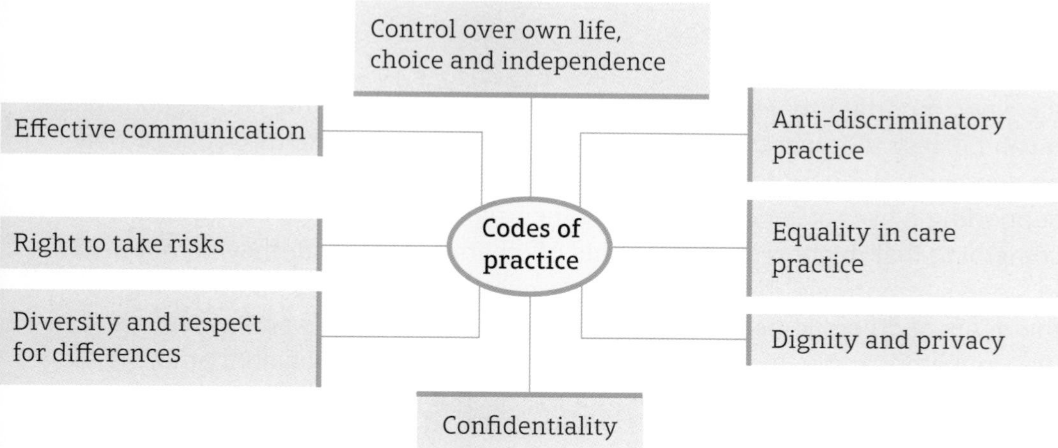

Figure 7: Rights covered by the codes of practice

As you can see, the rights covered by the code of practice also involve responsibilities. These responsibilities are linked to the rights of the users of service and to you as workers. Table 6 links to some of these responsibilities and rights.

Right	Responsibility
Diversity and the right to be different	Respect for diversity in others
Equality and freedom from discrimination	Respect for the equality of others and valuing members of other social groups
Control over life, choice and independence	Making choices that respect others' independence, choices and lifestyles
Freedom to choose lifestyle, self-presentation, diet and routine	The consequences of choices for the person and others around them
Dignity and privacy	Respect for the dignity and privacy of others
To be valued as an individual	Respect for the identity needs of others
Confidentiality	Respect for the confidentiality of others
To be safe and secure	To behave in a way that does not threaten or abuse the physical or emotional safety and security of others
To take risks, including taking risks as a matter of choice, in order to maintain the person's own identity or perceived wellbeing	Not to expose oneself or others to unacceptable risks, including a willingness to negotiate with respect to the impact of risk on others

Table 6: Rights and responsibilities

It is very important that you understand the link between rights and responsibilities. It can be easy to forget that one person's idea of rights might impact negatively on another's; the right to free speech is a good example of this. Imagine you are supporting a user of service, exercising their right to free speech. They could say something that might restrict the rights of others, such as that they do not believe in same-sex marriage. This would be unacceptable because it would infringe on the rights of others to be respected and valued as individuals and it would also be discriminatory and potentially homophobic. People might tell you that this is a right of free speech and they can say what they like, but it is **not** true.

6Cs

Commitment, care

Key term

Dilemma – a situation requiring a choice between equally undesirable alternatives

Addressing potential conflicts or dilemmas between rights and safety/duty of care

The concept of risk-taking is something you do on a daily basis; simply crossing the road carries an element of risk. For users of service this is no different. Exercising your duty of care does not mean preventing them from taking any risks, but there must be a balance and you must consider this. Your duty of care does not override the right of choice; the people you support have the right to make their own decisions regarding the actions they take. However, this can sometimes lead to a conflict or **dilemma**. How this is resolved depends to a large extent upon the legal situation of the person you are supporting.

Mental capacity

Some of the individuals you support will have the mental capacity to make their own choices regarding their lives. Your role, specifically relating to duty of care, is to ensure that they make these choices based on an understanding of the consequences and potential risk factors involved with what want they want to do.

When considering someone's capacity to make decisions, you must balance several different factors. This is particularly important when you might have concerns regarding a user of service's capacity to make such choices and to fully comprehend the risks and consequences. Understanding or making a judgment on someone's capacity to make decisions is highly complex and requires careful consideration. It is easy to make an assumption because a user of service has a learning disability, dementia or a mental illness. This does **not** mean that they lack the capacity to make decisions regarding important issues that affect their lives.

The capacity to make a decision will depend on how much help you have. For example, if you were going to buy a new car and you found two differently-priced models that you liked, you might seek help from:

- your bank
- your mechanic
- the car dealer
- your partner or spouse, or a friend.

You will ultimately make the final decision, but if you lack the skills or information to make this choice on your own, you seek advice. It is important to remember that capacity within decision-making is relative and depends very heavily on the circumstances.

Mental Capacity Act 2005

The Mental Capacity Act 2005 was passed to assist people to make decisions. Its framework supports this by highlighting how people can be supported to make their own decisions.

This Act is supported by five key principles:

- a presumption of capacity – every adult has the right to make his or her own decisions and must be assumed to have capacity to do so unless it is proved otherwise
- the right for individuals to be supported to make their own decisions – people must be given all appropriate help before anyone concludes that they cannot make their own decisions
- individuals must retain the right to make what might be seen as eccentric or unwise decisions
- best interests – anything done for or on behalf of people without capacity must be in their best interests
- least restrictive intervention – anything done for or on behalf of people without capacity should be an option that is least restrictive of their basic rights – as long as it is still in their best interests.

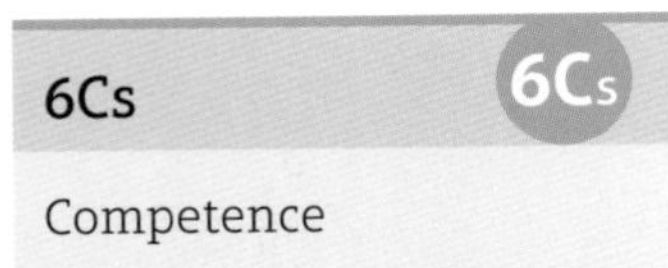

6Cs

Competence

The Act supports and describes exactly how to establish if someone is incapable of making a decision. The 'incapacity test' is only in relation to a specific decision. You cannot describe anyone as 'incapable' simply because of a medical condition or diagnosis. It is an offence to ill treat or neglect someone who lacks capacity.

The underlying principle with regard to the dilemma of risk and choice is simply that you cannot stop people doing what they want to do. You can simply give them advice and information so they have a better understanding of the risks involved and the consequences of their actions. There are, of course, situations in which you can and should take action, but they are limited. You should only intercede if someone is going to do something that:

- is illegal or criminal
- will deliberately cause harm to themselves
- will cause harm to others.

Managing the risk factors

The reason for undertaking risk assessments is not to remove the risk but to manage it and to take reasonable steps in doing so. As a lead adult care worker you may have already undertaken risk assessments with the users of service you have supported. Consider this assessment as a means to manage what can be done to make it less likely that the risk will become a reality. Encouraging managed daily risk is a positive way to promote choice, rights and personal control, as long as it is being managed with an understanding of the possible consequences and steps have been taken towards reducing or minimising harm to themselves and other people.

When you think about duty of care in relation to managed risk-taking, it is not about preventing people doing what they want to do but looking at and promoting the protecting factors. Resolving a risky situation may require that you add additional protecting factors to manage the risk effectively. If you have any doubt regarding this, consider engaging additional support.

Getting additional support with conflicts and dilemmas

There are different places you could go to seek advice or support with regard to exercising your duty of care. Your manager or supervisor would be a reasonable person to consult with regard to suitable action. You might choose to consult your regulator for advice about how to implement the appropriate codes of practice. You can also access written guidance that is produced with regard to implementing the codes of practice. All of these documents can be extremely informative in helping you verify the day-to-day implications of your work. Professional organisations are also a good source of support, as well as trade unions, if appropriate, when you have concerns or questions about any aspect of the duty of care towards users of the service.

Summary

There are many possible dilemmas that can occur between your duty of care and an individual's right of choice. However, there are clear guidelines, legislation and policies to support you with these dilemmas, so be sure to use them. Person-centred planning and intervention can be very helpful and if you are in any doubt, seek advice.

Conflicts or dilemmas between rights and duty of care

Activities

Rights and risks

Trevor is 22 years old and is a user of service who you have been supporting for over a year. He has a mild learning disability but is independent and works in a local charity shop two days a week. Trevor's friend, who also works at the same charity shop, has asked Trevor if he would like to go with him on holiday to Spain.

- As Trevor's adult care worker, what are the issues for you here?
- What do you think you should do?
- What is your duty of care?
- Can you do anything to stop him – should you stop him?
- What are the risks and what are the protecting factors?

Duty of care dilemma

A member of your staff has come to you, as lead adult care worker, with a duty of care dilemma because they need your support. Doreen is a user of service they are supporting who has mild dementia. She has recently been reported as becoming increasingly confused. She has allegedly been waking her neighbours at night and causing a disturbance. Her social worker has informed you that they could refer Doreen to supported housing but she has refused.

- Whose rights should take precedence?
- What could you do to help?
- What are the risks to Doreen?
- What are the risks and what are the protecting factors?

Code of conduct for adult social care in England

Look at the code of conduct for adult health care workers below and answer these questions:

- Do you comply with this code of conduct in your day-to-day practice?
- Does your employer comply with this code of conduct?
- Are there areas that need improvement?
- If the answer is yes, how do you think you could achieve this?

There is no legal requirement for employers to use this code of conduct. However, the code of conduct outlines 'best practice' and could be used to inform objective setting, personal development reviews, investigation and complaints procedures.

As a Healthcare Support Worker or Adult Social Care Worker in England you must:

1. Be accountable by making sure you can answer for your actions or omissions.
2. Promote and uphold the privacy, dignity, rights, health and wellbeing of people who use health and care services and their carers at all times.
3. Work in collaboration with your colleagues to ensure the delivery of high quality, safe and compassionate healthcare, care and support.
4. Communicate in an open and effective way to promote the health, safety and wellbeing of people who use health and care services and their carers.
5. Respect a person's right to confidentiality.
6. Strive to improve the quality of healthcare, care and support through continuing professional development.
7. Uphold and promote equality, diversity and **inclusion**.

(Source: www.skillsforcare.org.uk)

Key term 

Inclusion – place individuals at the centre of planning and support, regardless of their circumstances or background

Practice for professional discussion: Conflict dilemma

It is highly likely that you will have to negotiate conflict between your duty of care as a lead adult care worker and the rights and wishes of an individual you support. Decisions made in the best interest of the person you are supporting can only be finalised when it has been established that the person does not have capacity to decide matters for themselves at the time the choice is made. With that in mind, consider the following scenario and make notes for a professional discussion.

You are supporting an individual who is mildly obese, has recently been diagnosed with diabetes and is visually impaired. You have been working with this person for some time and have a good working relationship with them. Their support plan is focused on supporting them to lose weight and to reduce their alcohol consumption, which has been linked to their diabetes. The individual has told you that they would like to go to the shops alone to buy some groceries, but the shops are only accessible by crossing a busy road. You suspect that they might buy alcohol and have safety concerns regarding crossing the road. The individual is quite capable of making this decision. What would you do as their carer in this situation?

Think about your own work context and include evidence/experience from your own practice to support your discussion, for example:

- expert witness testimonies
- reflective accounts
- observation records.

Understand the principles of online safety

The principles of safeguarding apply when supporting users of service to access and utilise a variety of electronic communication devices, when social networking, and when using the internet. The same dilemmas that arise between a user of service's rights and their safety are just as important here. This unit will look at some of these dilemmas and potential risks, as well as measures that can be put in place to help address the situation.

The internet is an abundant source of opportunities for everyone, including users of service. This might include socialising, connecting with friends and family, shopping, banking or any other number of activities, all of which are actions that can promote independence and wellbeing for users of service. Unfortunately there are also potential risks with regard to the safety of the user of service. As a lead adult care worker, you need to be aware of how you can support individuals to be able to make use of online facilities while managing the associated risks appropriately.

For users of service with disabilities, accessing and utilising electronic media can have even greater value than for their non-disabled peers. This is because of things like assistive technologies that aid communication, and social networking, which helps and supports disabled or isolated users of service. As a lead adult care worker you will have to manage the dilemma of online safety against the benefits and associated risks involved with using electronic systems and devices.

Harassment and bullying	Cyberbullying includes sending hateful messages or even death threats, spreading lies online, making nasty comments on social media, or creating a website to criticise a person
Identify theft	Identity fraud or theft is a crime in which a person obtains key pieces of personally identifiable information, such as social security or driver's license numbers, in order to impersonate someone else
Fraud	Internet fraud is the use of internet services or software with internet access to defraud victims or to otherwise take advantage of them
Radicalisation	This refers to a situation in which a vulnerable adult is targeted or **"groomed"** to take part in abusive or potentially illegal activities
Abuse, illegal or inappropriate behaviour	Internet abuse refers to improper use of the internet and could include any of the above

Table 7: Potential online risks

Qualification mapping 

Unit 5 LO 2.1, 2.2 and 7.1

Key term 

Grooming – when someone builds an emotional connection with a user of the service to gain their trust for the purposes of exploitation

Qualification mapping 

Unit 5 LO 5.1, 5.3, 6.2, 6.3, 7.2 and 7.3

6Cs 

Competence

Key term 

Spam – irrelevant or unsolicited messages sent over the Internet, typically to a large number of users, for the purposes of advertising, phishing, spreading malware, etc.

How to reduce the risk of abuse

General precautions

- Do not give out personal information on every website you visit (this will also reduce the risk of **spam** e-mails).
- Use established and reputable sites; beware of sites that demand subscription.
- Block junk e-mails – most reputable sites will allow you to do this; you can also purchase security software (see below).

Protect the computer

- Ensure you have up-to-date security software installed on the computer and keep it updated.
- Automate software updates.
- Protect third-party connections, and make sure that security options are set on mobile phones or any other connectable devices.

Protect personal information

- Only create accounts with trusted parties.
- Only use secure sites when purchasing off the internet, and keep details secure.
- When buying online, make sure the page you are buying from is secure before you enter your payment details. This is easily done by looking at the address at the top of the browser. It should say, http**s**:// at the beginning. Non-secure websites only have http:// (without the **S**).
- Make passwords strong, secure and unique.
- Keep records of passwords safe and secure.
- Set any privacy and security settings where possible.

Here is a selection of the common anti-virus and internet security software available:

- Norton
- McAfee
- AVG
- Kaspersky
- AVAST.
- **If you wish to get the free versions for your computer, you can read this guide to the current free software versions:** https://www.moneysavingexpert.com/utilities/free-anti-virus-software/#

How can you balance the rights and needs of the user of service with the risks involved?

A significant factor in managing the dilemma associated between a person's rights and their safety is having robust policies and procedures in place. The government laid out its strategy regarding internet safety in the form of a green paper, 'Internet Safety Strategy'. However, organisations are encouraged to develop specific policies that support users of service with their use of digital technologies and the internet.

A typical policy should establish the rules and responsibilities, and detail how you can support both users of service and staff to safely manage the potential risks involved with accessing the internet and associated technologies. It should reflect on the needs of users of service, how they can be encouraged to learn about e-safety and how they can take responsibility, where appropriate, for themselves. These policies should also include other areas of acceptable usage regarding data protection, information sharing, and 'safe' sites. Other balancing measures should include regular awareness training for staff and users of the service, and regular policy updates to reflect the changing nature of the various technologies. Organisations could also appoint an e-safety co-ordinator to reflect the nature of the organisation and manage the needs of the users of service. Staff development programmes on safeguarding should include content on e-safety, linking with an individual's ICT training needs as addressed in their appraisal or review. Identifying a dilemma between a person's right of choice and their safety may not always be straightforward. In extreme cases, ethical issues are more clearly observed, but these are less common.

6Cs

Care

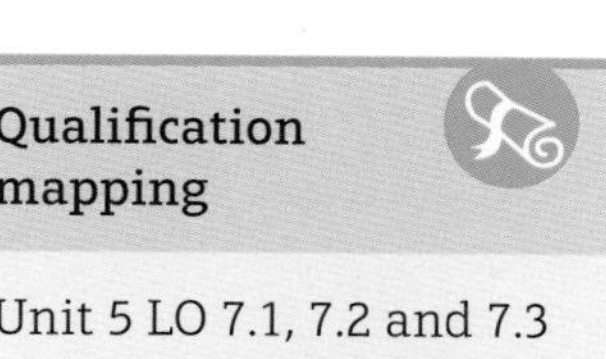

Qualification mapping

Unit 5 LO 7.1, 7.2 and 7.3

Summary

You have learned that safeguarding responsibilities include using the internet and associated technologies safely. As a lead adult care worker, you and other appropriate staff members have a duty of care to protect and support users of service with online safety. This should be considered on a number of levels, including both personal and professional use, the needs of the users of service and the identity of the organisation. It is important to remember that you are never alone in making such decisions regarding conflicts or dilemmas. You will be supported by an established procedure involving other staff members. This procedure will be clearly identified within your organisational policies and procedures.

Activities

Qualification mapping

Unit 5 LO 3.1, 3.2, 5.3, 6.1, 6.2, 6.3, 7.1, 7.2 and 7.3

Safeguarding policies

Write a safeguarding policy for an organisation that supports users of service to engage safely with the internet. It should include any specific responsibilities and appropriate procedures to safeguard and support users of the service.

Qualification mapping

Unit 5 LO 2.2, 7.1, 7.2 and 7.3

Meeting individual needs

You are responsible for two users of service – Anish is in his 20s and Mark is in his 60s. In your own words, answer the following questions:

1. What are the advantages and disadvantages of using the internet for a user of service?
2. What might Anish and Mark's internet preferences be?
3. What are the risks of using the internet for a user of service and how could you reduce them?
4. How could you develop a risk assessment to help both Anish and Mark remain safe and free from harm when online?

Qualification mapping

Unit 5 LO 1.2, 2.2, 3.1, 3.2, 5.3, 7.1, 7.2 and 7.3

Minimising online risks

You are supporting a vulnerable adult with a mild learning disability who also has mobility issues and lives in a remote area. Their partner has recently died and now the user of service feels lonely and cannot get to the shops to buy groceries and other essential items. They have asked for your support to buy a laptop computer so that they can use the internet to help with these issues. Whilst you are happy to do this, you have concerns regarding the possibility of risk of abuse to the user of service.

Answer the following questions in your own words:

1. What are the potential risks to the user of the service?
2. What could you do to minimise those risks?
3. What would you do to maintain their safety?

Situational judgement questions

1. You have thought of a new procedure that you believe would improve safeguarding and reduce the risk of unsafe practices. Some colleagues agree with the change but one staff member openly criticises the idea to your manager. What do you do?
   a. You decide not to respond to the critics in order to avoid unnecessary conflict
   b. You reprimand your colleague for going over your head to your manager and work to promote your idea with even more enthusiasm
   c. You meet the person for a talk and explain that bypassing your authority is unacceptable
   d. Your colleagues' trust in you is important so you decide to implement only some of the changes to keep everyone satisfied
2. Identify the correct term to describe a person who, due to their need for care and support, whether permanent or temporary, and whether or not the local authority is meeting any of those needs, is unable to protect themselves from either the risk of, or the experience of abuse or neglect.
   a. Vulnerable adult
   b. Adult at risk
   c. Needy adult
   d. Supported adult
3. The Mental Capacity Act 2005 means that adults have the capacity to choose how they live and to make decisions about their safety, even if you do not agree with them. Which of the following is NOT one of the five key principles that underpin the Act?
   a. Presumption of capacity
   b. Individuals being supported to make their own decisions
   c. Proportionality
   d. Less restrictive option
4. You may experience unacceptable or oppressive behaviour from your colleagues or other professionals in or outside of your workplace. Which one of the following would NOT be considered oppressive or unacceptable?
   a. Bullying or intimidating behaviour
   b. Removing someone's right to exercise choice
   c. Reporting client behaviour that you consider unsafe
   d. Failing to recognise individuality
5. Safeguarding adults is everybody's responsibility. All staff have a duty to help prevent abuse and to act quickly. There are four key principles with regard to safeguarding adults. Which one of the following does not describe a safeguarding principle?
   a. Protect
   b. Discuss
   c. Preserve
   d. Record
6. Whistleblowing about potentially abusive situations in the workplace can be difficult; and legislation is in place to protect whistleblowers. Which of the following is NOT covered?
   a. A criminal offence
   b. A danger to the health and safety of a person
   c. Staff disputes
   d. Damage to the environment
7. Whistleblowing law is informed by two specific pieces of legislation. Which of the following are those two items of legislation?
   a. Employment Rights Act 1996
   b. Health and Safety at Work Act 1974
   c. Safeguarding Vulnerable Groups Act 2006
   d. Public Interest Disclosure Act 1998
8. The complaints procedure is an important aspect of the monitoring process of an organisation. Which one of the following would NOT be considered appropriate?
   a. Listen to what the person is saying and do not interrupt them
   b. Be explicit about what you are going to do and then do it
   c. Try to resolve the complaint yourself
   d. Learn from what has been complained about and reflect in order to improve the practice

E

Championing health and wellbeing

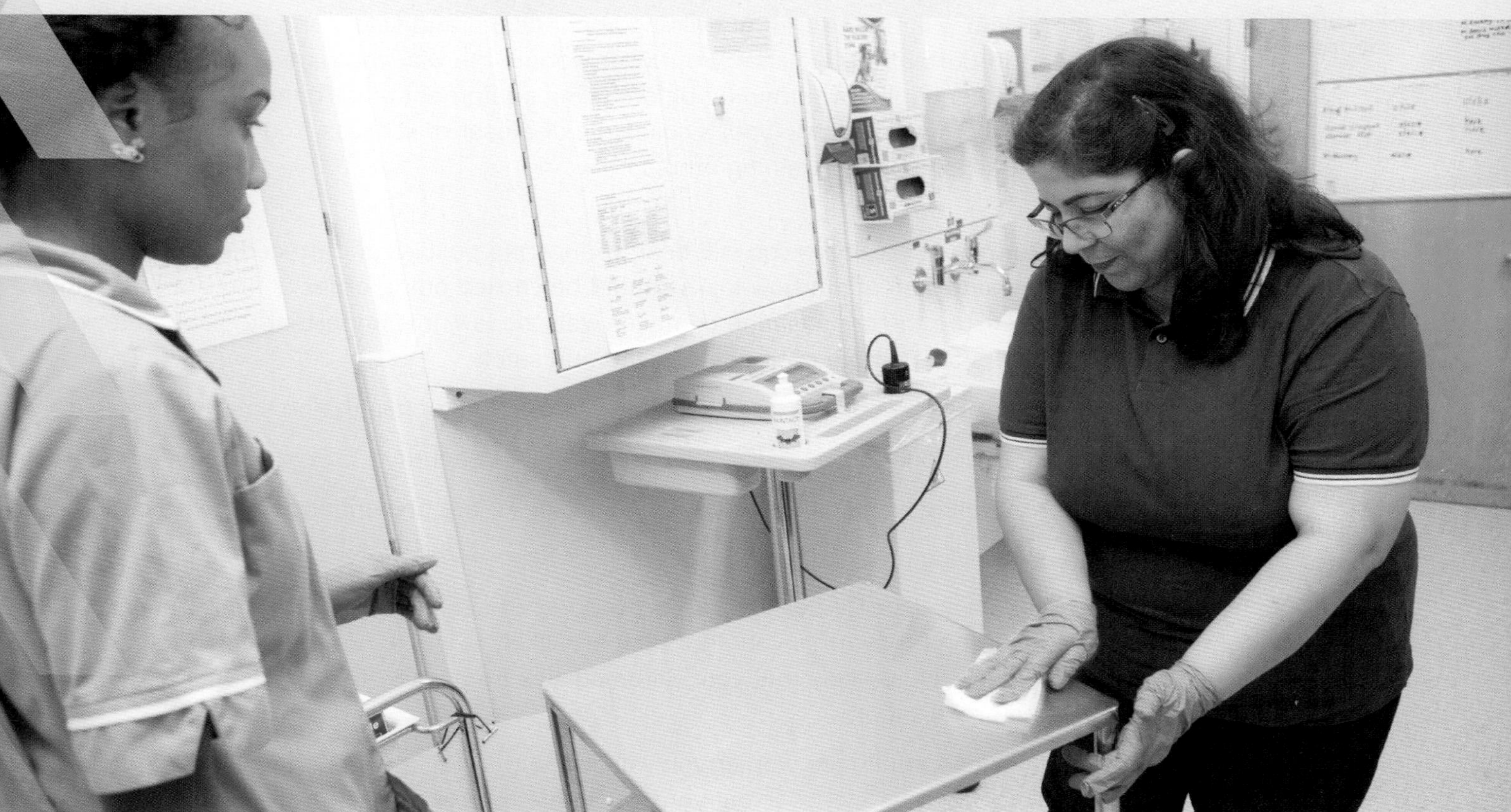

When people are being supported and cared for, they rightly expect to be kept safe from harm and protected from illness. Many illnesses and injuries can be prevented by working safely and you have a duty of care and accountability as a lead adult care worker to work with your colleagues to ensure safe working practices are followed.

This topic will cover the following areas:

- health and safety responsibilities in adult care settings
- keeping safe in the work environment
- responding to accidents and sudden illness
- dealing with hazardous substances
- promoting fire safety
- reducing the spread of infection
- promoting nutrition and hydration
- promoting and using risk assessments.

You will also learn about the skills you will need so that you can apply this knowledge in the care setting where you work.

Health and safety responsibilities

Qualification mapping

Unit 8 LO 2 AC 2.2

You will receive a lot of training about health and safety and it is very important that you carry out your work in the way you have been taught. It is essential to have training before using equipment or carrying out procedures to prevent harm to you, a colleague or a user of services. You will also be responsible for training others.

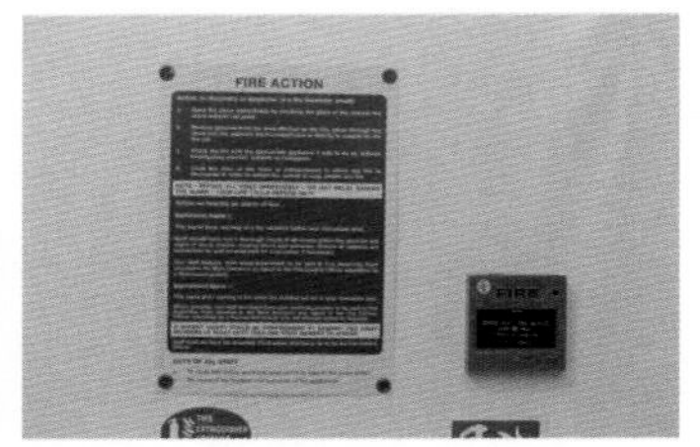

You must follow the given procedure if there is a fire

During your training you will be introduced to policies and procedures that are used to guide staff about how tasks should be carried out in order to prevent harm and to ensure the organisation complies with the law. It is important to cooperate with others to promote everyone's health and safety.

There will be policies and procedures on a range of health and safety topics, such as:

- infection control
- dealing with spillages of body fluids
- moving and handling
- security
- fire prevention and fire procedures
- food safety.

Health and safety policies and procedures are in place for everyone's benefit. By following procedures you are much less likely to get injured or catch an infection, making it less likely that you will be off sick from work. This is good for you as well as the organisation.

As a lead adult care worker you will also support less experienced staff to work safely. This might be by observing your colleagues carrying out a procedure, such as using personal protective equipment correctly, or carrying out an audit on hand washing to ensure staff are cleaning their hands thoroughly.

Key term

Calibration – checking that a monitor is working accurately

As a lead adult care worker, you may be given specific responsibilities to monitor potential health and safety risks. You may be given responsibility for checking that equipment is working properly, such as carrying out **calibration** checks on blood glucose monitors or checking when equipment is due for servicing. If this is not done, incorrect readings may be given, meaning that health problems could be missed.

Some health and safety responsibilities involve record keeping. Records can be used to prove that care was carried out correctly if there is a dispute.

The Health and Safety Executive (see www.hse.gov.uk) is responsible for the regulation of health and safety in the UK.

As a lead adult care worker you may be given responsibility for supporting less experienced staff to work safely. For example, once you are competent in using a hoist, you may be asked to supervise a new member of staff after their training to ensure they are correctly using equipment.

Professional working

It is important that all staff know the main points of policies and procedures that are used regularly, to ensure consistency of safe working practices.

It is very important that you communicate effectively any concerns about health and safety to ensure people are not put at risk. This might include reporting broken equipment, equipment that needs servicing, or concerns over colleagues not working safely. Communication must be clear and accurate when reporting concerns.

It is important that you know where to get health and safety advice and information from should you need it.

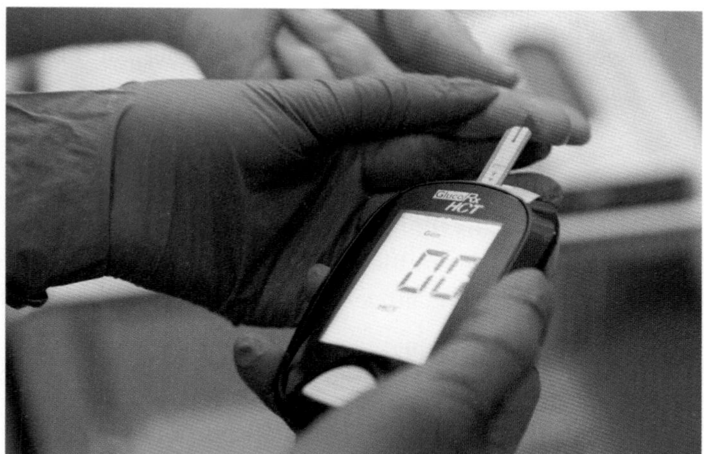
Equipment such as blood glucose monitors must be checked carefully

Professional working 

Reporting colleagues who are not working safely takes courage, as you may feel you are being disloyal. However, you may be saving them from harm.

Activity

Finding out information

Find out where you would look for the following information at your workplace:

- instruction manuals for equipment
- maximum weight limits for hoists and slings
- service due dates for equipment
- training courses available for infection control
- health and safety policies and procedures
- storage instructions for chemicals.

Familiarise yourself with the main points of the policies and procedures so that you could explain them to a new member of staff, and demonstrate to your assessor if asked.

You might need to show a colleague how to carry out a procedure such as correct hand washing

Responsibilities of employers

It is the responsibility of your employer to provide health and safety information, training and equipment, and to ensure the environment is spacious enough for staff to work safely.

Summary 

Policies and procedures are useful documents to guide you about safe working practices. Familiarise yourself with them, so you are always working safely.

Qualification mapping 

Unit 8 LO 1 AC 1.2, LO 2 AC 2.1, 2.2 and 2.6

Keep safe in the work environment

Qualification mapping

Unit 8 LO 1

Legally, health and safety at work is everyone's responsibility in a work environment. There are different laws and regulations setting out the actions that must be followed in a work setting in order to minimise the risk that you, your colleagues, users of services or visitors will come to harm.

Professional working

As a lead adult care worker you need to be observant and notice when any less experienced colleagues are putting themselves or others at risk of harm. You may need to stop them and show them how to work safely, or discuss with your manager the need for training and supervision.

Health and safety at work

The Labour Force Survey estimates that there are 192,000 incidents of work-related illness and 72,000 non-fatal injuries in the health and social care sector every year. See www.hse.gov.uk/statistics/industry/healthservices/index.htm for more information.

Health and Safety at Work Act 1974

Since the Health and Safety at Work Act was first passed in 1974, several more laws and regulations have been brought in that focus on particular aspects of potentially hazardous work. Figure 1 shows the important ones to know about when working in adult care.

Figure 1: Health and safety laws come under the umbrella of the Health and Safety at Work Act

The Health and Safety at Work Act 1974 requires everyone to take responsibility for health and safety. **Employers** must provide training, information and equipment, but **employees** are obliged by law to attend and follow the training when at work, and to use the equipment provided for their safety.

Employers must have insurance in case a member of staff is seriously injured at work. All accidents and health and safety incidents that do occur must be recorded in the accident book or online system.

You should never tamper with any equipment provided to reduce the risk of harm, and must always think about your colleagues' safety as well as your own.

Key term

Employer – the owner or manager of the setting acts as the employer

Employee – the workers at the setting are employees

Activity

Rubina has just arrived for the first day of her apprenticeship at Springfield Day Centre for individuals with learning disabilities. The front door is open so Rubina walks up the ramp and enters the building. Before she has got as far as the manager's office, she hears a loud bang and a squeal. When she turns round, Maxine, one of the users of the service has wheeled herself outside in her wheelchair and fallen off the edge of the ramp. Rubina goes to help but does not think it can be her fault as it is only her first day.

- Is she right? Look back at the Health and Safety at Work Act and see if you can decide who is at fault.
- Is it Rubina, other staff, the manager, or all three?

Qualification mapping

Unit 8 LO 1 AC 1.1

Management of Health and Safety at Work Regulations 1999

This law focuses on the use of risk assessments to anticipate where work tasks are potentially hazardous, and requires managers to carry out risk assessments to identify the risks that exist and the best ways to avoid harm. This might be by providing training for staff and equipment to use during tasks. As a lead adult care worker you may be asked to instruct a new member of staff. For example, you might show a member of staff how to assist a new user of services to go up a short flight of stairs safely. It is crucial that you instruct thoroughly and then watch your colleague to ensure they have fully understood the safe way of carrying out the task.

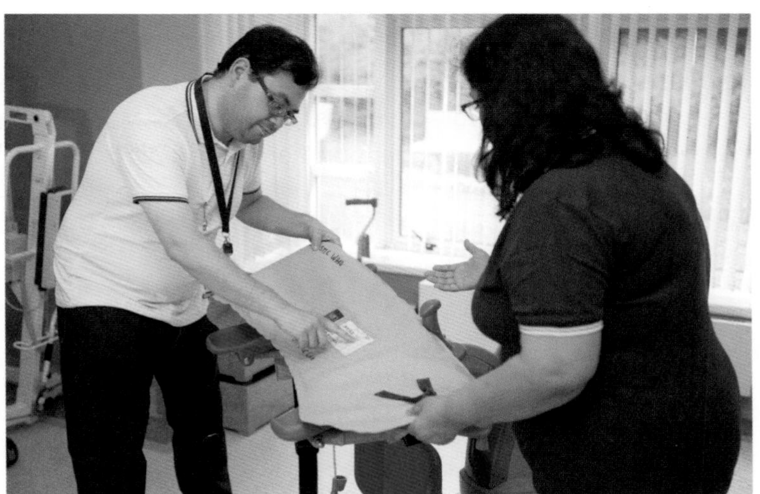

You might need to train a junior colleague on how to use lifting equipment

Professional working

Always challenge poor practice by colleagues, as this could prevent harm to yourself or users of your service.

Information must be available for staff to read in case they are unsure of safe ways of working. This would include instruction manuals, policies and procedures. You can read more about risk assessments on page 160.

Manual Handling Operations Regulations 1992

It is a legal requirement that you receive manual handling training as soon as possible after starting your apprenticeship. You will be taught how to operate the equipment used in your workplace. It is your responsibility to use the equipment and methods you have been taught in order to reduce the risk of an injury. Moving and handling methods will be covered on page 192.

Qualification mapping

Unit 8 LO 1 AC 1.4

Health and Safety (First Aid) Regulations 1981

As a lead adult care worker you may have the opportunity to train as a first aider. There must always be a first aider available at your workplace. Nurses are not necessarily first aiders. The first aider will be able to provide immediate first aid if someone is injured or becomes unwell. You will find information on dealing with accidents and sudden illness on page 164.

Professional working

The main reason for recording this information is to learn from incidents in an attempt to avoid the same mistakes being made in the future.

Reporting of Injuries, Diseases and Dangerous Occurrences Regulations 1995

These regulations are usually shortened to RIDDOR. At work there will be a system to record any incidents that have, or could have, resulted in injury, infection or a security breach. It is important to have a record of what happened and how it was dealt with in case there is an investigation. A near-miss still has to be reported, as another time it may result in harm.

Control of Substances Hazardous to Health

This is usually known as COSHH. Any hazardous substances that employees need to handle during their work must be covered by a risk assessment that informs staff about the safest way to handle, store and dispose of the substance.

In your work, you may have to handle:

- chemicals
- blood
- vomit
- soiled incontinence pads
- soiled dressings
- medicines.

All of these are potentially hazardous. You must receive training and be provided with the necessary equipment to protect yourself from harm. More information about dealing with hazardous substances can be found on page 173.

Activity

Working within the law

In the table below, the column on the left gives examples of actions that you might need to take when you are following health and safety legislation (laws) correctly. Read these examples of actions and identify which law or regulation each relates to. Some laws are used more than once.

Actions to meet requirements of the law	Relevant law or regulation
You explain to a person that you can't take them to the toilet on your own as they have been assessed as needing two people to assist them.	
Someone slips over on a wet patch on the floor. This is recorded in the accident book, even though there are no apparent injuries.	
You read the moving and handling risk assessment for a new user of your service and use the recommended equipment to transfer her into a chair.	
You are called to assess a member of the kitchen staff who has cut his finger, because you are the first aider on duty.	
You move some cleaning fluid that the cleaner has left in the toilet and lock it in the cleaners' cupboard.	
You are provided with, and use, protective gloves to wash a user of services.	
You encourage an individual to walk with a walking frame rather than pushing them in a wheelchair.	

You will need to put these laws into practice in order to prevent illness and injury.

Qualification mapping

Unit 8 LO 1 AC 1.1

Policies and procedures at work

Think about the health and safety policies and procedures at your workplace. You need to analyse the responsibilities of yourself, your employer and others for making sure everyone is kept safe and well. This means the actions each person takes to ensure the requirements of the laws are met. Who writes the rules? How do they know what to write? Who checks that everyone is working safely? How do they do this? How do others know what to do to be safe?

Qualification mapping

Unit 8 LO 1 AC 1.3

Summary

The consequences of breaking health and safety laws can be serious, with companies being fined or even closed temporarily or permanently. Always make sure you understand legal requirements and follow policies and procedures at your workplace. These are written around the laws, so following them will prevent you breaking the law.

Promoting and using risk assessment

Qualification mapping

Unit 8 LO 2 AC 2.3, 2.4 and 2.5

Key term

Hazard – something that could cause harm, such as illness or injury

Harm – the consequence if a hazard causes injury or illness

Risk – the likelihood that a hazard will cause harm

Risk assessments are used to identify work tasks that could potentially cause harm if they are not carried out safely. As a lead adult care worker you will be expected to promote the benefits of risk assessment in preventing harm.

A person-centred approach to risk assessment in adult care

Most risk assessments are done for all staff to follow with all users of services. However, some risk assessments are done as part of care planning and are only about one specific member of staff or user of the service. Examples include nutritional risk assessments to prevent choking and weight loss, and moving and handling risk assessments to prevent injuries to carers and users of the service. It is likely that there will be some compromise involved. Few people would choose to be moved by hoist, for example, but many people would prefer to get up in the daytime than stay in bed, and if this means hoisting to prevent carers hurting themselves, most people would accept this compromise.

The Health and Safety Executive recommends five steps to risk assessment:

1. Identify the **hazard**
2. Assess the potential **harm**
3. Calculate the **risk** and decide on the control measures
4. Document the findings from the assessment and the recommendations (there are several different formats for this)
5. Regularly review to ensure the control measures are still relevant; a new piece of equipment or service user may require a different approach.

Hazards include:

- excessive clutter or a loose rug on the floor causing a trip hazard
- a spillage or leaking radiator causing a slip hazard
- a cramped working space making it hard to get into a good position for moving and handling
- a person who is unsteady and prone to falls
- staff shortages
- an unlocked door.

Examples of **harm** include:

- incorrect use of a new piece of equipment that might cause falls, leading to fractures, head injuries or cuts
- twisting in a cramped working space or trying to stop a person falling over – may lead to muscle strains
- insufficient care staff – could lead to pressure ulcers and falls
- an unlocked door, which might give intruders an opportunity to get in, or allow a confused user of services to leave without being noticed.

Professional working 

When deciding whether something is too risky, consider whether the benefits of doing the activity outweigh the risks. Document the physical or psychological benefits in the document.

Calculating the risk

This involves estimating how likely it is that harm will occur and, if it did, the potential severity. To calculate the risk, multiply the likelihood by the severity, as shown in Table 1.

	Likelihood		Severity
1	Unlikely	1	No harm likely
2	Small chance	2	Minor injury (e.g. minor cut)
3	Medium chance	3	Significant injury (e.g. broken arm)
4	Highly likely	4	Serious injury (e.g. broken leg)
5	Almost certainly	5	Death or permanent disability

Table 1: Calculating the risk: likelihood multiplied by severity

Case study: What is the risk for John?

John has just been referred to a day centre for individuals who have had a stroke. While in hospital, he developed pneumonia from choking on his food. His swallow reflex is still poor. He chokes at almost every mealtime.

Anita is a speech and language therapist and is doing a risk assessment for John for eating and drinking. His likelihood of choking at mealtimes is 'almost certainly'; the consequences if he does choke could be another bout of pneumonia, which could result in death.

The risk is 5 x 5 = 25. This is too great a risk, but obviously John does need to eat.

To reduce John's risk of choking, Anita recommends that his food is puréed and his drinks are thickened. Using the table above this reduces the likelihood to 'medium chance'.

- Using the information above, what is the risk for John if his food is pureed?
- What are the potential consequences for him?

The findings will be recorded on a risk assessment form. There are many different versions of these forms and your workplace will have one for you to look at.

Qualification mapping

Unit 8 LO 2 AC 2.3, 2.4 and 2.5

Control measures

These are actions taken to reduce the risk, such as modifying the way food is prepared to reduce the risk of choking. There are several ways to control hazards:

1. Removing the hazard, such as taking broken equipment out of service.
2. Separating the hazard from people, such as locking away chemicals.
3. Using safety equipment, such as gloves and aprons to avoid infection.
4. Using safety strategies, such as safe methods of walking with an unsteady person.

Risk assessments are working documents, meaning they should be used regularly and reviewed to ensure they are still relevant.

There are many reasons why a risk assessment may need to be reviewed, for example:

- a new user of services has a visual impairment
- a new piece of equipment is purchased
- a staff member finds out she is pregnant.

Key term

Least restrictive – allowing as much freedom as possible without risking harm

It is not possible to prevent all accidents because you would have to stop all service users from doing anything that could result in harm. This would be too restrictive and infringe their rights. If you do identify that a person is at significant risk of harm, you need to think of ways to reduce risk that would be **least restrictive.**

Activity

Risk assessment for an outing

Alex and Sam are taking two users of their learning disability residential home to the seaside for a day. This is an annual trip. Last year they took Amil, who has epilepsy, and Conrad, who is allergic to nuts. Both were wheelchair users, and Conrad needed two people to transfer him onto the toilet.

This year they are taking Mo, who is mobile but has very poor eyesight, and Iolo, who has ADHD and can behave quite erratically, sometimes running off suddenly.

On page 163, Table 2 shows an extract from last year's risk assessment.

(A) means Amil; (C) means Conrad.

- What would need to change before they go on their trip this year?

Activity

Trip to seaside

Hazard	Potential Harm	Risk	Control measures
Food (A & C)	Choking	1x5	Keep conversation calm, avoid causing laughter Cut food into manageable size
Food (C)	Allergic reaction	2x5	Check ingredients with chef Take epipen in case of allergic reaction
Road traffic (A)	Seizure while crossing the road	2x4	Ensure medication has been taken Use pelican crossings so traffic has stopped
Sea (A)	Seizure while in the sea Drowning	2x5	Ensure medication has been taken Stay in shallow water Wear buoyancy aid
Transferring onto toilet (C)	Staff injury	2x3	Two staff to transfer using correct lifting methods
Unaccompanied user (A)	Getting lost	3x2	Take an extra member of staff to stand with A whilst C using toilet

Table 2: Risk assessment for an outing

Qualification mapping 

Unit 8 LO 2 AC 2.4 and 2.5

Summary 

A good risk assessment will anticipate all the possible ways that harm could occur, and suggest ways to reduce or remove the risk without restricting users of service more than necessary. Make sure staff know where risk assessments are stored, and encourage them to contribute ideas to improve safe working.

Accidents and sudden illness

Qualification mapping

Unit 8 LO 3

Under the Health and Safety (First Aid) Regulations 1981, first aid is only legally required for staff, but in a care setting it is appropriate that staff are trained to deal with situations that might arise from a user of service becoming ill or having an accident.

First aid

However careful staff are, there will be occasional accidents in a health and care setting. You may also have users of services who become suddenly unwell. While you are not expected to be able to diagnose illness, it is useful to have some understanding of potential signs and symptoms to look out for, and knowledge of first aid.

Working in adult care means that you will occasionally have to deal with accidents or sudden illness. Older people often have particular medical conditions, such as heart disease or high blood pressure, or you may care for people of any age who have conditions such as epilepsy or diabetes.

In order to be the first aider on duty, you must have good first-aid knowledge and the best way to ensure this is to hold a current first-aid certificate. Qualifications are only valid for three years so you would need to complete a new course when your certificate is due to expire. The Health and Safety Executive also recommend annual refresher courses.

There are three aims of first aid:

1. To preserve life
2. To prevent the situation worsening
3. To promote recovery.

It is not always possible to achieve these aims, but if you do manage to save a life you will have good reason to be proud of yourself.

The role of the first aider involves:

- assessing the situation
- protecting yourself and the casualty from danger
- preventing the spread of infection
- comforting and reassuring the casualty
- assessing the casualty
- giving first-aid treatment
- arranging for further help if needed.

(Source: St John Ambulance 2018, www.sja.org.uk/sea/first-aid-advice/what-to-do-as-a-first-aider/the-role-of-a-first-aider.aspx)

Assessing the situation

If you have to deal with an accident or the sudden illness of a user of service in your workplace, follow these guidelines:

- Never put yourself in danger, you are of no use if you become another casualty.
- Look for sources of help. Get colleagues or bystanders to do things for you.
- Check there is only one casualty. Quiet casualties are often more seriously ill or injured than noisy ones.
- Make space for yourself so you can get to work.
- Send for help straight away. You might ask someone to fetch the first aider or ask someone to dial 999, whichever you think most appropriate.

Protecting yourself and the casualty from danger

Do not move the casualty if you don't need to: you could make them worse.

Preventing the spread of infection

At work you should always have access to protective gloves and wound dressings in the first-aid kit. If you go out with users of service, take a first-aid kit with you.

Comforting and reassuring the casualty

You may be anxious as well as the casualty; reassuring them can also reassure you.

Try to keep calm as this will help you to think clearly and put your training into practice.

All of the above points will be carried out in a very short time, and can save time in the end.

Assessing the casualty

Try to work out what you need to do based on your observations.

Check for a response. If the casualty is talking or screaming, you know they are breathing. If they are quiet, shake their shoulders and speak to them to see if they respond. If not, you need to check whether the airway is blocked. This can happen if the tongue has fallen over the back of the throat. If there is no risk of neck injury, you can open the airway by tipping the head back placing one hand on the forehead and the other on the bony part of the chin.

Even if someone does not wish to be resuscitated, you should open the airway, as they may breathe without any further help.

Professional working

Some users of service may have a 'do not resuscitate' order in place, meaning the person has expressed a wish not to be given cardiopulmonary resuscitation (CPR) if their heart stops. It is important to know who has these orders in place. This is distressing but it is important to respect the person's wishes should their heart stop.

Qualification mapping 

Unit 8 LO 3 AC 3.2

If there is a risk of neck injury, do not tip the head back. Instead push the bottom jaw forward. This is known as the jaw thrust manoeuvre.

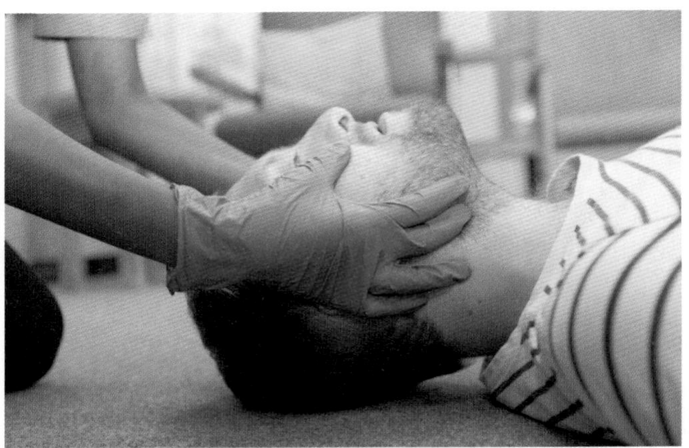

To do the jaw thrust, place your hands on either side of the face and with your fingertips gently lift the jaw to open the airway, avoiding any movement of the neck

Check the person is **breathing**. Look for the rise and fall of the chest.

Listen and feel for breaths for 10 seconds. If they are not breathing, start cardiopulmonary resuscitation (CPR). A first-aid course will teach you this skill.

If the person is breathing, check for signs of **bleeding**. If you cannot see any blood but signs of shock are present they could be bleeding internally.

Signs of shock

Signs of shock include:

- pale colour
- cold, sweaty skin
- fast breathing rate
- fast pulse rate.

Recovery position

If an individual is breathing but unresponsive, and is not thought to have a spinal injury, they should be placed in the recovery position to keep the airway open while waiting for an ambulance to arrive.

See the step-by-step procedure on page 167.

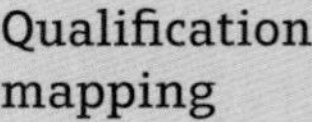

Qualification mapping 

Unit 8 LO 3 AC 3.2

Step by step

Recovery position

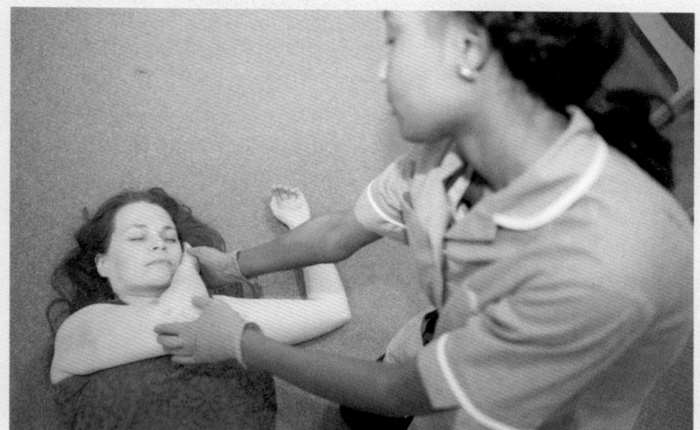

Step 1
Place the nearest arm at a right angle to the body and the back of the furthest hand under the nearest cheek.

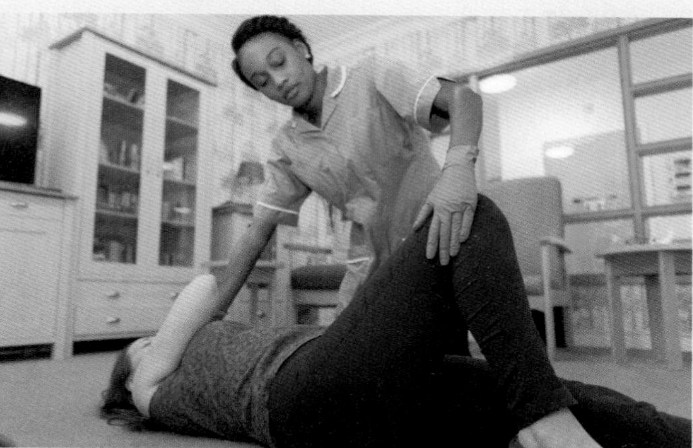

Step 2
Bend the furthest leg.

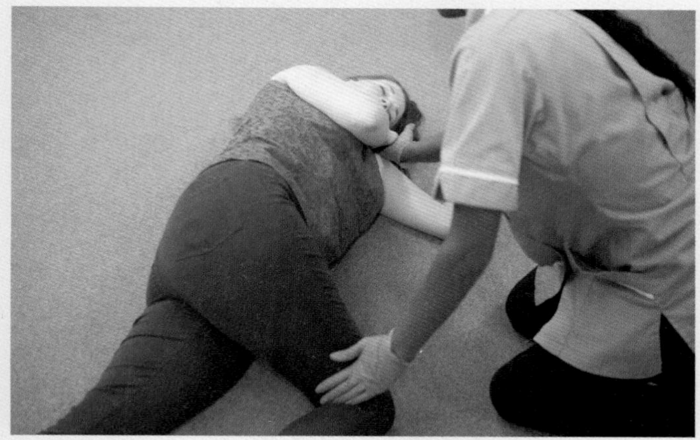

Step 3
Use the furthest knee to turn the casualty onto their side. Keep supporting the head as you turn them.

Step 4
Adjust the head to make sure the airway is kept open.

Professional working

Your workplace will have policies and procedures for dealing with accidents and medical emergencies, and you need to be familiar with these. For example, there may be an emergency button on the wall to summon help quickly, saving vital time compared with running for help.

Professional working

Always complete an incident form, even for a medical emergency, as these can help improve practice in the future.

First-aid treatment

Treatment will depend on your findings during the assessment. To prepare yourself for potential situations, you can familiarise yourself with the most likely incidents you will come across. This will depend on the setting you work in.

Activity

▶ Ask if you can look back at the accident book at your workplace to see what the most common accidents are, then research first-aid treatments for these.
Find out about the medical history of the users of your service and what types of sudden illness you are likely to come across. Research the first-aid treatments for these.

You could download a first-aid app on your phone or write notes in a pocket-sized notebook which you can refer to.

Reliable websites include www.sja.org.uk and www.redcross.org.uk

The injuries most common in adult care include:

- slips, trips and falls
- needle stick injuries
- burns and scalds
- moving and handling injuries
- skin tears.

Common illnesses include:

- heart attacks
- people with diabetes becoming low in blood glucose, known as hypoglycaemia or a 'hypo'
- epileptic seizures
- chest infections.

Once you have the situation under control it is important that someone stays with the casualty, providing comfort and reassurance until help arrives. If possible, use this time to take some observations of the individual's blood pressure, pulse, temperature and breathing rate, as this can be useful information for the paramedics. You should only do this if you are competent; incorrect information could result in the wrong care being given.

Summary

It is worthwhile taking the opportunity to become a trained first aider so you have the confidence to deal with emergency situations. It can also be useful out of work time as well.

Manage, monitor, report and respond to changes in health and wellbeing

Whether or not you are in an emergency situation, you should always be alert to signs that an individual is not well and report these to the person in charge of the shift.

Qualification mapping 

Unit 8 LO 3 AC 3.1 and 3.2

Signs and symptoms

A **sign** is something you could notice by looking at a person, or by taking observations. A **symptom** is something the person feels.

Signs

Signs you should respond to include the following:

- a pulse over 100 beats per minute or that beats irregularly
- breathing rate more than 20 breaths per minute
- temperature of 37.5°C or higher
- sweating
- shaking
- weakness down one side
- inability to speak normally or appearing confused
- offensive-smelling urine
- diarrhoea or vomiting
- blood in urine, faeces, vomit, or vaginally if periods have stopped
- a new break in the skin
- swelling, including lumps or swollen ankles
- changes in skin colour – a blue or grey tinge, a yellow tinge, paleness or a rash
- blood pressure greater than 140/90mmHg or lower than 100/60mmHg.

These are only some of the changes in an individual that you might notice; you should always report signs that you are worried about.

If someone has a medical condition where observations are always out of normal range, a GP can give you different measures to decide if the person needs medical attention. These are called parameters. You should also document what they told you and what action you took, including the name of the person you reported your concerns to.

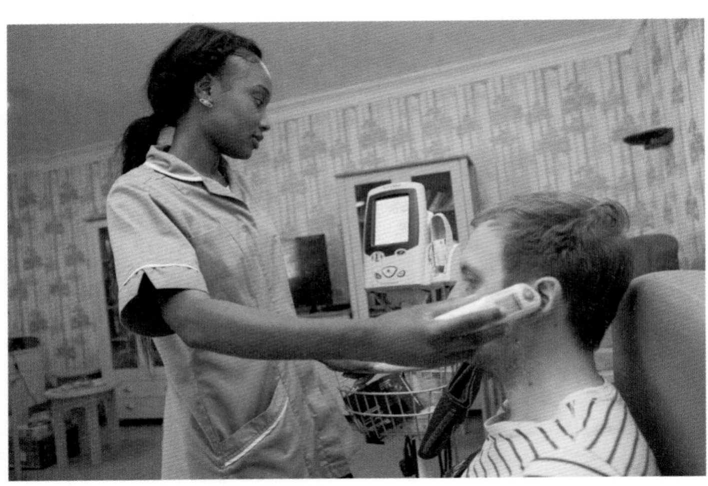

Observations can provide you with more information if you are concerned about an individual

Symptoms

Symptoms that should be reported include:

- pain, especially chest pain or severe headache
- dizziness
- shortness of breath
- feeling sick.

You should always listen to users of services and take seriously any symptoms they tell you about. Even if a person has dementia they may be able to tell you about their symptoms, so always report worrying symptoms.

Common medical emergencies in adult care settings

Heart attack

Symptoms to be aware of:

- feeling of pressure, tightness or squeezing in the centre of the chest
- pain travelling from the chest to the arms (usually the left arm), jaw, neck, back and abdomen
- feeling lightheaded or dizzy
- feeling sick, or being sick
- anxiety.

Signs of a heart attack:

- sweating
- coughing or wheezing
- a greyish tinge to the skin.

For more information go to: www.nhs.uk/conditions/heart-attack/symptoms/

First aid for a suspected heart attack

If you think there is a chance someone is having a heart attack, do not hesitate to follow the guidance below:

- Dial 999. Make it clear you think they are having a heart attack so they are made a priority. It doesn't matter if you are wrong.
- Position the person propped up, knees bent if possible.

- Give them a 300mg aspirin tablet to chew slowly if you know they are not allergic to aspirin.
- They could use a GTN spray (glyceryl trinitrate – diagnosed for angina), if they have one.
- The first aider should stay with the individual, in case their condition deteriorates. An ambulance should come quickly.

For more information, go to: www.sja.org.uk/sja/first-aid-advice/heart/heart-attack.aspx

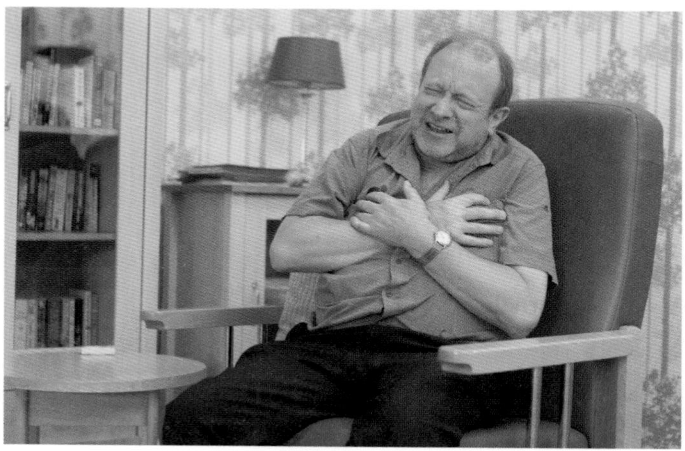

Act fast if you think someone is having a heart attack

Diabetic emergencies

Qualification mapping

Unit 8 LO 2 AC 3.2

People with diabetes do not produce sufficient insulin to control their blood sugar levels. Some people need insulin injections, some need tablets and some can control their blood sugar levels by changing their diet. Sometimes blood sugar levels can become unstable, for example, if the person has an infection or they forget to take their medication.

Most people with diabetes check their blood sugar levels regularly with a monitor. This is to ensure they are under control, as there can be serious side effects if levels are persistently too high. These include kidney failure, blindness and poor circulation.

Blood sugar levels can also drop too low and the person can quickly lose consciousness if they are not given something sugary to drink.

If you have a blood sugar testing monitor, this is the most accurate way to determine if a person with diabetes has too much or too little sugar in their blood.

First aid for diabetic emergencies

Anyone with a reading below 4 should be given something containing sugary to drink and a bowl of breakfast cereal, for example. Do not give diet drinks as these do not contain sugar. Test the blood sugar level again in about 20 minutes to check it has gone up.

If you do not have a blood sugar monitor, signs and symptoms to look for include:

- confusion
- sweating
- shaking
- aggression
- dizziness
- drowsiness.

Qualification mapping

Unit 8 LO 3 AC 3.1 and 3.2

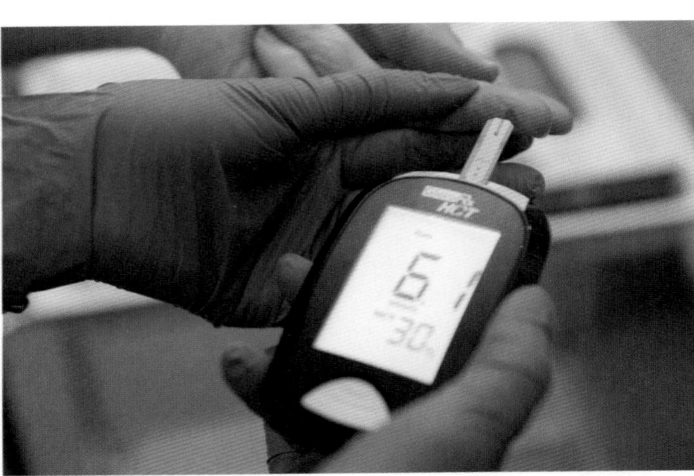

People with diabetes check their blood sugar levels regularly

If you know the person has diabetes, try giving them a drink and a snack to see if this works. It should make a difference within a few minutes.

Low blood sugar can soon lead to unconsciousness. If the person does not quickly improve, call an ambulance. If the blood sugar reading is high, but the individual seems all right, refer them to the doctor or diabetic nurse for a review.

Epilepsy

People who have epilepsy are prone to seizures. There is medication for this and many people with epilepsy have it well controlled and rarely or never have a seizure. It is critical that their medication is taken as prescribed.

There are two main types of seizures:

- absence seizures, where the person seems to be in a daydream
- convulsions, where the person's limbs shake and they lose consciousness.

Activity

▶ Changes in health and wellbeing: what to do

Prepare a presentation that would be suitable for a new member of staff to describe changes in health and wellbeing in the individuals you support. It should describe the different types of accidents and sudden illnesses that might typically occur at your workplace. You should include signs and symptoms, and how these might affect the users of service in terms of mobility, general wellbeing, special dietary requirements and any care needs.

You should include information in the presentation that explains the procedure at your workplace if anyone becomes suddenly ill or has an accident.

First aid for epilepsy

There is no need to worry about absence seizures; just stay with the person until they become responsive again.

If an individual has a convulsion you can protect them from harm during the seizure by:

- moving objects out of the way
- cushioning their head against hard surfaces
- putting them into the recovery position once the convulsion has stopped and staying with them until they regain consciousness.

It is useful to time a seizure and keep a record of the frequency of seizures in case the person's medication needs reviewing.

You should call an ambulance for any seizure lasting more than five minutes.

Dealing with hazardous substances

Hazardous substances include any substances that could cause harm if not handled correctly. This could mean poisoning, damage to the skin or eyes, infection or damage to the environment. If you have to handle hazardous substances as part of your role, you should receive appropriate training before carrying out such tasks.

Qualification mapping 

Unit 8 LO 6 AC 6.1

Hazardous substances include the following:

- acids, which can burn if they come into contact with skin
- irritants such as cleaning fluids, which can irritate skin or eyes
- substances that give off fumes, which can cause breathing difficulties
- poisons, including chemicals, plants or medicines swallowed by the wrong person, or an overdose
- flammable substances, which can be solids or liquids; these can catch fire easily
- chemicals that can cause harm to the environment if poured down the drain.

You may see the symbols shown in Figure 2 on labels and containers. See if you can match the hazard to the symbol using the bullet points above.

Figure 2: Can you identify these hazardous substances?

As a lead adult care worker you will come across many infection hazards, such as dirty dressings, used incontinence pads, blood and sputum. In addition, individuals with airborne infections such as flu, or diarrhoea and vomiting, are an infection hazard and will need to stay in their own rooms away from other people. You may also see injection needles disposed of at your workplace. These are classed as sharps.

It is important to know how to handle, store and dispose of hazardous substances. These are covered by COSHH regulations, and the policies and procedures at your workplace.

Storing hazardous substances

Chemicals and flammable substances should have the manufacturer's storage instructions on the container. There may be a temperature range for storage. Hazardous substances should always be kept in a locked room or cupboard when not in use, and never left unattended while in use.

Qualification mapping 

Unit 8 LO 6 AC 6.2

Medicines should always be kept in a locked trolley or cabinet, except when in use, and must never be left unattended. If you complete training for administration of medicine, you will sometimes be responsible for administering tablets to users of the service. Always make sure tablets are swallowed; do not leave them on tables or lockers as they could be swallowed by the wrong person or a visiting child. Some people may ask you to leave them for later. This is *not* allowed so you should ask them what time to bring them back and lock them away until the individual is ready to take them.

You should never transfer hazardous substances out of their original containers, as a confused person may mistake the liquid for a drink. Chemicals can burn the throat and gullet.

Store hazardous substances such as drugs in line with your workplace policy

Using hazardous substances

Protective gloves and clothing should always be worn when dealing with acids, irritants and potentially infectious substances. You should still wash your hands thoroughly after you remove your gloves.

Make sure there is plenty of ventilation when using substances that give off fumes or strong odours. Check if anyone is sensitive to these, as they can cause a range of symptoms including headaches, asthma or diarrhoea.

Medication is often dispensed in blister packs by the pharmacy, which reduces the risk of errors significantly.

Professional working 

Adverse reactions to medicines are sometimes reported by the doctor or nurse using the yellow card scheme, which gathers information to improve the safety of medicines in the UK.

Side effects

It is important to be aware of potential side effects that must be reported. Anyone who has started a new medicine may develop side effects. If a user of services reports new symptoms they were not experiencing before they started the medication, these should be reported straight away and advice sought about whether the new medication should be continued. You should report concerns to the person in charge, who will contact the on-call doctor.

Signs that might indicate an allergic reaction can be very severe or even life threatening. A rash might be the first sign, which is not life threatening but could indicate an allergy. The next time the medicine is taken, the reaction could be much worse, such as swelling of the tongue and throat, which can obstruct the airway. For this reason, you should always report a rash. Other side effects might include dizziness, nausea or low blood pressure.

If a user of service does develop a severe allergic reaction to a medicine, known as anaphylactic shock, this can cause obstructed breathing and is considered a medical emergency. Dial 999 immediately. Sit the person in the best position for them to help with breathing. Be prepared to start resuscitation if necessary.

Professional working 

If the person has had a reaction before, they may have an Epipen. Staff should have training so they know how to use this in an emergency.

Disposing of hazardous substances

To prevent harm to users of services, staff and the wider environment, it is important to dispose of hazardous substances correctly.

Infectious waste should be discarded in the correct bin, usually with a yellow or orange liner. These are dealt with separately by the council, not mixed with the household waste. Make sure you know where different types of waste should be discarded.

Sharps should always be discarded in a yellow sharps bin. The bin should be taken to the user of services to prevent needle stick injuries.

There may be documentation to complete when disposing of chemicals, so check if this is needed in your workplace policy or procedure.

You may also come across bins for disposing of waste tablets and medicines. Medicines should never be put down the drain as they could contaminate the water supply. If you do not have bins, return unwanted medicines to the pharmacy for disposal.

Qualification mapping 

Unit 8 LO 6 AC 6.2

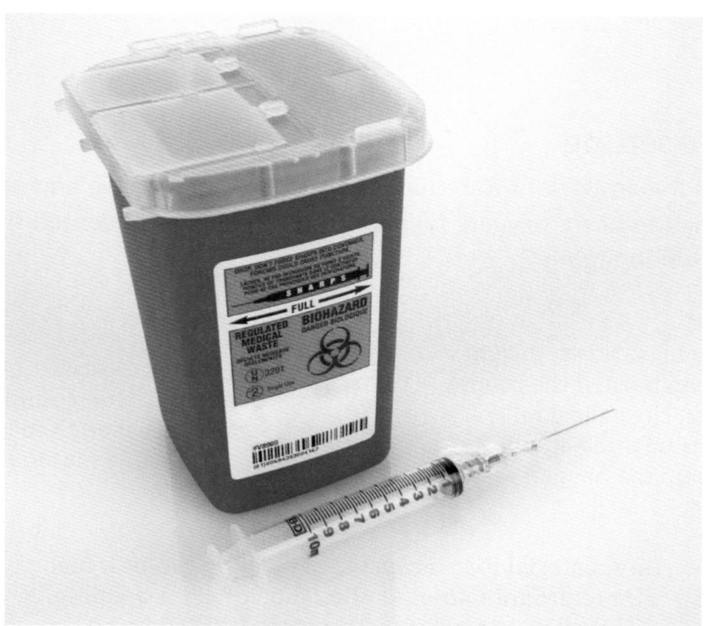

A sharps bin should be used to prevent needlestick injuries

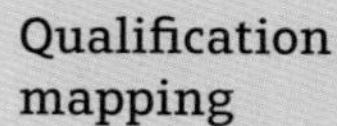 

Qualification mapping

Unit 8 LO 6 AC 6.1 and 6.2

Activity

▶ Information on hazardous substances

Spend time looking around your workplace to identify which hazardous substances are used. Find out about why they are hazardous and how they should be handled, stored and disposed of. Think about the most useful way this information could be presented for staff to be able to refer to if unsure. You may decide to make a poster, a leaflet, a pocket-sized booklet or a set of reference cards. You should describe each substance and explain to the reader the handling, storage and disposal requirements. Try to make the information concise, accurate and quick and easy to find.

Ask your assessor or a suitable colleague to observe you safely using, storing and disposing of hazardous substances so you can get a witness testimony for your evidence portfolio.

Summary 

It is essential to store, handle and dispose of hazardous substances correctly in an adult care setting. Never leave hazardous substances where they could be mistaken for drinks or sweets, and protect the environment by disposing of them correctly.

Promote fire safety

Qualification mapping

Unit 8 LO 7

You are legally required to undertake fire training as part of your workplace induction. You will learn the fire procedure and how to use any equipment you might need in an emergency. You must be confident that you would know what to do if a fire broke out and that you could direct others during a fire emergency.

Fire in a care setting

In care settings it is important to reduce the risk of fires starting and spreading. Fires need three things to burn: oxygen, fuel and heat. This is represented by the fire triangle, as shown in Figure 3.

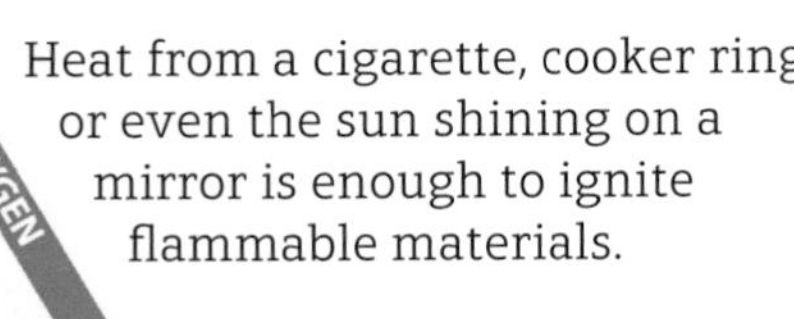

Figure 3: The fire triangle: fire needs all three of these elements to burn

A fire needs heat, fuel and oxygen to exist, so removing one of these elements will stop a fire from breaking out, or extinguish one that is alight.

Fuel

Fuel can come from a variety of sources, such as tea towels, bed linen, clothing or furnishing materials, such as curtains and sofas. Flammable liquids must be stored away from heat. Some skin creams are flammable and have been linked to fires, some of which have caused deaths.

Link to media story: www.bbc.co.uk/news/UK-39308748

A BBC investigation published in March 2017 found 37 cases where fires had been linked to the use of creams since 2010, but there could be many more.

If you work in the community you should advise anyone who is using paraffin-based creams to change their clothes and bedding daily, if possible, to prevent a build-up of cream. This is an example of removing fuel from the fire triangle, and so helping to prevent fires. People who use flammable creams should not smoke. There have been cases of people setting themselves on fire this way.

Oxygen

The air we breathe contains approximately 20 per cent oxygen. This can be used by fire to keep it alight. Some fire extinguishers work by removing oxygen from the fire. Carbon dioxide extinguishers work in this way.

Qualification mapping

Unit 8 LO 7 AC 7.1

Heat

Some fires start because fuel has been exposed to heat. A tea towel left next to a gas ring will soon catch fire. Some fires have started when a ray of sun has been directed onto curtains by a mirror. The risk is even greater with magnifying mirrors, used for putting on makeup. Sparks from faulty electrical equipment are another potential source of heat.

Activity

Fire prevention

Look at the actions below and decide which is removing heat, which is removing fuel and which is removing oxygen. There may be more than one correct answer; make sure you can justify your decision.

Closing doors and windows as you leave a building that will be empty overnight	
Advising a user of community care services never to smoke in bed	
Moving the armchair away from a gas fire in the home of a user of services	

Your fire training should ensure that you are fully aware of the fire procedure. However, your place of work will also display the fire procedure on the walls, and signs showing evacuation routes and fire-fighting equipment such as fire extinguishers.

Qualification mapping

Unit 8 LO 7 AC 7.4

Your employer must also remind staff of the evacuation procedure regularly, so that workers know what to do in case of a real fire. It will not be possible to practise with users of the service, as this could be distressing, but you may practise with colleagues taking the role of users of the service.

If you work in the community you will need to adapt to working in many different properties. It is much harder to insist that individuals living in their own homes do not behave in a way that puts visiting adult care workers in danger. If you feel that you are in danger when visiting specific properties, you must discuss this with your manager. If staff are at risk of harm then perhaps the service cannot be provided for that individual. For example, you may have to visit homes that are very cluttered, making the risk of fire greater and escape from a fire difficult.

Your workplace will have different types of fire extinguishers for different fires as well as displaying the fire procedure on the wall

A cluttered home can present a fire risk

There are services that will visit to assist with decluttering if family or friends are unable to do this, but, of course, consent has to be obtained. Sometimes cluttered houses are associated with mental ill health; decluttering can be very stressful for these individuals.

Fire-fighting equipment

Depending on your place of work, you may learn about the use of a fire blanket, fire extinguishers and evacuation chairs.

You would never be expected to put your own life in danger in a fire, but if it is safe to assist people to evacuate, or to extinguish a very small fire, then you should do so.

A residential or day care setting will have a fire risk assessment, identifying any fire hazards and how the risk of fires starting can be reduced. The most likely fire hazards in a care setting are:

- flammable substances, such as oxygen (in cylinders) or cleaning chemicals
- cigarettes, as care homes are exempt from the law banning smoking in the workplace, which means users of service may be allowed to smoke in their rooms
- electrical appliances, which can cause fires if faulty.

Community care managers would need to do individual fire risk assessments if properties are identified as a fire risk; for example, if a vulnerable person is a smoker. The person should be involved in the risk assessment. A fire could break out when they are alone, so knowing what to do, and what not to do, could save their life. Fire prevention is, of course, the main aim.

Summary

It is important that you know about what to do in case of a fire. It may not be possible to practise in the workplace, but you should know where fire exits are, how to raise the alarm and how to safely remove users of services from a building on fire without endangering your own life.

Fire safety procedures

As a lead adult care worker you will be expected to know what to do if there is a fire and be able to support other staff, visitors and users of the service during an evacuation. You are not, however, expected to put yourself in danger.

Professional working 

Always challenge any colleague who does not comply with fire policies, as vital seconds might be lost in a real emergency.

Check for hazards

In your role as a lead adult care worker you should keep vigilant for fire hazards as you may be able to prevent fires from happening. Move any flammable materials away from heat. Check electrical equipment on a regular basis to ensure that servicing and PAT testing is up to date. If you notice any frayed or damaged cables, remove the equipment from use, put a sign on it and report it for repair.

Keep alert to anyone placing objects in a fire evacuation route. Move these immediately and gently remind staff about the importance of this.

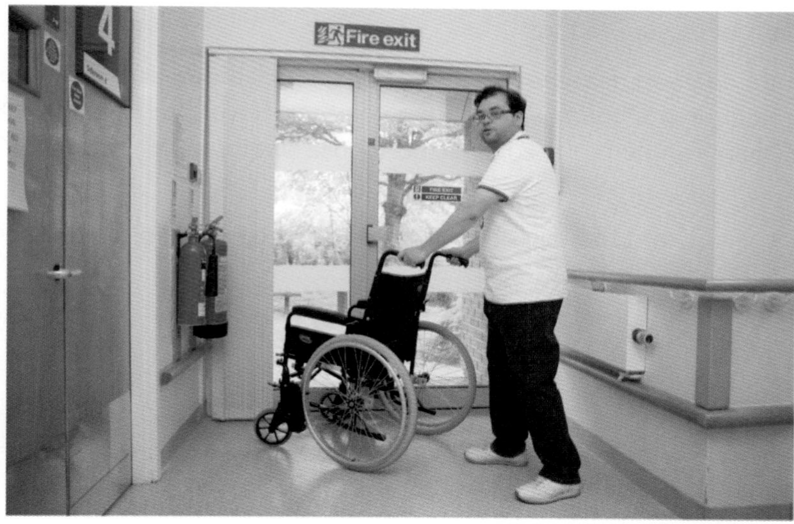

Always keep fire exits clear from any obstructions

Check smoke detectors are working on the first day of every month. Replace batteries on the same date each year. If you work in the community, the fire service will install smoke detectors for free in the homes of vulnerable people. You could phone on behalf of a user of service to arrange this.

Sounding the alarm

If a fire is discovered, the alarm must be raised before doing anything else, as you need to get the fire service on their way. Some settings have a fire button behind a glass panel on the wall that sounds the alarm and automatically calls the fire service. Others need a 999 call as well. Remember, if you need to dial 9 for an outside line you will need to dial 9-999. Learn the address and postcode of your workplace to save valuable time. If you are working at an individual's own home, you will need to have their address with you when you phone.

Staying calm is vital, as this will reassure everyone else that the situation is under control. Once you know the fire service is on the way, staff need to start moving users of the service and visitors to a safe place. Transfer people with mobility difficulties into wheelchairs as quickly as possible and evacuate if necessary.

In residential homes, housing complexes or day care settings, you need to know when to evacuate and when to just be prepared. Many settings have fire retardant doors inside to create safe zones, which can be used to safely separate people from the fire without the need for frail people to have to go outside. Cold, wet weather could in itself pose a hazard. Fire doors can hold back a fire for up to two hours, depending on their specification. Your fire policy should state how long the fire doors in your workplace can effectively protect people. If the fire is in your area, you may just have to move everyone to the next zone. If it is in an adjoining zone, you need to be ready to accept staff and users of service into your area. The fire service should arrive in plenty of time to deal with the fire within two hours. If the fire is substantial, and it is safe to do so, you should try to help to remove people from the safe zone in a calm way.

Your workplace will have specific places to assemble if you have to leave the area affected by the fire. A check should be made to identify whether anyone is still left in the building. For example, most care homes have a visitors' book where visitors sign in and out. If so, this should be collected so that visitors as well as staff and users of the service can be accounted for.

House fires are different as there will be no fire doors. You will need to assist the person to a neighbour's house or to wait in your car. Never go back for personal belongings; these can be replaced. It is sad to lose photographs but not worth losing a life for.

If a fire is very small and there is no danger to yourself, you could attempt to extinguish the fire.

Activity

▶ Reflection on fire practice

If it does not occur routinely, discuss whether it would be possible to have a fire practice using staff to represent users of the service. Notice how effective the procedure is in removing people to a safe area. Using the Kolb reflective cycle (see page v), consider the following points.

- What was your experience?
- How did you observe and reflect on that experience?
- What ideas did you come up with in order to act on your observation or reflection?
- How did these ideas work in practice?

Using a fire blanket

Kitchens in care settings usually have a fire blanket. These can be used to put out a fire in a frying pan or chip pan.

- Turn the heat off and remove the fire blanket from its container.
- Hold the blanket at the corners at arm's length with the top slightly higher than your head. Try to wrap your hands in the blanket to protect them.
- Gently place the blanket over the flames. Leave it there until the pan is cold.
- It is no longer recommended to use a wet tea towel if a fire blanket is not available because there is a risk of explosion if hot fat and water mix together.

There are several different types of fire extinguishers. You should never put yourself in any danger but fire extinguishers may be used to create an escape route.

Qualification mapping

Unit 8 LO 7 AC 7.3

Fire extinguishers

There are four types of fire extinguishers: water, foam, dry powder and carbon dioxide.

Activity

Identifying different fire extinguishers

Find out the types of extinguishers provided in your workplace.

Copy and complete the table below to improve your knowledge of what colour each extinguisher is and what they can and cannot be used for.

Type	Colour	Types of fires to use/not use on

Fire safety procedures

Read and familiarise yourself with the fire procedure at your workplace. Walk around the building to identify all the fire alarm points, exit routes and assembly points. During your training you should learn how to use any fire safety equipment that you might need to use in an emergency, and get the chance to practise using them if possible. Training will differ from one setting to another, but it is useful to know how to use a fire extinguisher, in case you ever need to use one to create an escape route.

Activities

Qualification mapping

Unit 8 LO 7 AC 7.3

Carry out fire safety procedures

With your supervisor or workplace mentor, carry out a tour of the building looking for fire hazards. Discuss with your assessor what you will be looking for. This could include:

- obstructed fire routes
- incorrectly stored items
- flammable items near heat sources
- people smoking in the wrong place, or without supervision
- smoke detectors that have been tampered with
- oven hobs left unattended whilst heat is turned on
- electrical equipment that has not been inspected within the last 12 months.

Make safe any hazards you identify. This is what you should do in your day-to-day work. Never leave a hazard for someone else to deal with. Explain to your assessor the importance of maintaining clear evacuation routes.

Finally, describe to your assessor the fire procedure, showing your assessor where the escape routes and extinguishers are, and demonstrate that you know how to use any special equipment used for evacuation at your workplace.

Preventing fires from starting and spreading

Select the correct answers below. Tick all that you think are correct.

1. To prevent a substantial fire in a bedroom from spreading you should:

☐ **a.** Open the window to cool the room down

☐ **b.** Close the door to stop the replacement of oxygen

☐ **c.** Pull all the contents of the room out to remove the fuel

☐ **d.** Tackle the fire with an extinguisher

2. To reduce the availability of fuel for fires in a care setting you should:

☐ **a.** Refuse to let residents have extra blankets

☐ **b.** Ensure the central heating fuel is not delivered until you have run out

☐ **c.** Store empty boxes awaiting refuse collection outside the building

☐ **d.** Make sure blankets are not touching radiators

Practice for professional discussion

Prepare for a 10-minute professional discussion on how you would minimise the risk if a user of your service wanted to smoke cigarettes in their room.

You could include the following points:

- Dealing with your own views and that of your colleagues on enabling a person to smoke while under your care.
- Your understanding of allowing people to make unwise choices if they have capacity.
- A description of the risk assessment process.
- How you would manage this situation.

Reducing the spread of infection

In adult care settings you will often be caring for people who are frail due to chronic ill health or disability. For these individuals, a simple infection could become a serious health challenge. It is essential to reduce the spread of infection as much as possible, and to support other staff and visitors in good infection control practice.

Qualification mapping 

Unit 8 LO 4 AC 4.1 and 4.2

How infection spreads

Infection is spread by bacteria, viruses, fungi and parasites transmitting from one person to another. Organisms can be spread by air, direct contact or indirect contact.

Airborne infections

Airborne infections are spread when organisms are released into the air and inhaled by a susceptible person. Respiratory infections, such as colds and influenza (flu) and the winter vomiting bug, *norovirus*, are all transmitted this way.

Direct contact

Direct contact is when people pass infections through very close contact. This includes sexually transmitted infections. Head lice, scabies and impetigo are all spread this way too.

Indirect contact

Germs spread by indirect contact have been left on an object or surface such as a door handle, which is then touched by someone else.

Case study: Dealing with *MRSA* and *Clostridium Difficile*

MRSA bacteria are resistant to many commonly used antibiotics. Between 2009 and 2016 the number of cases decreased by 61 per cent (Public Health England 2017). However, there have been slight increases in the last few years, so it is important to remain vigilant. Every new patient in hospital is screened for *MRSA* and, if found, the infection is treated with special shampoo, skin wash and nose gel to try to eliminate it. It is mostly harmless, but can prevent wounds from healing and make people seriously ill if it gets deeper into the body.

Clostridium Difficile (C.Diff) most often occurs when people have had several courses of antibiotics in a short space of time. This destroys other gut bacteria and allows *C. Diff* bacteria to multiply rapidly, causing inflammation and diarrhoea. People with chronic illness are more at risk.

- What do you know about *MRSA* and *C. Diff*?
- Carry out some research to find out infection rates in your local area.

Professional working

If anyone being cared for in your setting is infected with a superbug you need to ensure all staff are reminded about the importance of wearing gloves and aprons, and thorough hand washing. Bed linen and clothing should be washed separately from that of other users of services on a hot wash. They should not share a bedroom if they have a catheter or a wound. Always tell transport and outpatient departments that the individual is MRSA positive if they need to attend outpatients. Useful information for managing MRSA in the community can be found at http://mrsaactionuk

Professional working

It is good practice to be 'bare below the elbow' when at work. This means short sleeves, no wristwatch, and no jewellery except a wedding ring. Short nails without nail varnish or false nails are best to prevent harm.

Lead adult care workers should do everything they can to prevent infections spreading in a care setting. Infections can be extremely serious for frail people. Infection also means other workers have to take sick leave, which can affect levels of staffing in the setting. For example, if an adult care worker has diarrhoea and vomiting, they must stay off work until 48 hours after symptoms have gone.

Your organisational policies, procedures and training sessions will cover ways to reduce the spread of infections. You may become involved in delivering training on infection control once you are sufficiently experienced. If you can think of a way that a procedure could be improved to further reduce the spread of infection, make suggestions to the manager.

Importance of training

You and your colleagues should regularly update training on infection control. The Care Quality Commission carries out inspections on adult care settings and will assess whether the infection prevention procedures are adequate. There is no specific frequency of training required under the Health and Social Care Act 2008, because different settings have different needs depending on their users. The code of practice on the prevention and control of infections, and related guidance published by the Department of Health are useful reference guides.

Your organisation will have an infection prevention policy, which will state the frequency of training and updating.

General good hygiene practice

Everyone is carrying millions of organisms all of the time and the human body is designed to cope with this. However, good hygiene should always be practised when working with vulnerable people. You should be a good role model for staff and be observant for any staff who are not demonstrating high levels of hygiene. Adult care workers should always practise good hygiene and make sure to wash uniforms after every shift at a minimum of 60°C. It is a good idea to display hand washing guidelines above all sinks, as this reminds staff and shows visitors and users of the service how to wash hands thoroughly.

Your role in infection control

As a lead adult care worker you should be confident in your knowledge of the policies and procedures in your workplace that are relevant to preventing the spread of infection. You might have to demonstrate procedures to other staff. This might include:

- hand washing
- use of personal protective equipment
- dealing with spillages of body fluids using a spillage kit
- managing users of service with contagious infections
- correct disposal of contaminated single-use items
- decontamination of items that are to be re-used, using alcohol wipes
- effective cleaning routines for the setting.

Dealing with unsafe practice in infection control

If you witness any unsafe practice you would be expected to intervene, as it is crucial to prevent spread of infection from users of service to staff, as well as between service users.

Always be supportive and emphasise the importance of good practice. For example, you might witness a care worker not washing their hands thoroughly, or touching door handles with dirty gloves on. Speak to the person quietly and out of earshot of others, so they do not feel embarrassed. Demonstrate the correct procedures, and explain what you are doing at each stage and how this prevents infection spread. Using this method you are likely to get a positive response from the person, as they can see that you are only correcting them to avoid harm. As long as their practice improves, there is no need to take the matter any further.

Professional working

It is important to be diplomatic when dealing with staff who are not working safely. If they feel they are being 'told off' they will not respond as positively as if you explain in a supportive way how they need to improve.

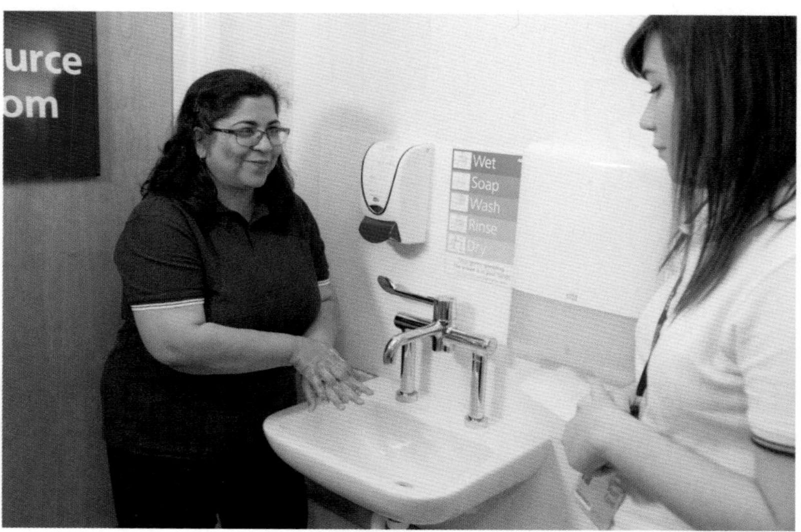

It can be important to demonstrate correct procedures

Case study: Hina

Hina lives in a small residential home for young adults with physical disabilities. She has cerebral palsy, but is able to mobilise using crutches. Hina is normally fairly independent, doing her own cooking, cleaning and laundry. In fact she often cooks for all four residents. When you visit, you find that Hina is unwell. She is lying on her bed, has a high temperature and feels sick. She says she has had diarrhoea in the downstairs toilet.

- Describe the causes and spread of diarrhoea and vomiting.
- Explain what you would do to prevent the spread of this infection to the other residents.

If you are not sure, research the way this type of infection spreads and consider the risk areas for contamination.

Qualification mapping

Unit 8 LO4 AC 4.1 and 4.2

Summary

Infection control policies and procedures are intended to prevent infections. Consequences of infections can be anything from unpleasant symptoms and staff shortages to serious illness or death. Caring for people with infections can also be unpleasant, so containing infectious outbreaks is important for everyone.

Demonstrate the management of the reduction of infection

Qualification mapping

Unit 8 LO 4 AC 4.3 and 4.4

Throughout your working day you should practise good hygiene and be a good role model to your colleagues. Good practice can be infectious!

The most important factor in infection control is **hand washing.** The World Health Organization recommends the 11-step method of hand washing, as shown in Figure 4.

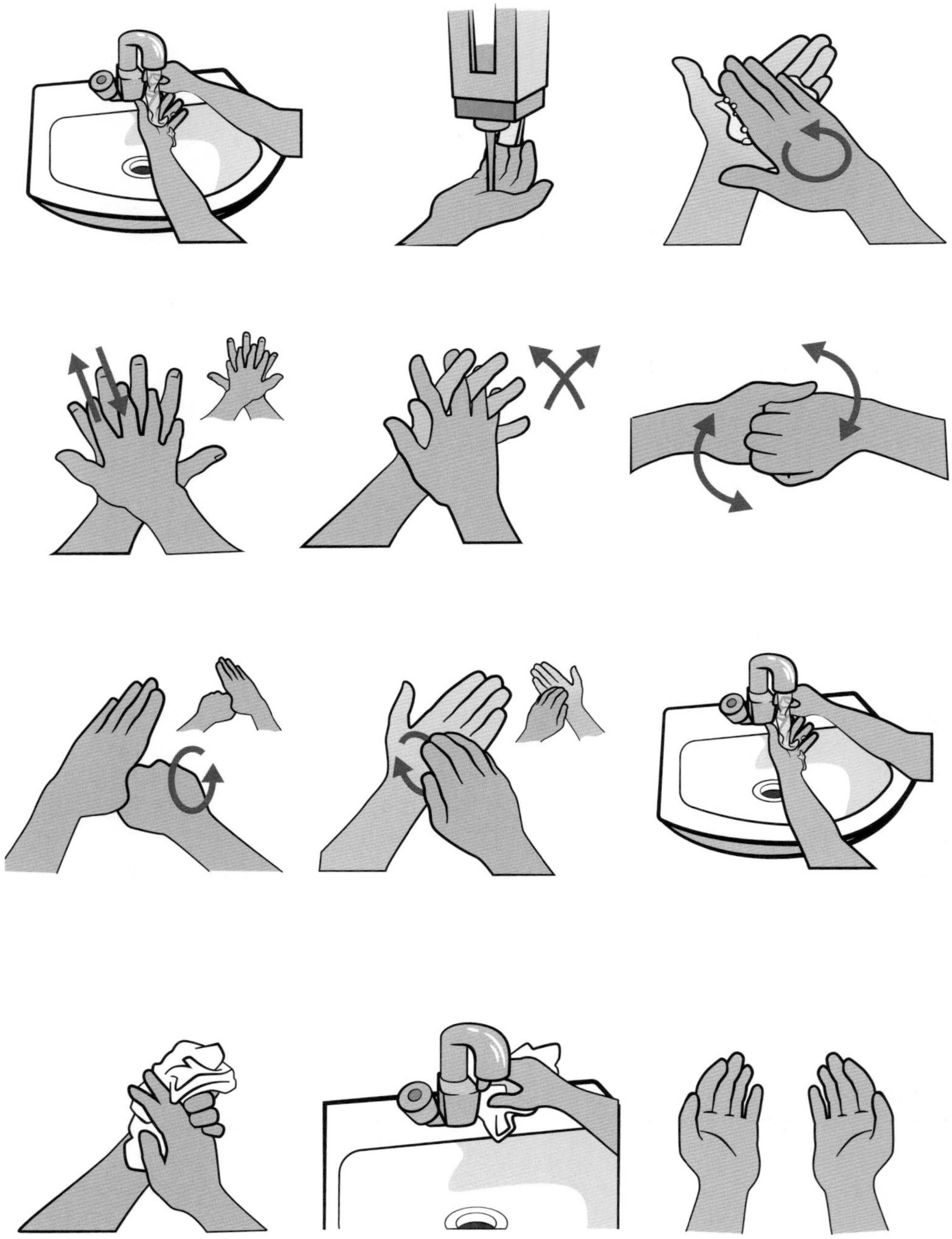

Figure 4: Step-by-step hand-washing guide

Hands should be washed at the following critical times:

- at the beginning of your shift
- between personal care interventions with users of service
- before serving food
- after using the toilet
- after using a tissue if coughing or sneezing
- after cleaning up blood or bodily fluids
- after removing gloves.

Hand gel should also be used regularly to further reduce the chance of spreading germs. If hands look dirty, they should always be washed. Hand gel will not remove visible dirt. Monitor staff to ensure they always maintain high standards to reduce the risk of spreading infection.

Many organisations carry out audits on procedures, such as hand-washing technique, where a senior member of staff will observe staff and record whether or not they are working safely. Anyone who is not doing this should be given immediate training and reassessment. This may be something you become responsible for. If so, it should be done in a supportive way, as this will mean that staff do not worry about audits, instead regarding them as a positive way of maintaining high standards.

Correct use of personal protective equipment (PPE)

Personal protective equipment (PPE) is the general term for the gloves, aprons and masks used to protect you from spreading infection, in addition to thorough hand washing.

Staff should always wear gloves and aprons for personal care, such as washing or taking someone to the toilet, and when dealing with soiled laundry.

Your service will have policies on when to use PPE. For example, some services do not require staff to use PPE for assisting with meals, or assisting with moving and handling, as long as hands are washed afterwards.

Remove PPE in the correct order: gloves, then apron, then mask, if worn.

- Non sterile gloves should be removed before touching surfaces such as door handles. To remove gloves pull the first one off by the outside and screw up into a ball. Then pull the second one off by hooking your finger inside the glove and turning it inside out with the first glove inside. Discard in the correct bin.
- Remove your apron by touching the side of the apron towards your body, break the ties around your back and screw the apron into a ball. Discard in the correct bin.
- If you are wearing a mask, this should be removed last. Untie the ties and pull it away from your face without touching the front. Discard in the correct bin.

Wash your hands thoroughly using the 11-step procedure shown in Figure 4.

Qualification mapping

Unit 8 LO 4 AC 4.3 and 4.4

Professional working

It is important to explain to a user of service why they need to stay in their room, and why everyone is wearing protective equipment.

Professional working

Examples of signs of infection include: a temperature over 37°C, confusion, feeling unwell.

Urinary tract infection: passing urine frequently, passing offensive or cloudy urine, or pain on passing urine.

Chest infection: increased breathing rate, coughing up sputum, breathlessness.

Skin infection: redness, heat, swelling, pus.

Activity

Witness testimony

When a new member of staff starts at your workplace, ask if you could be observed demonstrating to them the correct method of hand washing and use of PPE.

Ask the person observing you to write a witness testimony for your portfolio.

Dealing with infections

If a user of services has an infection, with symptoms such as diarrhoea or vomiting, you should ensure there are clear instructions on their door about precautions that are needed to stop the infection spreading. All staff and visitors must follow the instructions carefully. Masks are only needed for infections spread through the air and can be quite off-putting for the user of the service, so only use if necessary. Make sure the room is adequately ventilated without being too cold or draughty.

Precautions

Precautions to prevent the spread of infection depend on the way the infection spreads, so there will be different precautions for dealing with a person with diarrhoea, vomiting, a wound infection, a urinary tract infection or a respiratory infection. It is therefore important that you understand how different organisms spread in order to put in place the correct precautions to reduce the risk to staff and other users of your service.

Activity

Infection prevention and control

Many local authorities or community health services have an infection control advice team. Have a look on the Internet to see if you can find your local team and the service they provide. The NHS also provides advice and information on infection control, including resources you could use with staff.

https://www.infectionpreventioncontrol.co.uk and navigate to the section in resources on preventing infection – workbook guidance for care homes.

Familiarise yourself with these in case you have a user of your service with an infection that you are unsure how to manage.

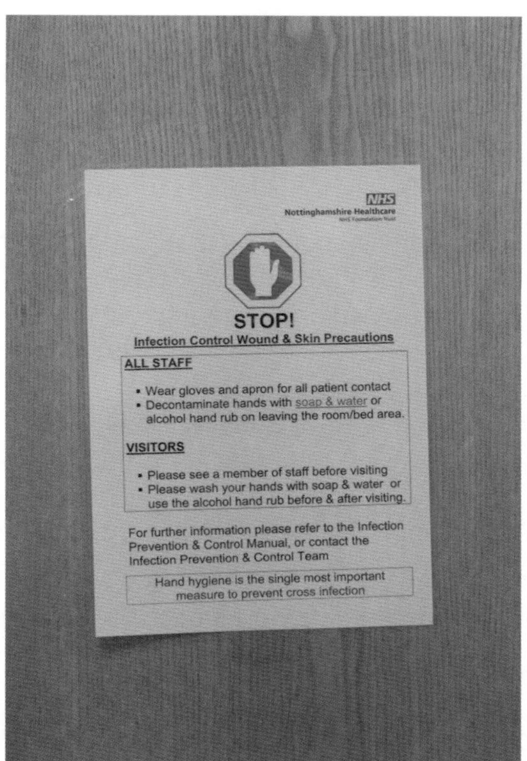

Instructions are displayed on the door if someone is isolated, to maintain infection control

Ensuring you do not pose a risk to others

If you have an infection yourself, it is important that you do not risk passing that infection to colleagues and users of your service. If you are feeling too unwell to work, that is an easy decision – just telephone to say you are on sick leave.

However, sometimes you feel well enough to work, and most care workers do not like to let down the team. If you are working with young people with mental ill health, it will be different from working with very frail elderly people.

It is always best to ring and discuss your situation with the manager, so they can arrange cover in good time, rather than arriving for work and being sent home. Here are some guidelines to help you. Your workplace will have guidelines too.

- If you have diarrhoea and sickness you should not return to work until you have been symptom-free for 48 hours.
- If you have a cold, you should avoid contact with vulnerable people, such as frail elderly people, young babies, or people with low immunity. Cover your mouth and nose with disposable tissues when coughing or sneezing. Discard them immediately and wash your hands.
- You should not go to work with a highly infectious illness, such as flu or chicken pox.
- If you have a cut, you should cover it with a blue waterproof plaster to avoid transmitting infection into or out of the cut.
- If you have a condition such as hepatitis or HIV, you will need to get guidance from occupational health about whether you can work in particular settings, and what precautions to take to ensure the infection is not transmitted to others.

Qualification mapping

Unit 8 LO 4 AC 4.5

Professional working

A good understanding of the way infection spreads will enable you to put into place effective measures to prevent cross infection. An infection that is mild in adults and young people can be very serious, or even life threatening, in people who are elderly, frail, or who have a long-term illness, so good infection control is essential when working in adult care.

Using risk assessments to support individuals to move safely

Qualification mapping

Unit 8 LO 5 AC 5.1

Every individual in a care setting should be assessed to identify the safest way for them to move as independently as possible. The person who carries out the risk assessment should be trained and competent to do so.

Legislation

The laws relevant to moving and handling are:

- Health and Safety at Work Act 1974
- Manual Handling Operations Regulations 1992
- Management of Health and Safety at Work Regulations 1999.

Health and Safety at Work Act 1974

Under this law, employers must provide training, information and equipment, and employees are obliged by law to attend and follow the training when at work and to use the equipment provided for their safety.

It is therefore a legal requirement that all staff should receive manual handling training when they start a job and be assessed as competent. Equipment must be provided to enable staff to avoid having to manually lift users of service who are unable to move themselves. Staff must use the equipment provided.

Manual Handling Operations Regulations 1992

The Manual Handling Operations Regulations state that staff should:

- avoid hazardous manual handling operations so far as is reasonably practicable
- assess any hazardous manual handling operations that cannot be avoided
- reduce the risk of injury so far as is reasonably practicable.

(Source: Health and Safety Executive, 2018)

This means that staff should always encourage users of service to move themselves if they can, and use equipment to move people if they are unable to move independently.

Management of Health and Safety at Work Regulations 1999

This law requires managers to undertake risk assessments for any hazardous tasks. Moving and handling risk assessments may be generic, meaning that they are relevant to day-to-day working, or they may be completed for one specific individual.

Moving and handling risk assessments

You may come across users of service with a range of levels of mobility during your career in adult care. You may have users of service who can walk independently, but have cognitive impairments such as dementia, meaning they are not safe to leave the building unaccompanied. At the other end of the spectrum, you might care for a person who is unable even to turn over in bed and relies entirely on care staff to move them many times during the day.

It is very important that users of service are encouraged to maintain their mobility as much as possible. Although there are risks associated with moving independently there are also risks associated with immobility.

Immobility can lead to:

- loss of muscle strength – increasing the risk of falls
- loss of bone strength – increasing the risk of fractures
- urinary tract infections caused by reluctance to drink, due to not wanting to have to keep asking for the toilet
- breaks in the skin or even pressure ulcers from poor blood supply as a result of staying too long in one position
- constipation
- cognitive decline or low mood due to lack of stimulation and boredom.

A risk assessment is not intended to prevent users of service moving independently, but to identify the safest way for them to do so. Risk assessments should be carried out by a person who is competent. You may be offered an opportunity to do extra training to give you the skills to be able to do this task.

Each user of service should be assessed as an individual to determine how mobile they need to be to be able to enjoy a fulfilling life.

Look back at the section on risk assessment on page 160.

The hazards related to moving and handling can put staff or users of the service at risk. The risk assessment should be person-centred, but staff safety should not be compromised. There is always a risk that a person will still fall, but this usually outweighs the risks caused by preventing users of service being able to move around.

Assessing hazards

To produce the risk assessment, the health care professional will consider what hazards exist:

- Is the person unsteady?
- Would they be able to get up again if they fell?
- Would they be able to summon help if they fell?
- Is the person unable to move at all independently?
- Is the person able to stand?
- Do they suffer from dizziness?
- Do they have visual, hearing or cognitive impairment?
- Are there trip hazards in the environment?

Qualification mapping 

Unit 8 LO 2 AC 2.3 and 2.4

Professional working 

Any person who spends much of the day sitting or lying in bed should have their risk of developing pressure damage reviewed at least weekly, and more often if damage is observed. The Braden Scale is one assessment tool that can be used for this purpose. See: www.bradenscale.com

Professional working

The Health and Safety Executive provide clear guidance on risk assessment in health and social care settings. Visit http://www.hse.gov.uk/healthservices/moving-handling-do.htm

Identifying risks

Risks might include:

- injuries such as fractures, lacerations or head injuries if a fall occurred
- having to wait a long time for help, increasing the risk of pressure ulcers or pneumonia developing
- staff muscular injuries, if the person stumbles or collapses during a manoeuvre.

Reducing the risk

The following are measures that reduce the risk of the potential injuries identified:

- Select appropriate equipment to allow the person to mobilise independently, such as walking sticks, wheeled zimmer frames and wheelchairs.
- Make sure that chairs are the right height to enable people to get from sitting to standing. Install a raised toilet seat if needed.
- Install grab rails in bathrooms and handrails in hallways. This can also be arranged in the community.
- Make sure that footwear fits well and is supportive, with non-slip soles.
- Remove any trip hazards, especially if working in the community. Rugs, clutter and waste bins can easily be tripped over, especially if a person's eyesight is poor.
- Request a medication review by the pharmacist or doctor to ensure the medications are not causing dizziness or low blood pressure.
- Check the person has the correct glasses on and they have had a recent eye test.
- Staff must have training before assisting with moving and handling.
- Make sure the user of service has heard and understood any instructions.
- Select the right equipment for staff to use to transfer the person, or move up the bed, such as a hoist, rotunda, standing hoist or slide sheet.
- People with cognitive impairment may need to be accompanied but allow them freedom to decide where they want to go as far as possible.

Qualification mapping

Unit 8 LO 5 AC 5.2

Principles for safe moving and handling

The key principles for safe moving or handling of people or objects is firstly to avoid manual handling if possible and secondly to take measures to reduce the risk of injury if manual handling cannot be avoided.

Avoiding manual handling

You should always encourage individuals to move themselves without any physical effort if possible, using equipment if necessary.

Teach people how to get from sitting to standing. They should push up with their arms on the arms of the chair, or the mattress of the bed. They should never pull up on a walking frame or trolley, as these are unstable. A rotunda can be used for pulling up, as they are designed to be used this way.

Ensuring a user of services is sitting in a chair of the correct seat height can also help them to stand up unaided. When seated, the hips and knees should be at right angles, with the feet flat on the floor.

Reducing risk

Where it is impossible to achieve independence, it is important to choose equipment that can make moving and handling safe for users of the service and their care workers.

Aids and equipment

If someone is not able to move themselves there are different aids you can use, such as a standing hoist and a slide sheet. A slide sheet is made of slippery material and is a simple way of assisting a person to move up the bed. Sometimes the person can move themselves once the sheet is in place.

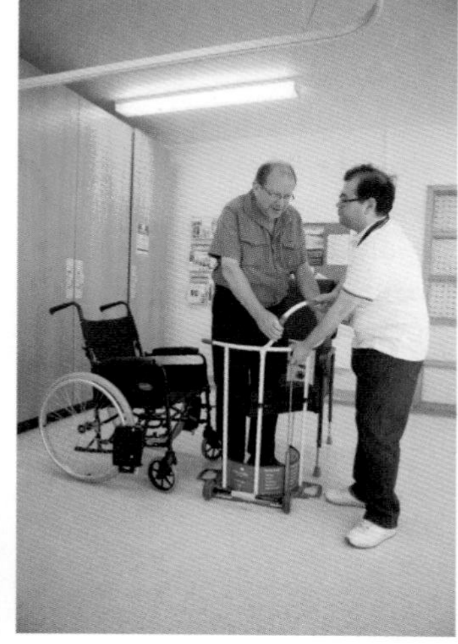

A user of services can pull themselves from sitting to standing using a rotunda without any physical effort by the adult care worker

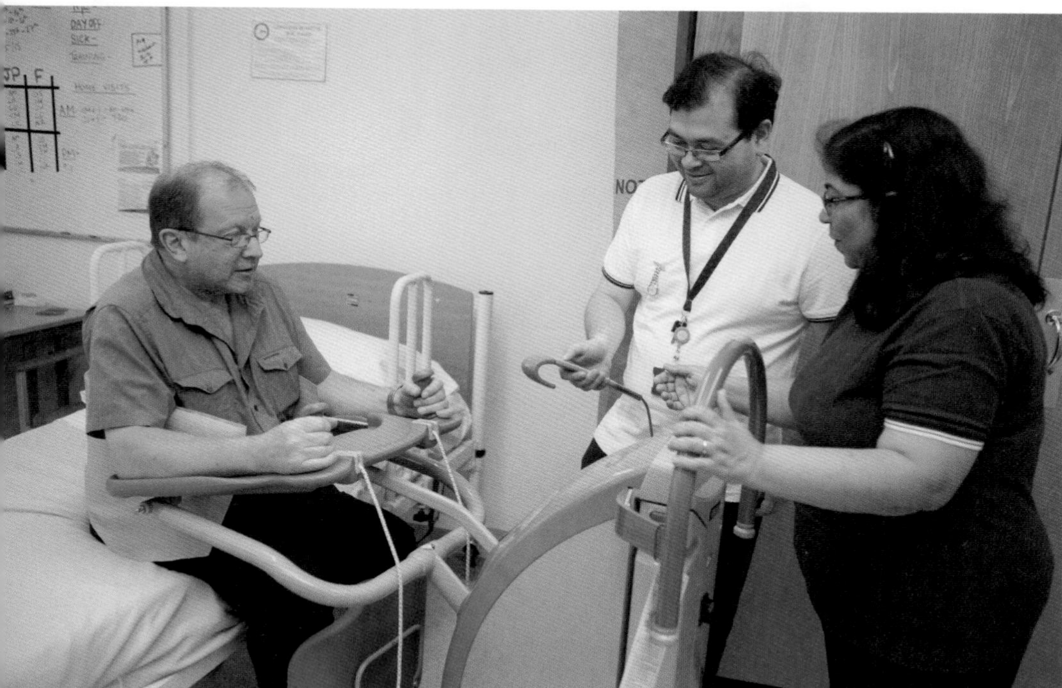

A standing hoist provides support and security but still allows weight to be put on the legs

Professional working

One of the biggest risks for frail people is falling over. If you can prevent slips, trips and falls, you can prevent serious injuries that could be fatal. Always be alert for hazards that could lead to falls.

Ensure your users of service have well-fitting shoes and use their walking aids correctly.

Be tidy, mop up spillages and remove any trip hazards. Encourage people who live at home to do the same.

If anyone complains of dizziness, have this checked out by a nurse or doctor.

Professional working

You should not expect staff to attempt to move anyone until they have attended a moving and handling training course.

Professional working

A hoist should only be used if a user of services is unable to be safely moved by any other means. Most people find a hoist uncomfortable. It is also quite undignified to be moved in this way, so it should be a last resort. If a hoist is used, it is essential to use the correct size of sling, as there have been incidents where people have fallen out of a hoist because the sling is too big.

Qualification mapping

Unit 8 LO 5 AC 5.1, 5.2 and 5.3

Professional working

Never feel under pressure to ignore policies and procedures. Always support staff to follow risk assessments.

All members of staff must be competent to use any equipment that is chosen before they are expected to use it to move a user of service. Training should be provided if a new piece of equipment is brought into the setting.

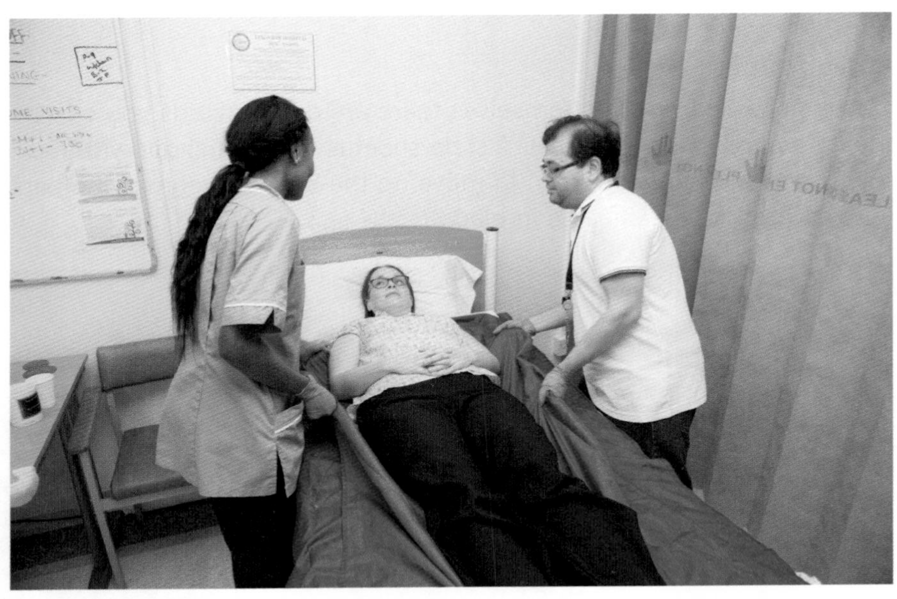

A slide sheet helps to reposition someone in bed

When carrying out any moving or handling manoeuvre, observe the following points:

- keep your feet stable; the foot furthest from the load should be in front
- have a firm hold
- keep any weight close to your body
- keep your back straight and bend your knees
- point your feet in the direction you are moving towards
- lift as smoothly as possible.

The same principles apply when moving objects. Try to avoid lifting things from the floor, but, if you do, keep your back straight and bend your knees. Your thigh muscles should do the work. Avoid twisting during lifting. Always ask for help if the object is heavy and use equipment, such as a wheelchair, whenever practical for transporting heavy loads.

Activity

Safe moving and handling

- Identify which laws and regulations are relevant to moving and handling people and objects in an adult care setting, and explain the main points.
- Select a user of your service who requires assistance to move. Explain to your supervisor or assessor the principles you use when assisting them to move. Alternatively, you could create a written account for your portfolio.
- Demonstrate your ability to move and handle equipment and other objects safely to your assessor or a suitably experienced and competent colleague. You would need to ask a colleague to provide a witness testimony.

Promoting healthy eating and wellbeing

It is very important that users of services are well-nourished and hydrated. This will help them to maintain good health, prevent ill health and aid with recovery from ill health and injury.

Qualification mapping 

Unit 43 LO 1 AC 1.1 and 1.2

You and your users of service need to eat a range of foods for a balanced diet. The bulk of it should be made up of vegetables, fruits and wholegrain cereals, as shown in Figure 5.

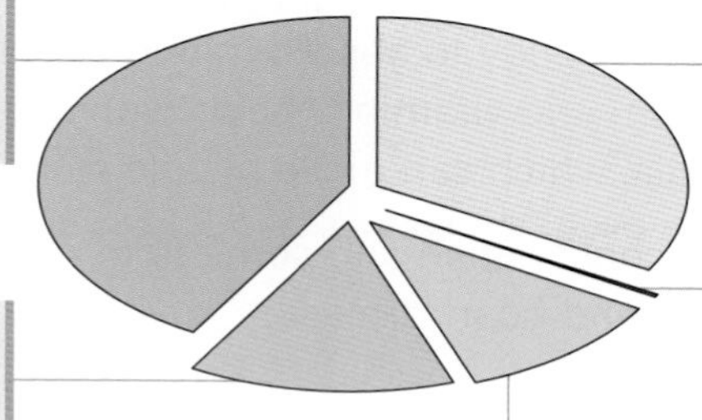

Fruit and vegetables provide vitamins, minerals and fibre

Carbohydrates provide energy, and wholemeal carbohydrates provide fibre and vitamins

Meat, fish, eggs and pulses provide protein

High sugar, high fat foods are not needed for a healthy diet

Milk, cheese and yoghurt provide protein, calcium and vitamin D

Figure 5: The balance of foods needed for good health

Qualification mapping 

Unit 43 LO 2 AC 2.1

The NHS promotes eight tips for healthy eating, as shown in Figure 6.

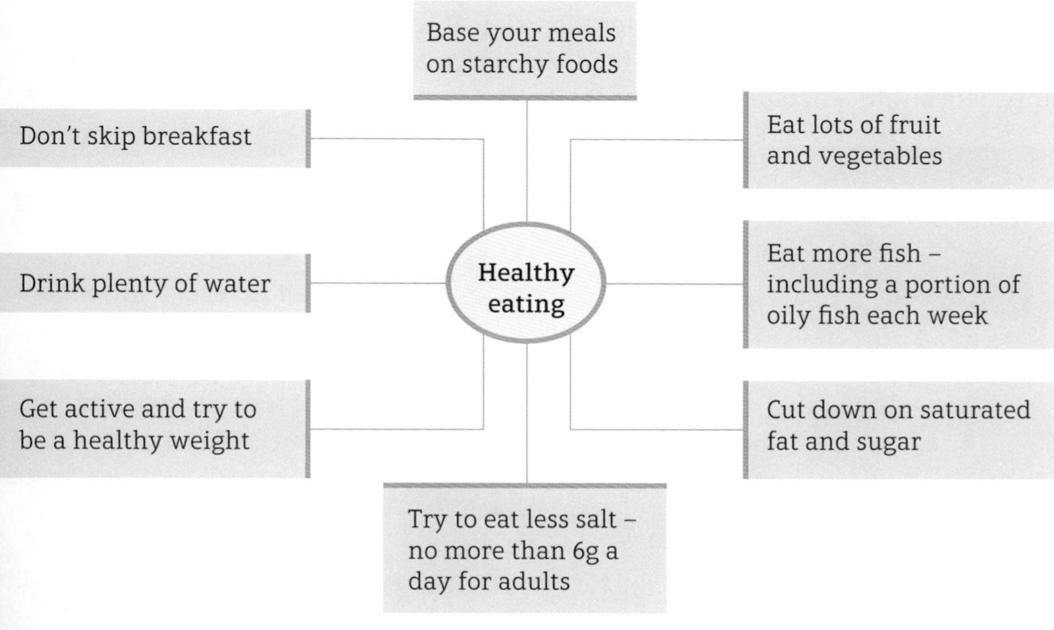

Figure 6: Top tips for healthy eating

Healthy eating and nutrition

It is important to identify any user of services who is not eating sufficient calories. You should encourage staff to always report if individuals are regularly leaving or refusing meals. This can lead to weight loss and muscle weakness, increasing the risk of falls. Weighing users of your service on a regular basis may also identify if someone is not eating enough. However, you need to be aware of people with heart failure, who may gain weight through fluid retention, so do not rely on weight loss alone to highlight an inadequate diet.

A healthy diet should contain calcium and vitamin D, which are important for bone strength, helping to prevent fractures. Protein is needed for healing and renewing cells. Muscles are made of protein, so a good protein intake is again an important factor in keeping people mobile and reducing the risk of falls.

Vitamins are important for many reasons, including maintaining good eyesight, healthy skin, good healing, fighting infections and a healthy nervous system. Some vitamins are needed to help the body to absorb minerals. For example, vitamin D helps the body absorb calcium and vitamin C helps with iron absorption. Iron is important to prevent anaemia, which can make people feel dizzy and weak.

Fibre is essential to prevent constipation and some fibre can lower cholesterol, which reduces the chance of stroke and heart disease.

Qualification mapping

Unit 43 LO 4 AC 4.1 and 4.2

Fluids

It is very important to ensure that individuals drink enough fluids. Insufficient fluid intake can increase the risk of urinary tract infections, constipation, kidney damage, confusion and low blood pressure – another cause of falls. Extra fluids are needed in hot weather or if the person has a fever. Signs of dehydration include low blood pressure, dark urine, low urine output, dry mouth and constipation.

Encourage fluid intake by offering varied drinks, making sure a drink is always in reach and prompting people to have a drink. Some individuals are reluctant to drink as they do not like to keep asking for the toilet. Always reassure users of the service that no one minds taking them to the toilet, and make sure staff never show signs of impatience with a person asking for the toilet.

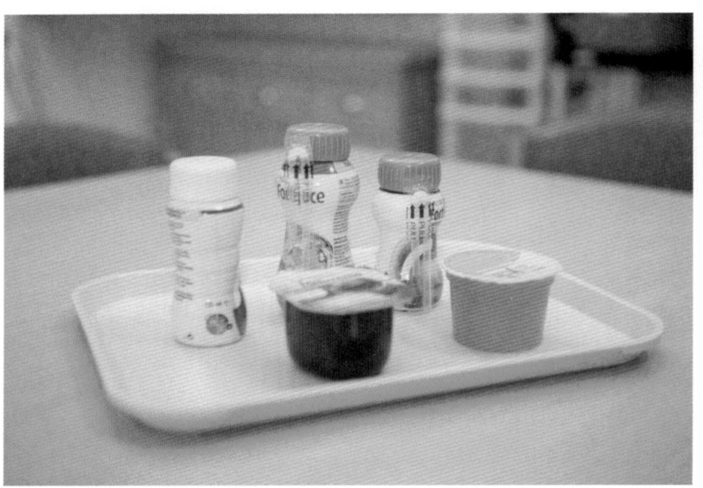

Food supplements can help with nourishment for a vulnerable individual

If you are told that an individual is not eating or drinking enough, but they look otherwise well, ask staff to record what the person eats and drinks over a two-day period to get a good idea of their total intake. Always ask for a medical review if you are concerned. A dietician can prescribe food supplements if necessary.

Malnourishment

Studies, such as Hungry to Be Heard (Age Concern, 2006) highlighted the fact that, in the past, some older people became more malnourished while they were in hospital than they were before admission. This was followed up in 2011 (Still Hungry to be Heard, Age UK, 2011) and many hospitals and care homes now have protected mealtimes, where all staff stop doing other jobs and concentrate on making sure everyone gets their meals.

There are several reasons why some individuals do not eat properly. These can include:

- difficulty managing cutlery, making it hard to cut up food
- mental illness, such as depression
- drug addiction or alcoholism
- poorly fitting dentures, or dentures not put in
- chewing and swallowing difficulties
- poor vision
- dementia
- poor appetite or feeling sick
- pain or chronic illness
- difficulty getting to the shops or being unable to afford nutritious food.

If you understand the reason for poor intake of diet or fluids, measures can be put in place to deal with the issue. Adapted cutlery, medication to reduce nausea and arranging for the meals service are all examples of strategies to improve food intake.

Qualification mapping 

Unit 43 LO 5 AC 5.1 and 5.2

Adapted cutlery and crockery can help if individuals are not eating properly

Professional working

If a user of service keeps coughing when eating and drinking, they should be assessed by a speech and language therapist. Frequent choking can cause pneumonia. Thickened drinks and a soft or pureed diet can reduce choking episodes.

Support at mealtimes

Always make sure people are offered a choice of meals so they can choose foods that they like. Make sure the food is served at the right temperature, and that individuals use adapted cutlery and crockery if needed. You should always provide a drink and put it within reach if the person is unable to move independently. If a person has poor vision, ensure they know their meal has arrived and the position of both the plate and their drink.

Some people need a care worker to sit with them throughout their meal to ensure that they eat sufficient food, and that they are offered a supplement if they have not eaten sufficiently.

Those requiring full supervision would include:

- individuals who are unable to physically move the food from the plate to their mouth, such as a person who is paralysed or who has a severe physical impairment, like multiple sclerosis
- individuals who have a cognitive impairment, such as dementia, who do not recognise hunger or the fact that the meal is in front of them.

If a person has swallowing difficulties they should *never* be left alone to eat and drink. They may need their drinks thickened to prevent choking. You will need special training before you can assist a person with swallowing difficulties to eat and drink.

If you are interested in learning more about nutrition and hydration you might like to choose Unit 43 as an option unit for your Level 3 Diploma in Adult Care: Promoting Nutrition and Hydration in Care Settings.

Monitoring nutritional needs

It is good practice to monitor the weight of users of service to check they are receiving adequate nutrition. If you weigh people on admission, you have a baseline to work with. If you then weigh individuals at least once a month, you will know if they are losing or gaining weight. If a user of services is gaining weight they may be eating portions that are too big; however, if they have heart problems they may gain weight because they are retaining fluid. The doctor may want them to be weighed more often to check for this. You might also notice signs such as swollen legs and breathlessness.

Weight is always recorded in kilograms, but many people think of their weight in stones and pounds. A conversion table can be used to convert weight so that users of service will understand whether they are gaining or losing weight.

You may also monitor an individual's body mass index (BMI), and for this you need to know the person's height in metres. There is a tool that is used in health and care settings that estimates a person's height by measuring the length of the bone in the forearm, which is called the ulnar length.

Activity

Promoting healthy eating

You are working in the community with young adults with learning disabilities. You notice that one of the users of service appears to only eat crisps, chocolate and cake.

- Which nutrients are they getting too much of and which too little in their diet?
- Think of three reasons why they might be eating this diet.

Choose one of the reasons you have identified and come up with a plan to improve this person's diet. You should also think about your communication strategy when making your plan.

Estimating height from ulna length

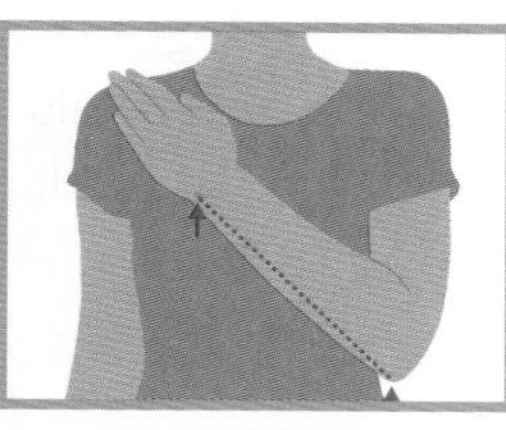

Measure between the point of the elbow (olecranon process) and the midpoint of the prominent bone of the wrist (styloid process) (left side if possible).

Height (m)	men (<65 years)	1.94	1.93	1.91	1.89	1.87	1.85	1.84	1.82	1.80	1.78	1.76	1.75	1.73	1.71
	men (≥65 years)	1.87	1.86	1.84	1.82	1.81	1.79	1.78	1.76	1.75	1.73	1.71	1.70	1.68	1.67
	Ulna length (cm)	32.0	31.5	31.0	30.5	30.0	29.5	29.0	28.5	28.0	27.5	27.0	26.5	26.0	25.5
Height (m)	Women (<65 years)	1.84	1.83	1.81	1.80	1.79	1.77	1.76	1.75	1.73	1.72	1.70	1.69	1.68	1.66
	Women (≥65 years)	1.84	1.83	1.81	1.79	1.78	1.76	1.75	1.73	1.71	1.70	1.68	1.66	1.65	1.63
Height (m)	men (<65 years)	1.69	1.67	1.66	1.64	1.62	1.60	1.58	1.57	1.55	1.53	1.51	1.49	1.48	1.46
	men (≥65 years)	1.65	1.63	1.62	1.60	1.59	1.57	1.56	1.54	1.52	1.51	1.49	1.48	1.46	1.45
	Ulna length (cm)	25.0	24.5	24.0	23.5	23.0	22.5	22.0	21.5	21.0	20.5	20.0	19.5	19.0	18.5
Height (m)	Women (<65 years)	1.65	1.63	1.62	1.61	1.59	1.58	1.56	1.55	1.54	1.52	1.51	1.50	1.48	1.47
	Women (≥65 years)	1.61	1.60	1.58	1.56	1.55	1.53	1.52	1.50	1.48	1.47	1.45	1.44	1.42	1.40

Figure 7: You can estimate an individual's height from their arm length

The BMI can be found by finding the square on a BMI chart (as shown in Figure 8) where the height and weight meet.

Weight	**Ibs**	90	100	110	120	130	140	150	160	170	180	190	200	210	220	230	240	250	260	270	280	290
	kgs	41	45	50	54	59	64	68	73	77	82	86	91	95	100	104	109	113	118	122	127	132
Height																						
ft/in	**cm**																					
4'8"	142.2	20	22	25	27	29	31	34	36	38	40	43	45	47	49	52	54	56	58	61	63	65
4'9"	144.7	19	22	24	26	28	30	32	35	37	39	41	43	45	48	50	52	54	56	58	61	63
4'10"	147.3	19	21	23	25	27	29	31	33	36	38	40	42	44	46	48	50	52	54	56	59	61
4'11"	149.8	18	20	22	24	26	28	30	32	34	36	38	40	42	44	46	48	51	53	55	57	59
5'0"	152.4	18	20	21	23	25	27	29	31	33	35	37	39	41	43	45	47	49	51	53	55	57
5'1"	154.9	17	19	21	23	25	26	28	30	32	34	36	38	40	42	43	45	47	49	51	53	55
5'2"	157.4	16	18	20	22	24	26	27	29	31	33	35	37	38	40	42	44	46	48	49	51	53
5'3"	160.0	16	18	19	21	23	25	27	28	30	32	34	35	37	39	41	43	44	46	48	50	51
5'4"	162.5	15	17	19	21	22	24	26	27	29	31	33	34	36	38	39	41	43	45	46	48	50
5'5"	165.1	15	17	18	20	22	23	25	27	28	30	32	33	35	37	38	40	42	43	45	47	48
5'6"	167.6	15	16	18	19	21	23	24	26	27	29	31	32	34	36	37	39	40	42	44	45	47
5'7"	170.1	14	16	17	19	20	22	24	25	27	28	30	31	33	34	36	38	39	41	42	44	45
5'8"	172.7	14	15	17	18	20	21	23	24	26	27	29	30	32	33	35	37	38	40	41	43	44
5'9"	175.2	13	15	16	18	19	21	22	24	25	27	28	30	31	33	34	35	37	38	40	41	43
5'10"	177.8	13	14	16	17	19	20	22	23	24	26	27	29	30	32	33	34	36	37	39	40	42
5'11"	180.3	13	14	15	17	18	20	21	22	24	25	27	28	29	31	32	33	35	36	38	39	40
6'0"	182.8	12	14	15	16	18	19	20	22	23	24	26	27	28	30	31	33	34	35	37	38	39
6'1"	185.4	12	13	15	16	17	18	20	21	22	24	25	26	28	29	30	32	33	34	36	37	38
6'2"	187.9	12	13	14	15	17	18	19	21	22	23	24	26	27	28	30	31	32	33	35	36	37
6'3"	190.5	11	13	14	15	16	18	19	20	21	23	24	24	26	28	29	30	31	33	34	35	36
6'4"	193.0	11	12	13	15	16	17	18	19	21	22	23	24	26	27	28	29	30	32	33	34	35
6'5"	195.5	11	12	13	14	15	17	18	19	20	21	23	24	25	26	27	28	30	31	32	33	34
6'6"	198.1	10	12	13	14	15	16	17	18	20	21	22	23	24	25	27	28	29	30	31	32	34
6'7"	200.6	10	11	12	14	15	16	17	18	19	20	21	23	24	25	26	27	28	29	30	32	33
6'8"	203.2	10	11	12	13	14	15	16	18	19	20	21	22	23	24	25	26	27	29	30	31	32
6'9"	205.7	10	11	12	13	14	15	16	17	18	19	20	21	23	24	25	26	27	28	29	30	31
6'10"	208.2	9	10	12	13	14	15	16	17	18	19	20	21	22	23	24	25	26	27	28	29	30
6'11"	210.8	9	10	11	12	13	14	15	16	17	18	19	20	21	22	23	25	26	27	28	29	30

Underweight **Healthy** **Overweight** **Obese** **Extremely Obese**

Figure 8: You need to know an individual's height and weight to calculate their BMI

Key term 

Body mass index (BMI) – a measure of body fat based on your weight in relation to your height, calculated by dividing a person's weight in kilograms by the square of their height in metres.

Activity

Calculating BMI

Find a BMI chart at your workplace and ask for permission to practise using an individual's details.

Find the height in metres using the ulnar length, and the weight in kilograms.

Use the BMI chart to calculate the body mass index, and notice whether the person is under weight, a healthy weight, overweight, or obese.

Professional working 

It is crucial to identify any user of service who is not eating or drinking adequately, and take action to prevent this leading to ill health. Always offer choices and have a few spare healthy alternatives to offer, such as soup, if a meal is refused.

Lead and mentor the promotion of the wellbeing of individuals

As a lead adult care worker you should always lead by example and practise working in a way that promotes the wellbeing of those receiving care in your work setting. This means working to support good health and minimise the risk of harm.

It is not always possible to prevent ill health, but you can improve the chances of maintaining good health and wellbeing for individuals by:

- ensuring access to healthy food choices
- encouraging people to remain mobile
- providing an environment where people can enjoy socialising
- practising good standards of hygiene
- responding promptly to early signs of illness
- ensuring the environment is safe and secure for the users of service
- anticipating potential risks and putting in place measures to prevent hazards causing harm
- having well-trained staff.

Professional working

Remember, individuals with mental capacity are allowed to make unwise choices, just like you are. For example, they may choose to eat chips every day. As long as there is a healthy alternative available, that is their choice.

Person-centred care

It is very important that all staff within a setting have a positive attitude to creating an environment in which the users of service are put at the centre of the organisation.

Encouraging users of the service to maintain control over as many aspects of their lives as possible will improve their experience of receiving care. This also means that they will be more satisfied with the care they are receiving, and this in turn makes staff satisfaction better (The Health Foundation, 2018).

Always support staff to encourage users of your service to do as much for themselves as they can, even if it takes longer to complete tasks. Keeping mobile is also very important for wellbeing. People who do not walk quickly lose muscle strength, and are at greater risk of falls, constipation, chest infections and depression (Arora, 2017 www.england.nhs.uk/blog/amit-arora)

Those who are not mobile must have their position changed regularly to prevent pressure ulcers. Remind colleagues to use pressure-relieving cushions when individuals sit for long periods during the day. Examine pressure areas daily to quickly identify any signs of pressure damage.

According to Age UK, loneliness can be as harmful as smoking 15 cigarettes per day (see www.ageuk.org – navigate to sections on information and advice, then health, wellbeing and loneliness). As a team, think about strategies to combat loneliness.

- Consider the seating layout: is it easy for individuals to chat socially during the day?
- Sit people near others who have similar interests.
- Can they eat meals around a table?
- A **reminiscence** box can be a good way to get people chatting to each other. Photographs or objects can be used to remind people of their early lives.

Key term 

Reminiscence – activities to encourage older people to think about something familiar from their past

Health and hygiene

As a lead adult care worker you can promote wellbeing by encouraging staff to maintain high standards of hygiene through the correct use of PPE and hand washing. Lead by example and demonstrate correct techniques if anyone is unsure, or not using the correct technique.

Set up precautions if any user of service develops diarrhoea or vomiting. Keep them separated from other users of service to prevent germs from spreading. Your good hygiene should also protect you from becoming infected.

If a colleague alerts you to any changes in the condition of a user of services, tell a senior member of staff. Carry out their observations to see if there are any signs that they are becoming unwell, so that treatment can start early.

Safety and security

Make sure all staff work tidily, keep all doors and corridors clear to prevent trips and falls, and ensure the escape routes are not blocked in case of a fire.

Qualification mapping 

Unit 8 LO 8 AC 8.1, 8.2 and 8.3

Any user of the service who smokes should have a risk assessment to make sure they are not putting themselves or others at risk. Remember that in a residential care setting smoking is allowed, but it is important that it is managed safely.

It is important to ensure the setting is secure. There should only be one way in and out of the premises and this should be kept locked, but be quick to open by staff in case of an emergency. Ensure all staff are following security procedures, such as asking all visitors to sign in and out, and checking the ID of visiting professionals and contractors. Have a system so staff can easily check the visitor is expected. Confidential information must be securely stored and password protected if electronic.

Remember to review any risk assessments for tasks you are doing, to minimise the risk of harm to you and your colleagues as well as your users of services. Always discuss with your line manager any concerns or suggestions you have about further reducing risk.

Take any opportunities offered to attend training sessions. You may be offered the opportunity to become a lead practitioner in a particular area, such as dementia care. This will enable you to develop an in-depth knowledge and to be able to advise colleagues about best practice.

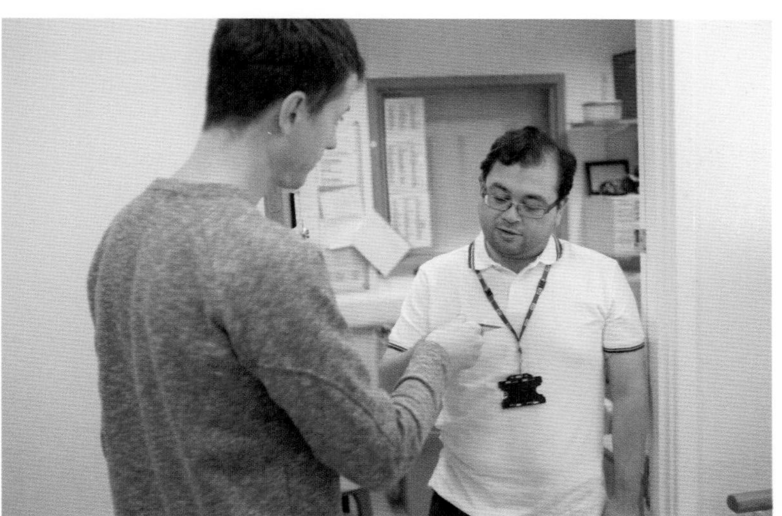

Check ID for all visitors – personal, professional and contractors

Situational judgement questions

1. You notice that some of the newer staff are not using the hoist safely. What is your responsibility as a lead adult care worker?
   a. Stop them, demonstrate the correct method and observe them to check they have understood
   b. Report them to the manager
   c. Ignore them; they must have been taught how to use it so it's their responsiblity
   d. Shout at them and tell them to use the hoist properly
2. You are caring for a 43-year-old woman with multiple sclerosis who is unable to move independently from bed to chair. She tells you she hates being hoisted. She finds it frightening and undignified. What do you do?
   a. Respect her wishes and ask her to hold her hands behind your neck so you can move her without the hoist
   b. Tell her she will have to stay in bed
   c. Tell her she will have to be hoisted due to the manual handling regulations
   d. Explain to her the reasons why you are not able to move her manually and reassure her that she will be moved safely and in privacy
3. An adult care worker reports that a user of services in a mental health day service has collapsed in the lounge. What do you do as lead adult care worker?
   a. Go to the lounge, provide first aid, check for airway, breathing and circulation, send for an ambulance if needed, stay and observe until ambulance arrives, hand over to paramedics and complete an accident report
   b. Go to the lounge, check for safety, check for airway, breathing and circulation, send for an ambulance if needed, provide first aid, stay and observe until ambulance arrives, hand over to paramedics and complete an accident report
   c. Go to the lounge, check for safety, check for airway, breathing and circulation, send for an ambulance if needed, stay and observe until ambulance arrives, hand over to paramedics
   d. Go to the lounge, check for safety, check for airway, breathing and circulation, provide first aid, send for an ambulance if needed, stay and observe until ambulance arrives, hand over to paramedics and complete an accident report
4. An elderly user of your service has cut themselves on a wheelchair foot rest. There is blood on the bathroom floor. How do you advise staff to clean this up?
   a. Mop and bucket
   b. Disposable gloves, toilet paper and flush down the toilet
   c. Disposable gloves, plastic apron, spillage kit, infectious waste bin
   d. Disposable gloves, mask, spillage kit, general waste bin
5. A user of community services is a heavy smoker. One of the adult care workers is concerned about the fire risk at the property. As a lead adult care worker, what would you do?
   a. Tell the manager and offer to do a risk assessment with the user of services.
   b. Tell the manager and leave him to deal with it
   c. Use your initiative and go round to tell the user of services that she must not smoke again as it is dangerous
   d. Ring the fire and rescue service and ask for a smoke detector to be installed
6. A user of community services has had a positive screen for MRSA while in hospital. Despite applications of body wash, hair wash and nose gel, he is still positive in his groin area. He is being discharged home. How would you manage this if you were a lead adult care worker at a community care provider?
   a. Tell the staff not to worry – MRSA is not particularly infectious and as long as they are well there is no real risk
   b. Carry out a risk assessment to include personal care and laundry; advise the user of service to use a hot wash, and the care staff to use gloves and aprons for personal care, as they should for all users of service
   c. Inform the hospital that you cannot accept the person into your service as they pose a risk to other users of your service
   d. Tell staff to wear gloves, gowns and a mask when dealing with the user of service, and dispose of these at the local health centre

F

Professional working and professional development

Your profession as a lead adult care worker is well regarded and you have a responsibility to maintain high personal and professional standards. You are trusted to care for and support the most vulnerable members of society, so it is vital that you work in a professional way that respects this position. This section will cover the following areas:

- professional relationships and boundaries
- working with other professionals
- reflective practice
- the value of receiving and giving feedback
- planning personal and professional development
- research around supporting individuals' specific needs
- mentoring and supervision
- recruitment of new staff and induction.

You will also learn about the skills you will need so that you can apply this knowledge in the care setting where you work.

Professional relationships and rules

Qualification mapping

Unit 2 LO 1 AC 1.1, 1.2 and 1.3

What does it mean to be a professional lead adult care worker? Being professional is about working to standards and rules, and consistently behaving in an appropriate manner with those who you support and work with. As a lead adult care worker you will guide others in their role, so always be a positive role model.

The lead adult care worker role

Individuals who access social care services are usually vulnerable, which is why they need support. You will make a positive difference to people's lives when they are faced with challenges such as physical, practical, emotional, social and intellectual difficulties. You will not only give direct care and support yourself, you may have extra responsibilities and autonomy to supervise and mentor junior, less experienced, colleagues to ensure that they work to the expected standards and provide high quality care. You will be accountable for your own work as well as for the work of those who you instruct to carry out tasks.

Your job description

The first step to being professional in your role as a lead adult care worker is having an understanding of the job that you have agreed to do. Your job description will list the responsibilities required of you; for example, expectations of how you support both users of the service and colleagues who you work with. It will also include such details as how many hours and shift patterns you are expected to work and who you report to. You and your employer will both sign the contract, which is a commitment between you both. Job descriptions can be updated from time to time as the needs of the service change; your employer will make you aware of any changes that are made.

Look at the list in Figure 1. It includes some examples that may be on your job description.

Your organisation will have a vision or statement of purpose that outlines what it aims to achieve in order to provide the best possible support for those who use your service (an example is shown in Figure 2). Your role as a lead adult care worker is to work in a way that helps to achieve these aims. You will need to work with colleagues in your workplace as well as external professionals and agencies; you may be the point of contact, liaising with social workers and other multi-health and social care professionals like nutritionists, counsellors and other therapists. It is likely that you will contribute to the assessment and ongoing care, as well as supporting review meetings. You will also guide new and junior colleagues.

Duties

- Provide support and guide others to support the holistic needs of users of the service
- Delegate tasks and supervise the work of junior care workers
- Plan work effectively to ensure the smooth running of a shift
- Support your manager in organising the staff rota
- Contribute to the recruitment of new staff
- Keep up-to-date with changes to policies and procedures
- Support your manager in reviewing and updating current procedures
- Communicate changes and developments to others within the team
- Keep up-to-date records of your continuous professional development

Figure 1: Some of the responsibilities that might be in your job description

You will all work together to achieve your organisation's aims in order to provide the best possible support to meet the needs of those who use your service.

As well as meeting the requirements of your job description, and working to your organisation's vision, you will need to follow professional standards and rules. It is likely that you will have an active role in supporting and monitoring colleagues to ensure that the required or higher standards are consistently met.

Code of conduct

This is a set of rules around how you should behave as a lead adult care worker; for example, you must work together with your colleagues and with external agencies, such as GP surgeries, to deliver high quality care to users of your service.

Professional working 

Take time to read through your job description and agreed ways of working so that you know what is expected of you, as well as the limits around what you can and should not do.

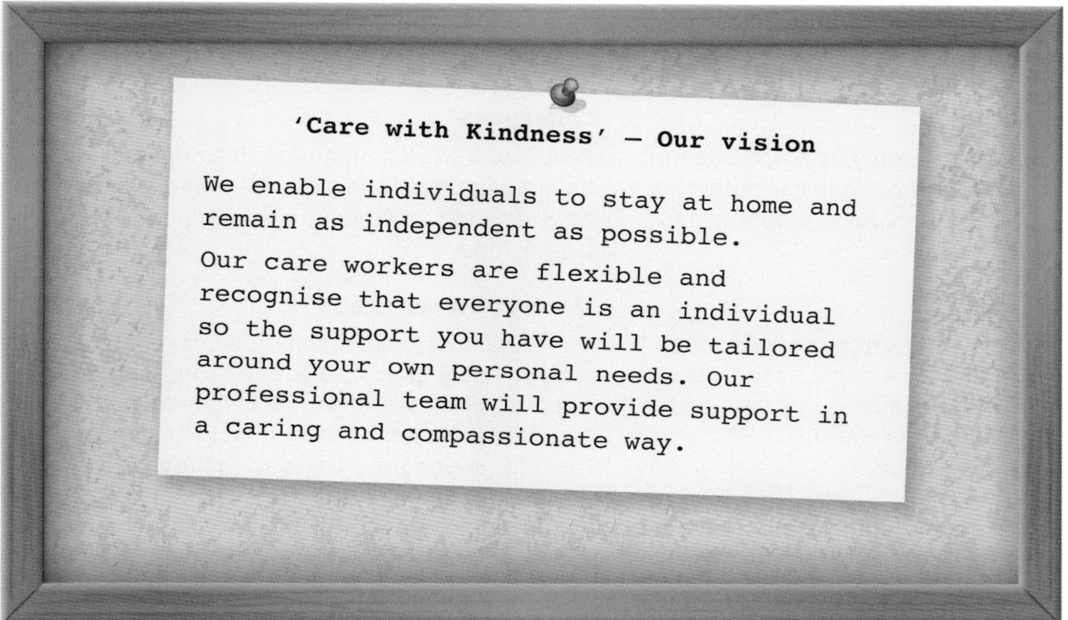

Figure 2: Your organisation will have a mission statement or vision setting out its aims

The Care Quality Commission (CQC)

The CQC inspect settings regularly to make sure that specific standards are met. The inspections focus on five areas to check that the organisation is safe, effective, caring, responsive to people's needs and well-led. For more information, see Topic A (Job role and responsibilities) page 12.

An inspector might ask you how you contribute to these five areas or how you think that the organisation meets the different areas. They will observe how care workers carry out their duties and speak to users of the service to see if they are satisfied with the care and support they receive.

Qualification mapping 

Unit 2 LO 1 AC 1.2

National Occupational Standards for social care

These are standards of performance expected from those who work in the sector. Skills for Care have developed National Occupational Standards for the care sector. Managers, supervisors and assessors will work with individuals to ensure that these standards are met. Your qualification in care will be based on the national occupational standards; these are standards that are expected of an individual working in your sector and at the level of the role that they are working at.

Link 

Topic A: Job role and responsibilities

Professional working

Some individuals may work alone, e.g. in domiciliary settings. This can make them feel isolated. As a lead adult care worker you may be responsible for monitoring individuals who work on their own. It can be a challenge to build relationships with people who you do not see often, but make a point of setting up regular contact so that the individual feels supported and part of the team. Regular phone contact and planned face-to-face meetings will help to build and sustain relationships.

First impressions count

When you first meet someone, such as a user of service or a new colleague at work, they will form an opinion of you. These first impressions are important. So make sure that people see you in a positive way right from the start because the relationship that follows will be shaped by that first encounter.

The importance of relationships

As human beings we need to interact and connect with other people. You will have relationships with different people in many different circumstances, for example, users of the service and their families and friends. You will also form relationships with those you work with, for example, senior colleagues such as your manager and junior care workers you may supervise. It is crucial that you build and maintain positive appropriate working relationships so that you can all work effectively together.

Family Bonds connected by blood or a unit that is committed to each other for the long term, for example, a civil partnership	**Colleagues** People you work with and with whom you have a common bond; you will spend a lot of time working together so may develop friendships
Friends People you choose to spend time with and to be part of your life; you will socialise and share personal information	**Users of the service** A professional relationship in which you are paid to support the person; it is a trusting relationship but different from a friendship; you do not share personal information even if you have known them for a long time; there are boundaries.

Professional relationships have a positive impact on users of the service because the individual will have confidence in the care and support that they are receiving. It puts the individuals at the centre of care whilst their holistic needs are being met. It also results in a more 'joined-up' way of providing care and support, and prevents gaps.

A professional relationship is different from a friendship. Imagine if your friend sat with you while you used the toilet or helped you to bath or shower; you would probably feel embarrassed. A professional relationship creates a safe distance so it is less likely that the individual will feel embarrassed while being supported.

6Cs

Communication, commitment

Professional relationships work best when you show that you are:

- trustworthy
- honest and fair
- flexible
- positive
- appreciative of others and what they do
- supportive of others in their work
- making time to build the relationship by getting to know the person.

Summary

A lead adult care worker will have an understanding of their job role, and build and maintain professional relationships with users of the service, their colleagues and outside agencies.

Identify and form professional relationships

As a lead adult care worker it is part of your role to take the initiative and be proactive in identifying and forming professional relationships. These might be with other people within your organisation but also externally.

Activities

Identifying professional relationships

Marek is an adult care worker. He used to work in a large nursing home but has recently changed employment to work for a domiciliary care provider. Marek now supports individuals who live in their own homes.

- What difficulties do you think Marek might face now that he mainly works alone without other team members around him?
- If you were leading a team of individuals who worked alone, explain how would you build a relationship with them so that they felt supported and part of a team?

Qualification mapping

Unit 2 LO 1 AC 1.1, 1.2 and 1.3

Professional working relationships

Go to the Skills for Care website (www.skillsforcare.org.uk) and follow the link to the code of conduct for Healthcare Support Workers and Adult Social Care Workers in England.

Read through the code carefully.

What does it say about professional relationships and working collaboratively with other people and organisations?

Copy out the table below to record your response.

Section of the code	Which point?	What does it say?

Give an example of how you have worked professionally and followed the code when working:

- with users of the service
- with colleagues
- as a supervisor to junior colleagues
- with external agencies.

Qualification mapping

Unit 2 LO 1 AC 1.1 and 1.2

Qualification mapping

Unit 2 LO 1 AC 1.3

Representing your organisation

Imagine your manager has asked you to represent your company at a local care provider's network event.

How will you present yourself so that you come across in a professional manner?

As part of the event you are asked to think about and feedback on the following questions:

- What is your workplace vision?
- How do the individuals in your organisation work together to achieve the aims and objectives?
- How do you contribute to helping other team members to achieve your workplace vision?

Make notes that you could use to help you to feedback your thoughts.

Identifying training needs for staff

Your organisation may not have the expertise to offer the full breadth of necessary training needed so will often work with external training providers.

- Make a list of specific training that is needed for staff who work in your organisation.
- Find out which training providers your organisation uses for different training needs.
- How do your organisation and external training providers communicate to plan how to meet the training needs of staff?

Carry out research and make notes that you can keep for future use.

You will need to work with other individuals and professionals to provide for training needs

Professional relationships and boundaries

Professional boundaries are about knowing the limits of the relationships that you will have with those you support and work with. Professional relationships are different from personal ones – at work your focus must be the person being supported. Having clear boundaries will protect both you and others.

Qualification mapping 

Unit 2 LO 1 AC 1.2 and 1.3

Keep relationships professional

The nature of your work as a lead adult care worker means that you support vulnerable individuals. You work closely with users of your service and will create a feeling of mutual trust. They must feel confident that you have their best interest at heart. Over time you will learn a lot about them as people – for example, their likes, dislikes and different aspects of their personality – and you will feel comfortable with each other.

However, if you are not careful, professional relationships can turn into inappropriate friendships. Imagine if, as part of your job, you visit an individual who is lonely and sees few people. They could start to rely on you too much and this can lead to all sorts of problems. For example:

- the emotional involvement can make you see things differently and inaccurately
- unrealistic and increased demands on you can result in added stress
- you could prioritise and favour the individual over other users of the service
- over-reliance on you could lead to difficulties for the individual and other adult care workers when you are not there
- there are likely to be difficulties managing expectations and behaviour.

Professional relationships do not have to be dull!

6Cs

Care, competence, commitment

Always maintain safe boundaries

While it is important that you connect with individuals and build trusting relationships, it is essential that you are both aware of the boundaries of the relationship. Boundaries are about limits to what both parties can or cannot do in the relationship. Keep a professional distance; for example, do not give out personal information and keep your personal and working life separate. Boundaries give safety, security and stability as well as protection to both parties.

What about people you work with?

Professional relationships are not just about how you work with users of your service – they are also about working with colleagues. As a lead adult care worker you should always maintain an appropriate professional distance. If you don't maintain boundaries with colleagues, it makes it difficult if you need to challenge their work practices and you may appear to favour one worker over another. Look at Figure 3 to see how lead adult care worker Samina is aware of her professional boundaries.

Samina is a lead adult care worker. She is aware of professional boundaries and is careful not to cross them.

Samina and her junior colleagues
Samina works well with her junior colleagues; she is fair when delegating tasks. When they go for a break, they share experiences and have a good laugh. Sometimes the team will organise a night out. Samina goes along and enjoys herself with the team but is always aware of her responsible position at work. She may need to challenge poor working behaviour from one of her colleagues when they are next at work.

Samina respects the relationship with her manager
Because Samina is aware of boundaries with her junior colleagues, she understands that her relationship with her manager should also be a professional one. Samina respects the boundaries between them and they have a good working relationship. They both attend and enjoy work social events. Samina tries not to be over-friendly; for example, she does not pry into her manager's personal life nor invite her on social media sites. Samina would not want to be treated more favourably than others and realises that if she needed to be corrected in her work, it would be difficult if they were too friendly.

Samina works professionally with others from outside her organisation.
Hari Khan is a solicitor; he visits the organisation quite regularly as he represents two individuals there. Although she has heard some senior managers referring to him as Hari, Samina addresses him as Mr Khan until he suggests otherwise.

Figure 3: Samina knows how to work within professional boundaries

Professional working

Other colleagues may need to be given advice and support about boundaries. You will need to be sensitive in how you approach this and explain why boundaries are so important. The use of social media means that it can be easy to cross boundaries without realising. Remember to be careful about what you post and check your privacy settings to restrict access to your information.

Activity

Val's physiotherapy visits

Val is a physiotherapist and goes into different care settings to help individuals who have limited movement. Val notices the differences in professionalism between two adult care workers she works with, as shown in the table below.

Sea View	Drake Court
Jan is a lead care worker in charge of the shift. Mrs Ling has a physio appointment at 10.30. In the morning, Jan made sure that she instructed staff to have Mrs Ling dressed and ready for Val's visit and to have her notes ready. Jan spoke to the physio afterwards, read the record and made a note of the next appointment. Jan thanked the staff afterwards for being so efficient.	Barney is a lead care worker at Drake Court. Barney instructs staff at handover to check the book to see if anyone has appointments that day. Val arrives to see Mr Ali for his appointment at 11.00. Mr Ali is being supported by a new care worker, Josie; he is still in bed. Barney is having his break. He is cross with Josie and explains to Val that it is Josie's fault. Mr Ali's treatment was delayed again.

Jan had a professional approach to her work; she was organised and worked effectively with the external agency. Jan gave a positive impression to the visiting professional.

- How do you think that a visiting professional would see you?
- Do you know anyone who works like Jan and Barney?
- Who is the most effective and professional?

Summary

Professional relationships will help you work within safe boundaries and work well with others to provide good quality care.

Work within safe professional boundaries

It is important to demonstrate how you work within safe professional boundaries and that you manage and support others to do the same.

Activities

Qualification mapping

Unit 2 LO 1 AC 1.2 and 1.3

Identifying boundaries

Building and maintaining relationships is an important part of working in social care, but relationships will be different depending on who they are with. Copy and complete the table below to demonstrate the differences around conversations and sharing of information in different relationships.

	Information that you would feel comfortable sharing about yourself	Information that you would not share with them nor expect them to share with you	Explain your answer
Friend			
User of your service			
Junior colleague who you supervise			
Manager			
Professional from outside your service			

Professional boundaries and social media

Jack is a new adult care worker in your organisation; you are his supervisor. The users of the service and the staff really like Jack and often comment on how much fun he brings to the place. Jack works hard and has fitted into the team well.

Jack is raising money for a local charity by carrying out a sponsored event. To raise money, Jack has put up a poster in the office and asked staff to sponsor him.

However, it has become apparent that Jack has shared information about his charity event and given some users of the service and their families his personal phone number. He has also invited them to join his social media sites to keep them up-to-date with what is happening.

- What is positive about how Jack is performing at work?
- What is wrong with what Jack has done?
- What could be the outcome of Jack's actions?
- As Jack's supervisor, how would you deal with the situation?

Reflective account

As part of your job as a lead adult care worker, it is likely that you will work with individuals from other organisations; for example, social workers, occupational therapists, doctors, dentists and faith leaders. They may visit individuals in your organisation or you may escort users of service to visit them.

Write a self-reflective account that shows how you have worked with individuals from other organisations and behaved in a professional and supportive manner.

You could use the Kolb reflective cycle – see page v.

Qualification mapping 

Unit 2 LO 2 AC 2.2

Support staff to maintain safe boundaries

It can be easy to forget about the importance of safe boundaries. These boundaries can sometimes be crossed without you even realising it; for example, when working with individuals for a long time, the relationship can start to become over-friendly.
When the relationship strays from a professional to a personal one, it can be easy to share inappropriate personal information. But sharing information and photos on social media can also be risky because it is then readily available by others unless strong security settings are applied.

Make some notes and produce a small information poster on the *Do's* and *Don'ts* to inform new staff about safe boundaries at work.

Sharing information

Nikita is an adult care worker and works for a social care organisation. The organisation has been short staffed recently and the manager has resigned. The deputy manager is struggling to cover shifts and has asked existing staff to help out if they can.

Nikita agrees to cover some shifts but, while she is supporting users of the service, she tells them about the manager resigning because her job became too stressful for her and that they are short staffed. She also says that she would rather not work extra shifts but feels as if she has to.

Explain why it was not professional for Nikita to share this information with users of the service.

If you were Nikita's supervisor, how would you handle the situation?

Prepare for personal development

Qualification mapping

Unit 2 LO 2 AC 2.1 and 2.3

Have you ever thought about how things were done years ago? Being reflective is a good starting point when determining the knowledge and skills that you need to develop.

Things change over time

The needs of individuals change over time and so does the way we do things as we learn about new and more effective ways of working. Consider how differently we support individuals who are living with dementia compared with twenty years ago. A lead adult care worker's knowledge and skills should continually develop in order to keep up with changes. You will also need to support others, for example, new and junior staff, to help them to develop their own skills. To be able to plan your development, you need to think about what you know already and what you need to learn and develop; this is being reflective.

The way in which people with dementia are supported is very different now

Professional working

For reflection to be effective, it is important to be very honest with yourself. This process is personal and private to you so you won't be judged by others. You can of course share your thoughts and ideas with others, especially if you think that they may learn from your experience.

Sometimes you may do things because that is the way you have always done the task, without giving much thought to it. However, this might not be the best way. If you think carefully about how you do things, you may find a different, and more effective or efficient way. There may also be times when you carried out a task that has not worked well and thought 'I will definitely approach this differently next time'. You may also identify gaps in your knowledge and skills.

Reflection is a straightforward and effective way of learning and developing. If you supervise others, you will need to support them to reflect; for example, when you have your supervision or mentor meetings, or informally on a day-to-day basis while you are working together. This will help them to learn and develop.

Lead adult care workers are expected to work in a reflective way so that they give good quality and up-to-date care. If you do not reflect, you could repeat mistakes and not work in the most safe or efficient way.

How to learn by being reflective

Some people are naturally reflective in their everyday life and work, while others are less so. If reflection is new to you, you will need to make a conscious effort to reflect on your work. A structured approach, such as the Kolb model, will help with your reflections. Look at the example below.

How Jacob used the Kolb model to reflect and learn

Experience

I arranged a doctor's appointment for Elena who is a user of my service. Elena speaks very little English so I spoke really slowly, formed my words properly and tried not to let my accent be a barrier. I used an app but it wasn't very good. I simplified my words and spoke in a slow and clear way, without using complicated language. After a few attempts, Elena nodded as if to say she understood; I felt relieved, only to find out later that she did not go to her appointment and when she spoke to an individual who spoke her native language, she had not understood what I was saying.

Reflection and observations

I tried my best to communicate the message but I had not given full consideration to how little Elena understood of the English language. I presumed that she could understand more English than she could and I could build on that understanding to make myself understood. I think that my body language was good but I do feel awful because Elena then had to wait another week for an appointment.

Development of ideas

Next time I will speak clearly as I did before and use gestures to help. I will research the use of a reliable translation application as I have heard that some are very good. I could also use images (I could draw a clock face and a simple image of a doctor).

Testing out new ideas

Elena had a visit from her social worker arranged so I tried out my new ideas. I spoke clearly and used gestures. I did find a good application that worked well. I will definitely use this again and tell others about it. I also drew a clock face with the time with what I thought could be a social worker – this ended up confusing Elena. Overall, the app was a real success.

The benefits of reflection

Reflecting helps you to look closely at what you are doing; it can identify learning and development needs for you to work on, which will lead to better performance. It will also help you develop good problem-solving skills. It's important when you reflect to be honest with yourself otherwise it will have no value at all. It's a good idea to make some notes so that you don't forget any details. Remember though to keep your notes secure and to maintain confidentiality.

Your own personal values and beliefs

It can be difficult when another person's views and beliefs are very different from your own, especially if you feel really strongly about something, such as being vegan, caring for the elders in your family yourself or recycling to preserve the earth's resources. If you are not careful, these beliefs can get in the way of the care that you give. You may need to learn how to put your own views to one side. Reflect on your own specific values and beliefs; this will help you to be mindful not to let them negatively influence how you work with others.

6Cs

Courage, competence

Professional working

As a lead adult care worker you need to ensure that others don't let their own values and beliefs affect their work.

Summary

Keep up-to-date and ahead of changes by reflecting on your knowledge, skills, values and beliefs; this will help you with your personal development plan. Help your junior colleagues to reflect as well in order to support their personal development.

Improve your skills by being reflective

You can evaluate and improve on your own skills and knowledge through reflective practice and by taking the initiative to make the most of learning opportunities.

Activities

Qualification mapping 

Unit 2 LO 2 AC 2.1, 2.2 and 2.3

▶ Personal skills audit

Find and read your job description and agreed ways of working.

Highlight the areas that you feel confident about and the areas where you are less confident.

Copy and complete the table below to record your ideas about how you could build confidence in your weaker areas.

Ares where I don't feel confident yet	Ideas that could help me gain confidence
1.	. . . .
2.	. . . .

This activity is a good starting point to help you to improve your knowledge and skills.

Link 

Topic A: Job role and responsibilities

▶ Effective communication

Look back at the scenario about Elena on page 215. Jacob suggests some ideas that could help him to communicate with Elena in the future. It is often helpful to ask other people for their ideas because they can sometimes see things from a different perspective. Make a list of your ideas that could help Jacob to communicate more effectively with Elena.

Ideas that could help Jacob to communicate with Elena	Is this a method that you have tried successfully? (yes /no)
. . . . .	

Benefits of reflective practice

Abbey Care is an organisation that provides care for individuals. It has recently received an excellent inspection report and it was clearly evident that there was a highly reflective workforce. This suggests that the staff try to improve practice.

The manager and supervisors encourage the staff to share their experiences and ideas during one-to-one supervision meetings as well as small team meetings. The team strive to constantly improve on the service they provide.

- Explain the benefits of a reflective workforce.
- How can reflection help you and others with personal development?
- How can you support junior colleagues with reflective practice?

Attitudes and behaviours at work

Your own attitudes and behaviours can influence how and why you do things.

Being self-aware can help you to work in a fair way.

Look at these values and beliefs. Do any of these relate to you?

I think that everyone should contribute to society and pay their taxes

It's ok for people to claim benefits – the rich should pay for the poor

Spend the money that you have today, you may not be here tomorrow

It's important to save money and not to squander it

I don't believe in any religion or faith; it makes no sense to me

My faith will help me through difficult times

Copy and complete the table below, listing five of your own values and beliefs then explaining how they could influence how you work.

Value / belief	How it could affect others I work with
1.	
2.	
3.	
4.	
5.	

Link 

Topic B: Values and beliefs

Qualification mapping 

Unit 2 LO 2 AC 2.3

Time to reflect for personal development

Qualification mapping

Unit 2 LO 3 AC 3.1

Reflection is something that you probably do without thinking. Some people make a conscious effort to reflect but you may also reflect while you are doing something – especially if it does not go to plan. In these situations, you need to 'think on your feet' and change what you are doing.

Reflecting on action

In the previous section, you used Kolb's model to reflect on an activity after it had happened. Reflecting after an event is called reflecting on action. Reflecting will help you to learn. Reflecting regularly on what you do at work will help you to become more competent and efficient in your job. You do not have to write about every event that happens but do make a point of reflecting on significant, memorable or unusual events where you feel that you have learned something. Keep a record of your accounts so you can revisit and maybe share your learning experiences with others. Some details can be easily forgotten if you do not keep a note of them.

Models of reflection

There are many models of reflection. You have learned about and applied Kolb's experiential model of reflection. Using Kolb's model will give you an opportunity to reflect in detail and will demonstrate learning. However, it is not all about filling in templates. The most important thing is for you to reflect on and not forget what you have done and learned. Table 1 shows a very quick and simple method of reflection.

<table>
<tr><td colspan="2">Event: The activity
I was leading a shift at work; I am new to this role.</td></tr>
<tr><td>What went well?
We had a full team, no one was off sick.
Everyone seemed comfortable about me giving instructions and being the team leader.
When I asked the users of the service, they said they were happy with how they had been supported.
I had encouraging feedback from the team.</td><td>What didn't go so well?
I forgot to say when the team members should go on their break. 'J' did not have a break. She is new and didn't like to ask.</td></tr>
<tr><td colspan="2">What would you do next time?
Next time I will plan breaks with the team when we have finished handover. I will also tell the team to let me know if there is a problem with getting their break and I will do something about it.</td></tr>
</table>

Table 1: A quick and simple method of reflection

A simple reflection exercise, like the one shown in Table 1, is quick to write – you can use short bullet points. Keeping a record like this will demonstrate your development over time and be helpful to show to your supervisor. But it is best for you to use a model such as Kolb's for deeper learning, especially when reflecting on significant events.

Reflecting in action

Sometimes you may be in the middle of an activity and things do not go to plan, requiring you to change your approach. For example, imagine you are supporting an individual who can usually walk with a little assistance but on this occasion, halfway to the lounge, her legs become weak. You call for assistance and a wheelchair, and safely help her to sit in the wheelchair. You prevented her from falling to the floor. This is called reflection in action. You reflected during the activity and responded to the situation. Some would describe this as 'thinking on your feet'.

Professional working 

You could take the opportunity to reflect on your learning experiences during a professional discussion with your assessor. This would be useful to help identify your next steps for development.

When do you reflect?

Reflection is a valuable tool and there are many opportunities to reflect. For example, you might reflect on practice during your day-to-day work and on study days, as well as reading articles and journals.

6Cs 6Cs

Competence, communication

Study days and learning programmes

You will have the opportunity to attend study sessions, at which you will learn about a range of interesting subjects. Study sessions are only valuable if you learn from them and use the information. Be sure to complete any evaluations that you are given by the trainer so that they can develop and improve how they deliver future sessions. Following a training session, you should reflect on what you have learned and think about how you can apply what you have learned to your own practice. You can also identify further developmental needs.

Reflecting on study days and programmes does not have to be a lengthy process. You could simply use the template in Figure 4 to structure your reflection.

Reflection following a study session

- Title of study programme and date
- Why you attended
- A brief overview of the content
- What did you learn?
- How could you apply what you have learned to your practice?
- Is there anything that would help you to learn more about the subject?

Figure 4: Template for reflection after a study session

Qualification mapping 

Unit 2 LO 2 AC 2.2, LO 5 AC 5.1

Articles and journals

As a lead adult care worker you should be keeping your knowledge up-to-date. You can do this by reading articles, journals and updates relating to your area of work. You can also subscribe to electronic journals and updates. Keep a record of literature that you are reading relating to your work because you may need to use and share the information with others, especially if you are guiding others in their work. Remember to use reliable sources, for example, those from government and NHS publications. Use the template in Figure 5 to evidence your learning from articles and journals.

Reflecting on articles and journals

- Name and date of article / publication and reference
- Date that you accessed it
- Why is it of interest to you?
- Summarise the basic overview of the content
- What have you learned?
- How can you use the information in your practice?
- Is there any further information that would benefit you relating to this subject?
- Include reference to the source of information

Figure 5: Template for reflecting on articles and journals

Summary 

Reflection is a valuable tool for learning. Try to get into the habit of regular reflection and use every opportunity that you can; this will help you to become more competent and confident in your work.

Demonstrate your reflective skills

You can evaluate and improve on your own skills and knowledge through reflective practice. It is also useful to demonstrate your reflective skills in order to be a good role model for others.

Activities

Qualification mapping

Unit 2 LO 3 AC 3.1, LO 5 AC 5.1

Reflection after the event

Sometimes it is useful to complete a quick reflection after an event so that you can keep the main points of the event in your mind. Think about a recent activity at your setting and use the example in Table 1.

Using Kolb's reflective model

Often you will benefit from a more in-depth reflection. Think of a situation in which you reflected in action and use Kolb's model of reflection to demonstrate your learning (see page v).

Reflection after study sessions

You can learn a lot from study sessions and learning programmes. These may be face-to-face or electronic. For your most recent study activity, use the template in Figure 4 to reflect on your learning from the experience.

Reflection using apps

Keeping yourself up-to-date by reading articles relating to your area of work can help you to give high quality care and guide others in their work.

There are many applications that you can subscribe to, some of which are free of charge.

- Search for electronic applications relating to your work that are free of charge. See what information they offer. If they will be useful to your area of work, you could download them. Always check the security before downloading information and applications to maintain the safety of your information and device.
- Check to see if your employer has access to applications or subscriptions that you could use.

Reflecting after reading articles and journals

Find an article of interest and, using Figure 5 as a template, reflect on your learning.

Develop and sustain a positive attitude

Qualification mapping

Unit 2 LO 1 AC 1.1, 1.2 and 1.3

A positive attitude makes you feel better both physically and emotionally, and helps you to deal with pressures at work. It also means you will be a good role model.

Positive workers

Every day you make a difference to people's lives when you work in adult care: for example, when you demonstrate care and sensitivity to users of your service, and in the support that you give to the colleagues you work with. You might never know how much your support meant to them. A happy and positive lead adult care worker is more likely to be successful, give quality care and lead an effective team.

Professional working

Preventing stress and building resilience will help you to be strong both mentally and physically. This will help you to stay healthy, so that you can maintain a long and rewarding career in social care. Make a note of what works for you when reducing stress and how you have built resilience. Share your ideas with other team members.

Case study: 'Liam's positivity is a delight'

Ace Care is a domiciliary care provider and is rated 'Outstanding'. The manager sought feedback from users of the service and adult care workers about their experiences at Ace Care. Liam's name was frequently mentioned. Here are some extracts from what people said.

'Nothing is too much trouble for Liam; he brightens up my day.'

'Liam is always smiling; he makes me happy when I am feeling low.'

'Liam always looks on the bright side, his positivity is a delight.'

'I am new to care work and I struggle with the pressures. When I work with Liam, his positive and happy nature makes me feel like I want to do the job and makes me want to be like him. He is a great role model.'

Liam was nominated for a Care Worker's Award for his positive attitude at work and the difference that he makes to people's lives and experiences.

- How do you think that Liam's positivity helps new workers to do their own job well?
- What are the benefits to the organisation if staff have a positive outlook?
- What do you think users of your service would say about how positive you are?

The demands and pressures of care work

Adult care work can be satisfying but also demanding; it will sometimes test you to the limits. It is mentally and physically exhausting, and you may sometimes feel that you are working under great pressure. Some pressure in life is positive. For example, it is what gets you up to go to work and the pressure of deadlines can quickly turn to satisfaction if you meet them. However, too much pressure over a long period of time is unhealthy and can damage your physical and mental health (as shown in Figure 6).

Resilience

To sustain a long and happy working life, you need to cope under pressure: this is called resilience. If you are not resilient, you can become stressed and burnt out. Try to change any negative behaviours into positive ones, as this will help you to be more resilient. You may also need to support junior colleagues to be positive in their work and to be resilient. A positive work environment with resilient staff will improve the overall feeling and culture of the organisation. This will mean staff are less likely to leave and new workers will be attracted to work there. Some examples of how you can build your resilience are shown in Figure 7.

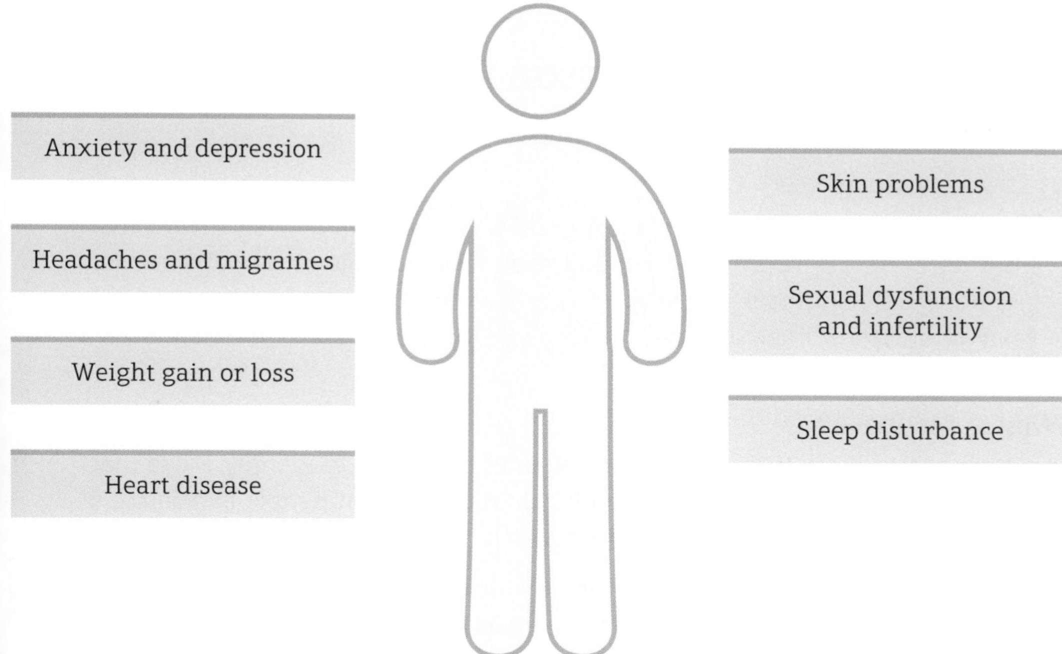

Figure 6: Some negative effects of stress

Build and sustain resilience to prevent and manage stress

Here are some tips for building your resilience:

- Supervision – reflect on situations and discuss them with your supervisor.
- Keep a reflective diary. This will help you to put issues in perspective and highlight the positives.
- Build up your problem-solving skills. Reflect on what has worked in the past and try out new ideas. You can ask your colleagues and supervisor for advice.
- Download an app – there are several that help to build resilience and reduce stress.

Make sure to do some exercise regularly, eat a healthy diet and get enough sleep. Keep watch for the signs of stress: headaches; digestive problems; poor sleep; excessive sweating; and a pounding heart.

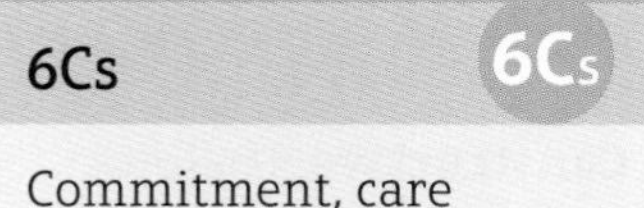

6Cs

Commitment, care

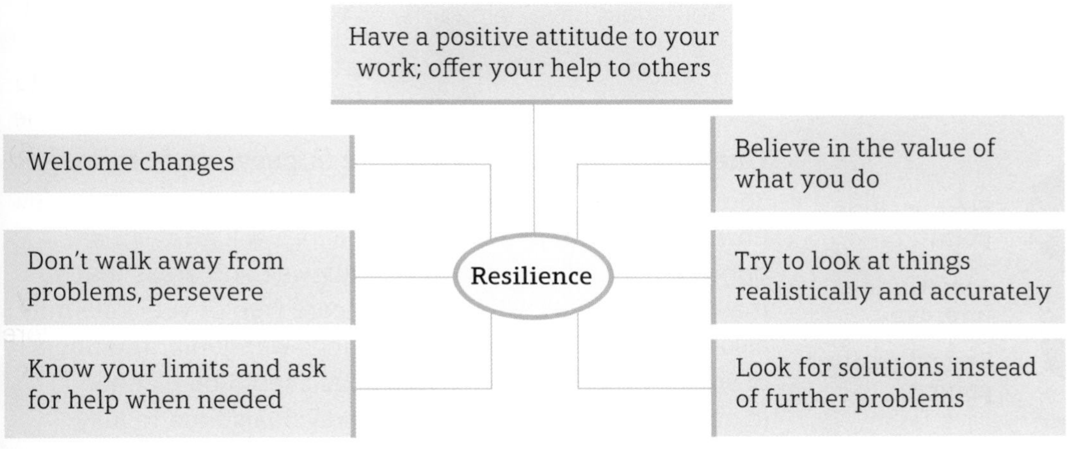

Figure 7: You need to be resilient to manage pressure and support others to do so

Summary 

Working in adult care is a rewarding job, but it can be tough at times. Watch your own and others' physical and mental health. This will help you to build and maintain resilience in order to meet the demands of the job.

Use feedback to help personal development

Qualification mapping 

Unit 2 LO 3 AC 3.2

Professional working 

You may need to give feedback to junior colleagues who work with you. This may be informal on a day-to-day basis but your role might also require you to give more formal, documented feedback. Your supervisor might also ask you for general feedback on how junior colleagues are doing in their role at work to help anticipate any potential difficulties there may be in the running of the organisation.

Key term 

Constructive – helpful, useful

Receiving feedback from people is a good way of getting actively involved in your personal development. It can help you to feel confident about what you are doing well and help you to identify any areas you need to improve. As a lead adult care worker you may need to give others feedback on their work.

What is feedback?

Feedback tells you what you are doing well and helps you to identify areas that you could improve. You will receive feedback from different people in a range of situations. Feedback can be formal or informal.

Formal: for example, from your assessor, or your manager or employer; formal feedback is official and documented but is usually discussed with you verbally as well.

Informal: for example, from your colleagues, saying how well you have managed a situation; informal feedback is more casual and not usually documented.

Feedback will only help if you use the information you are given. It can feel uncomfortable sometimes but try not to take it personally; it is intended to help not criticise.

How to make feedback supportive

Think of a time when you received feedback and it left you feeling useless or inadequate. Many people have had experiences in which they were given feedback that focused on what they did not do very well. This type of feedback is damaging because it can reduce your confidence and self-esteem. Even when you are not successful in doing something properly, there will almost always be something positive about the situation. It is important that any positive aspect is acknowledged. Receiving feedback should be a positive and valuable experience, so how you go about giving feedback is important. Remember that it should always be **constructive** (see Figure 8).

- Start with something positive: 'I like the way you gave Jessie a choice for her meal'.
- Area for development – 'You could have helped her to be more independent'.
- Finish with a positive – 'It was good to see you taking an interest in her conversation'.

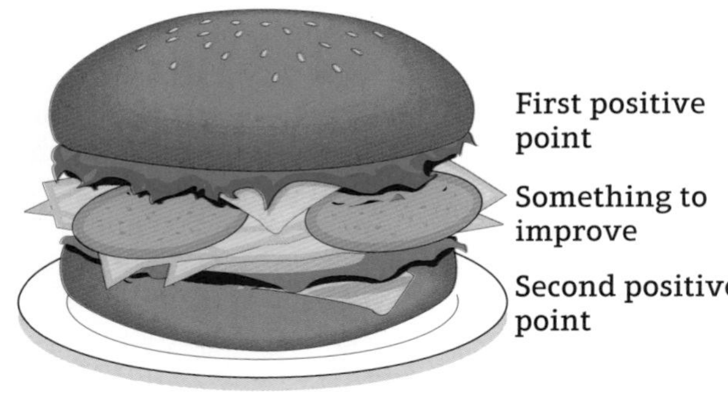

Figure 8: The feedback sandwich

One-to-one meetings with your supervisor or manager

You will have regular meetings with your supervisor to review how you are getting on. These meetings will give you an opportunity to discuss what is going well and areas that you may need support with. As a lead care worker your role may also involve organising such meetings with junior members of staff. Formal one-to-one meetings should be planned in advance in order to give both individuals time to fully prepare. The meetings should take place where there are no interruptions.

Professional working

There is a lot of information available outside your organisation covering work-related questions and concerns. ACAS (Advisory, Conciliation and Arbitration Service) provides lots of information sheets, such as absence, being monitored at work and mental health. You can find information by accessing www.acas.org.uk and following the links to advice A-Z. Professional information can help during supervision meetings (both your own and when you lead others).

Supervision meetings

Supervisions are one-to-one meetings with your supervisor. These supportive meetings will enable you to discuss issues that are impacting on your day-to-day work. For example, you might be finding a particular area of work difficult, such as supporting an individual at the end of their life, or work allocation schedules may be causing some difficulties. Your supervisor will be experienced in the role and can often offer support and advice. Your supervisor will also give you feedback on how they feel that you are getting on from their perspective.

Appraisal

Your appraisal is a formal review of your performance – usually carried out with your manager. You will both prepare beforehand by reflecting on your practice and you may have a set structure to follow. Dates will be agreed for each stage to be completed. You will need your job description, detailing your agreed ways of working, so that you can judge your performance against your job role.

You will usually complete an initial self-assessment and submit this to your appraiser, who will make notes to contribute to your appraisal. This ensures that both of you are fully prepared. You will then meet to go through each stage.

As a result of your appraisal, you are likely to agree targets that will help you with your progression. These targets will contribute to your future development.

Both supervision and appraisal can identify areas of knowledge and skills that you need to develop. From this, you can create a plan for your development. It is likely that you will be set targets to achieve. You will learn about preparing for your personal development plan on pages 230–231. The progress of your plan will be discussed in subsequent appraisal meetings.

Summary

Feedback is valuable in helping you to judge how you are doing in your job. It will also help contribute to your future personal and professional development. As part of your role you may need to give feedback to others, so make sure that it is supportive.

Professional working

One of the most valuable types of feedback is from users of the service as they are the direct receivers of care. It can take courage to ask others for feedback on how you are doing, but look on the experience positively as it will help you to continually improve and do a great job.

Professional working

Some organisations have an electronic system for recording appraisals where you both have access to the document. When you have finished your part you can confirm that it is complete. Your manager will then be alerted to complete their part in preparation for your appraisal meeting.

6Cs

Competence, courage

Feedback and team/partnership working skills

In your role as a lead adult care worker you must demonstrate good team/partnership working skills. Giving feedback can be an important element of this.

Activities

Qualification mapping

Unit 2 LO 3 AC 3.2

Giving and receiving feedback

How you give feedback is important if it is to help the individual receiving it. The feedback sandwich structure can help to make feedback constructive.

Think of a time when you received feedback and answer the following questions:

- What was the purpose of the feedback? For example, was it following a piece of work that you had recently submitted for a course that you are doing, for example, your Diploma?
- How did the feedback fit the structure of the feedback sandwich?

Think of a time when you gave feedback to an individual about something they had done. Compare how you gave the feedback to the 'sandwich' structure.

- Have you ever received feedback that was *not* constructive? How did it make you feel?
- How could you improve the feedback that you received and gave?

Constructive feedback

Giving good constructive feedback can take practice – especially if you need to give feedback to a colleague whose work is not reaching the required standard.

Read the scenario below.

Kristine has been working in your organisation for about six months; she works hard and the users of the service like her. Kristine carries out her work to a high standard. Kristine lives nearby and walks to work, but she often arrives late for her shifts. She is also late returning from her breaks while at work. Other members of your team are complaining.

Your manager has asked you to speak to Kristine about her punctuality.

Using the feedback sandwich as a guide, suggest how you would approach the situation with Kristine.

Responding to feedback

Ask your supervisor or manager to give you feedback on an activity that you have recently carried out. Then copy and complete this table to record your response.

Activity:	
Positive feedback	Areas to develop
Ideas that will help you to develop	

Qualification mapping 

Unit 2 LO 3 AC 3.1, 3.2 and LO 4 AC 4.1

Feeding back to a team member

You practised giving feedback to Kristine in the activity on page 226. Now it is time to put your skills into practice.

Discuss this activity with your supervisor or manager before carrying it out.

- Identify an opportunity to give feedback to a junior colleague on how they carried out an activity.

Your manager or supervisor could suggest an individual to ask.

- Ask them how they felt following your feedback.

Team/partnership skills audit

An important part of your role is developing and demonstrating good team/partnership working skills. Ask for feedback from some of your colleagues, then copy and complete the table to record the areas where you feel confident and the areas where you are less confident.

Think about how you could build confidence in your weaker areas.

Areas where I don't feel confident yet	Ideas that could help me gain confidence
	· ·
	· ·

This activity is a good starting point to help you to improve your team working skills.

Qualification mapping 

Unit 2 LO 4 AC 4.1 and 4.2

Excellent core skills

Imagine if a junior colleague asked you to check their time sheet to make sure they had calculated their hours accurately but you were not confident using numbers. How would you feel? Confident and accurate skills in writing, number and information technology are essential for lead adult care workers.

All adult care workers need to have good core skills in writing, number and information technology (IT) in order to be able to do their job properly and safely. A high standard in these core skills is expected of every lead adult care worker.

The following adult care workers were asked to give one example of how they had used writing, number and IT the previous day. This is what they said.

Jack – domiciliary care worker
Writing – I documented the care I gave to 'X'.
Number – I completed my travel claim, logged the miles that I drove then added them for the month.
IT – I am completing an online safeguarding course.

Bec – support worker, supported living
Writing – I helped 'A' to complete an application form for a college course.
Number – I helped 'B' to work out his weekly budget.
IT – I completed my pre-appraisal assessment online.

Jess – personal assistant
Writing – I helped 'L' to write a letter to her sister.
Number – I worked out if 'L' had enough medication for when she goes on holiday.
IT – I helped 'L' to order her repeat prescription using the app on her phone.

Sally – support worker, residential home
Writing – I wrote a performance report for a work placement student.
Number – I organised the off duty and made sure everyone's hours were correct.
IT – I used an electronic communication device with a user of our service.

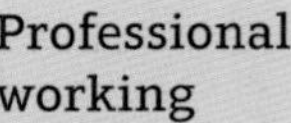

Professional working

Poor record keeping has led to individuals and organisations facing legal proceedings; do not let this happen to you or your workplace.

Writing skills

Although a lot of information is transferred electronically, you still need to make sure that your spelling and grammar are accurate. You may also support others in developing their written skills. Accurate writing skills are essential. Care is often dependent on messages conveyed through writing, for example, instructions within care plans. If they are not written clearly and accurately, things can get missed. Records will be checked by external inspectors and, in some cases, by legal teams and the police if there are criminal investigations. Your records must be written to a high standard in order to protect users of the service, yourself and your organisation. Poor spelling and grammar can give a negative impression of the organisation.

n law, if a care activity is not documented then it will be presumed that it has not been done. For example, if you forget to write that Mrs M would not allow you to change her position and she developed a pressure sore, you could be accused of neglect. Important decisions are made as a result of written records.

Number skills

You will not be able to support individuals properly, and you may even put them at risk, if you do not have accurate number skills. For example, consider the use of both traditional and 24-hour clocks, working out travel times using timetables and checking the accuracy of your pay slip.

Number skills are essential for food safety. Imagine the consequences if you did not understand how to read, interpret and record safe temperatures of the fridge or freezer for raw or cooked food. People could become very ill or even die. You and your organisation could be held responsible for food poisoning. You might also need to use fractions to document the quantity of food consumed by an individual. Your calculations must be accurate or a vulnerable individual might not receive the nourishment they need.

Information technology

We live in a fast-growing digital world; you cannot get by without using IT confidently. IT is a quick and efficient method for recording and communicating information and most non-human contact involves some use of IT. However, using IT is not without dangers, especially for individuals who are not confident in its use, for example, exposure to scams and computer viruses. Refer to Topic D (Safeguarding) to learn more about e-safety.

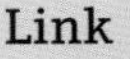

Link

Topic D: Safeguarding

Case study: Alex gets the conversions wrong

Alex is an adult care worker in an eating disorder clinic. As part of his role he monitors the weight of individuals who use the service. Alex asked an individual if he could check their weight. They were reluctant but stepped on to the scales then quickly stepped off. Alex made a note of their weight in stones and pounds but it needed to be documented in kilograms.

Fortunately, the lead adult care worker, Jo, noticed when checking the charts that Alex had made a mistake in his conversion.

- What could have been the consequences if Jo had not noticed the mistake?
- Imagine that you do not have access to a phone or the internet. One stone is equal to 6.35 kg. An individual weighs 7 1/2 stone. What is that in kilograms?
- Why are number skills so important in social care work?

Summary

To be a safe and effective lead adult care worker, you must keep your writing, number and IT skills up-to-date. In doing so, you will protect individuals, yourself and the organisation.

Figure 9: Can you quickly convert from one to the other?

Access specialist knowledge

Qualification mapping

Unit 2 LO 4 AC 4.1

As a lead adult care worker, you will never stop learning and developing. The adult care sector constantly changes and develops. You need to learn new skills and make sure that you regularly refresh your knowledge and skills on things that you have already learned.

Your personal development plan

This is a document to help plan for your personal and professional development. You have a responsibility to be actively involved in the plan and you may have to support others with their plans. You will need to reflect and use feedback; for example, from your manager during appraisals and supervision, your mentor and users of the service. You should refer to your job description and have an idea of your career progression plans.

Professional working

Your code of conduct clearly outlines your responsibilities in relation to keeping your knowledge and skills up to date. You may also be responsible for the developmental needs of less experienced care workers.

Step 1 is to judge your current knowledge, skills, opportunities that you have and things that might get in the way. Look at the SWOB analysis in Table 2, where a few examples have been included.

Strengths What are you good / confident at? *Communicating, verbally and writing* *Supporting new members of staff*	**Weaknesses** What areas do you still need to develop? *Maths and number work* *I am still unsure about some of the IT systems at work*
Opportunities What opportunities are there to develop? (e.g. shadowing others or attending training) *I could attend a mentor training programme at work* *I could attend maths sessions at my local learning centre*	**Barriers** What could get in the way of your development? (e.g. shift patterns or money) *Time, I work full time and feel tired when I get home* *I am also completing my diploma at the moment so have little time for anything else*

Table 2: An example of a SWOB analysis

Professional working

When you undertake training, remember to reflect on your learning and link it to your work place practice. Keep a record of your reflections for your professional portfolio.

You could review your SWOB analysis with your manager or supervisor when you complete your personal development plan; they may suggest specific targets for your development. Your development plan does not finish when the activities have been completed as you will review and evaluate it regularly. It will continue with you in your journey as a social care worker.

As the needs of your organisation, laws, policies and procedures change so too should your plan; this will ensure that you fully meet the requirements of your job. Continuous professional development will help in your career journey and provide evidence of your knowledge and skills.

Personal development plan

Knowledge or skill to develop	How will this help you do your job better?	How this will be achieved	Will any extra support be needed?	When will this be achieved?	Evaluation date/ How has this improved my work?
Mentoring skills	I will be able to support and mentor new members of staff	Ask my manager if I can attend the next available course	I will need cover for my shift that day	The course will be completed on 19 April 2019	19 May 2019 Course successfully achieved; I am a mentor for a new member of staff

Table 3: Your personal development plan might be similar to this

Workplaces will differ in how personal development plans are recorded and stored. They can be paper-based or stored electronically but must comply with confidentiality rules.

Being independent in your learning

As a lead adult care worker, you will likely be responsible for the training and development of junior colleagues. However, being in a lead and supervisory role, you may need to be more autonomous and take responsibility for your own learning. You may have limited access to supervision meetings so you will need to be more proactive in working out your own learning needs and what you need to do to develop your knowledge and practice rather than relying on others to plan it for you.

6Cs 6Cs

Competence, communication

Specialist knowledge you might need for your role

You might have worked in an adult care environment previously but find that the skills and knowledge required in your current job are very different. It is important to develop specialist knowledge and skills within your personal development plan.

Qualification mapping

Unit 2 LO 5 AC 5.3

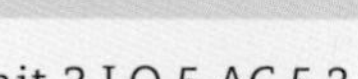

For example, lead adult care workers may require specialist knowledge about:

- supporting individuals who are living with dementia
- effects of addiction on individuals and how to offer support
- housing and benefit advice
- specialist communication techniques, such as Makaton.

Your manager or supervisor can help you to plan how to gain the necessary knowledge and skills so that you can do your job competently.

Recording your continuous professional development (CPD)

It is advisable that you keep your CPD records organised in a folder or portfolio. This can be paper-based or electronic and will demonstrate ongoing personal and professional development. Remember to be careful about how you record reflective accounts and ensure that individuals are not identifiable in order to maintain confidentiality. You can bring your portfolio to your appraisal meetings and if you apply for promotion or employment elsewhere, take it with you to show the interviewer.

As part of your role you may also need to ensure that the training needs of other staff members meet the requirements of their job role and are up to date.

Summary 

Reflecting and using feedback will help you to develop in your work. Targets in your personal development plan will help keep you focussed on your progress. Remember to keep a record of your continuous professional development.

Demonstrate continuous professional development

You must demonstrate continuous professional development in your work as a lead adult care worker and your personal development plan is an important part of this.

Activities

Qualification mapping

Unit 2 LO 4 AC 4.1, 4.2, 4,3, LO 5 AC 5.4

Demonstrate continuous professional development

Complete the mind map below to show who can help you to plan for your personal and professional development. Explain the support that they could give.

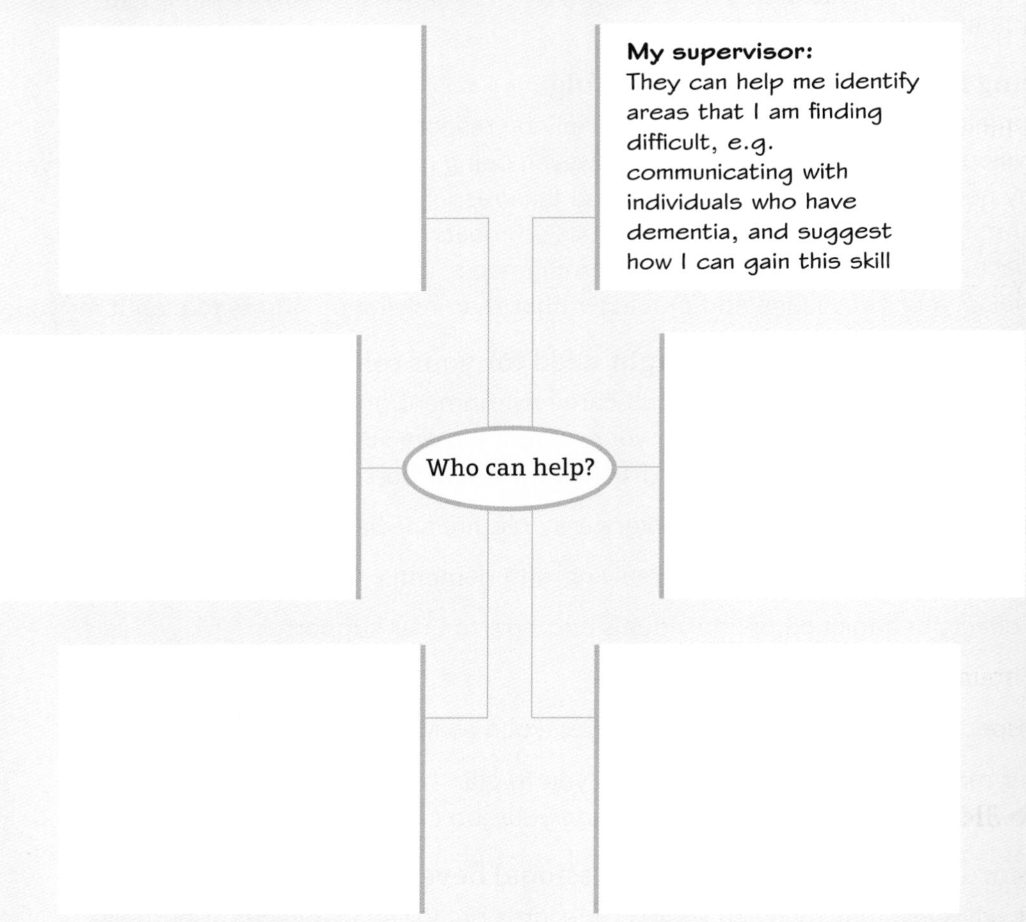

Assessing your core skills

Adult care workers need excellent core skills, for example, writing, numbers and information technology (IT).

As a lead adult care worker you may need to support others to use these skills.

It is likely that as part of your apprenticeship you have undertaken diagnostic assessments in English and number skills and you may have achieved national certificates of achievement. Having achieved a certificate does not necessarily mean that you are confident in using the skills.

Copy and complete the table to assess your skills.

	Relevant subject / grade achieved	Diagnostic assessment result if appropriate	What areas am I confident in?	Which areas am I less confident in?	Action plan / next step needed
Number					
Writing					
Information technology					

Qualification mapping 

Unit 2 LO 3 AC 3.1

SWOB analysis

You will have been given feedback from different sources; for example, from users of service, appraisals, supervision, mentor meetings and colleagues. You also completed self-reflective activities and self-assessed your core skills in the previous activity. Copy and complete the SWOB analysis below to show an overall assessment.

Strengths What are you good / confident at?	**Weaknesses** What areas do you still need to develop?
Opportunities What opportunities are there to develop? (e.g. shadowing others or attending training)	**Barriers** What could get in the way of your development? (e.g. shift patterns or money)

How has feedback helped you to develop your knowledge and skills?

SMART plans

You need to complete a personal development plan to help you to progress in your role. You must also demonstrate that you have contributed to your plan. Use the feedback you have been given to help form the plan.

For plans to work properly they need to be agreed and SMART as shown below:

Specific – to the point, precise (not vague)

Measurable – able to clearly measure and see progress and achievement

Achievable – possible to do

Realistic – sensible

Timed – dates of targets clearly stated.

Qualification mapping

Unit 2 LO 4 AC 4.1, 4.2 and 4.3

With your assessor or manager, copy and complete this guide to create your personal development plan – remember to keep it SMART.

Personal development plan for: **Date:**

Knowledge or skill to be developed	How will this help you do your job better?	How this will be achieved?	Will any extra support be needed?	When will this be achieved?	Evaluation date How has this improved my work?

Qualification mapping

Unit 2 LO 5 AC 5.4

Creating your portfolio

Create a portfolio that demonstrates your continuous professional development. This can be electronic or paper-based.

You could include the following:

- up-to-date Curriculum Vitae
- personal development plan
- record of CPD activities
- records of feedback
- self-reflective accounts
- witness testimonies
- any other evidence that you feel it would be beneficial to include.

Practice for professional discussion

Prepare for a 10-minute professional discussion on how your personal development plan will help you to progress in your current role and future career plans.

You could include the following points:

- your overall aims and goals
- strengths and areas for development
- your plans for how you will achieve your aims and goals
- what might get in the way of your success
- how you could overcome any barriers that you face.

Research and share information with others

How do you know if you are giving the best type of support? Usually you can ask the person but sometimes you may need to look for more detailed information, especially if their needs are complex and you have not supported a person with those needs before. You may need to research and share information with your colleagues so that you can all give the best possible care.

Qualification mapping

Unit 2 LO 1 AC 1.2 and 1.3

Link

Topic A: Job role and responsibilities

All the individuals you support are unique and this should be reflected in the personalised support they receive. You have learnt more about this aspect of planning care in Topic A (Job role and responsibilities). You can usually find out this information from the individual or someone who knows them well. Look at the examples in the case study below: Jack and Ramon have similar physical needs. You may be a key worker to both but you will need to find out how each wishes to be supported then share the information with those who will be involved in their care. You will usually gather the information from, for example, the person themselves, their family and other practitioners involved in their care, such as nurses and physiotherapists.

Case study: Jack and Ramon

Jack and Ramon are both in their 80s and have had hip surgery following a fall. Both are in a local care home to help with their rehabilitation. They require physiotherapy and have support from an occupational therapist; their physical needs are very similar.

Jack does not like eating in the company of others. He has a specific routine and does not feel comfortable accepting personal care support from a female care worker. However, Ramon likes to be with other individuals. He does not like being alone. He feels 'hemmed in' if he is in his room and he likes the door left open so he can see people around him.

Luca is key worker to both Jack and Ramon and has the responsibility of finding out and sharing information with the team about Jack and Ramon's needs. Luca spent time finding out about each of their individual needs and:

- recorded his findings in each of Jack and Ramon's care plans
- shared his assessment findings in a group team meeting
- reviews their care plans regularly and records any changes.

Now think of two individuals that you support who have similar needs but different wishes and preferences.

- How could you research what their individual support needs and preferences are?
- Where could you find information about best practice on how to support each of them as an individual?
- How would you share the information with others who need to know?

Professional working

When you share information with others, think about how you present it. It may not be obvious, for example, if a person is dyslexic and finds reading information difficult or if English is not their first language. If you use an electronic presentation programme, think about the use of colour as it can be difficult for some people to read black text on a white background.

Specific support needs

Sometimes individuals have specific support needs that you and your team may not be familiar with. For example, you may have a new user of your service who has autism, diabetes, or dementia or mental health difficulties. You will want to give them the best possible care so will need to find out how best to support them and share this information with your colleagues.

Professional working

When you research and use information, always state where you found it. If you do not acknowledge the source, you are claiming that the information is yours and this is plagiarism. Plagiarism is serious because the information belongs to the author or the organisation. You can find out more about how to acknowledge the sources that you use from 'how to reference' sites on the internet, your assessor and teacher.

6Cs

Competence, communication

Case study: Sharna is worried about Bill

Sharna works in a hostel for individuals who have nowhere to live and is a lead adult care worker to Bill. Bill has type 1 diabetes. Bill sometimes becomes quite angry and appears drunk even when there is no evidence of him having alcohol or using other substances. Sharna does not know much about diabetes but is aware that it can affect a person's mood and can be dangerous if blood sugar levels are unstable.

Sharna formed a plan to find out more about type 1 diabetes and how best to support Bill. She:

- searched on the internet to find out what type 1 diabetes is
- found out how to live healthily with diabetes
- researched potential difficulties people who have diabetes may experience
- asked Bill how he manages his diabetes and what works well and what doesn't
- made contact with a local specialist diabetes nurse
- found out how to recognise and respond to low and high blood sugar episodes
- requested specialist information from the local health centre and from a specialist diabetes organisation.

Sharna also arranged for the specialist diabetes nurse to come and talk with the team. In the meantime, she summarised the key important points from her research and shared them with her colleagues.

- Think of an individual you support who has a specific need that you or your colleagues may be unfamiliar with.
- Make a plan, like Sharna did, so that you can research their specific need.
- How would you choose to share the information with others?

Sharing information with others

You can carry out research and gather lots of information but it is important that it is shared effectively so that individuals can understand and use it. It is also important to know who you need to give information to and what they need to know. Think about how you choose to present and share your information, maybe via a short training session or during a 'slot' in a planned team meeting.

Some information you find will be written in a technical or academic way; this may not be right for the people you are sharing the information with. You need to bring out key important points and present information in a way that all individuals will understand.

Tips on how to share information using a presentation

First, decide on the information that you want to share. Then:

- set objectives about what you would like individuals to gain from the session
- present information in a logical and straightforward way – try to link to real workplace examples so that they can see the relevance and how to apply the information
- invite and ask open questions throughout (avoid closed 'yes and no' answer type questions)
- assess if they have met the objectives – you could do this by asking questions or giving them a short quiz.

Sometimes you will be able to share your research information in a team meeting

Sharing information using posters and leaflets

Not all information has to be shared in a formal presentation. There may simply not be the time to arrange for your colleagues to get together so you may choose a different method. For example, you may find information in leaflets and on posters that you could source from specialist organisations; for example, step-by-step instructions on what to do if a user of your service has a seizure.

You could present information in a poster format yourself; this is good for bringing together the necessary key information.

Tips for creating a good poster or leaflet

If you are creating a poster or leaflet:

- make it visually appealing
- ensure it is easy to read
- make it clear, to the point and organised
- ensure it is not too cluttered
- check your spelling and grammar
- state where you have found the information.

Summary

As a lead adult care worker you will research information about how to best support users of your service. Information needs to be shared with others in a way that they will understand and use.

Carry out research relevant to individuals' support needs

As part of your role as a lead adult care worker you may need to carry out research into the different support needs of individuals and share this information with your colleagues so that you can all give the best possible care.

Activities

Qualification mapping

Unit 2 LO 1 AC 1.3

Research information into individuals' support needs

As a lead adult care worker, you are responsible for making sure that users of the service have their support needs met. Think about the individuals you are responsible for; you may be their key worker. Check through each individual's care plan and make sure that it is up-to-date. Seek information on any areas of assessment that are not fully complete. Remember to include the user of the service when you review their support needs.

- Fully document the updated information.
- Share information about the updated support needs of each individual with the user of the service to confirm accuracy, and share the plan at your next appropriate team meeting.

Case study

Create a case study about an individual who has a specific support need in relation to a physical or mental health difficulty. Ask permission from the individual first, then complete the following plan.

- a brief history of the individual – relevant to the difficulty
- information about the disorder/difficulty and how it affects the individual
- research into current up-to-date practice around how individuals with the disorder/difficulty can be supported (make sure to use UK research and guidelines, and reference your sources)
- comparison of the management of the support needs of your individual against the published guidelines: Are there similarities? Are there any differences?
- if there are any differences, why do you think this is?
- what other needs must you consider for your individual: for example, emotional, social and spiritual?

Share your findings with your supervisor or assessor.

Information for research

Adult care work is varied. There are many specialities and the specialist knowledge that you need will vary greatly depending on where you work.

Sometimes a user of your service will need specific care and support that you are not used to dealing with. For example, you may work with individuals who have learning difficulties but one person has type 1 diabetes or dementia.

There is a lot of information available, especially via the internet, but remember that it may not always be reliable or accurate because anyone can post information online. You must always make sure to use reliable sources, such as the NHS or other official sites like Diabetes UK and MIND.

It is always a good idea to use more than one source because you can verify the information that you have gathered more effectively. When looking at how to manage and support individuals, use sites from the country that you work in so that it is relevant to your area.

Look at the following list and choose two areas of interest, then identify where accurate specialist information could be found (alternatively, you could choose two areas of your own): mental health, older people, end-of-life care, dementia care, addictions, learning disability, communication differences.

Specialist area	Current and reliable information Find at least 3 sources: for example, books, professional journals, internet

Carry out research into specialist areas

Now you have found some reliable sources, you can prepare to carry out some of your own research.

- Choose a specialist support need that you are interested in (it could be one of the above or a different one).
- Carry out some research on how best to support an individual with that need.
- Collect literature and summarise the information that you have found.
- Choose a method to share your information with others.
- Share your information and provide links to sources that you have used.
- Seek feedback from those who you shared the information with.

Use the feedback you receive to consider your strengths and areas for development. You can use this information to inform your personal development plan.

Good practice: mentoring and supervision

Qualification mapping 

Unit 2 LO 1 AC 1.3

Professional working 

Some organisations will want you to keep a record of mentor meetings so that the mentee can look back on what was discussed. A record of when meetings have taken place will also act as evidence that the organisation is providing support for their workforce.

Think about how you felt when you first started working for your organisation. Did you ever want to discuss any difficulties that you were facing with someone in a safe and private environment? Mentoring and supervision can help.

The new person

You will once have been the new person in an organisation. Everyone seems to know what they are doing and you can feel lost and ineffective. An experienced colleague as a mentor can be a great support and help with the professional development of new members of staff. A mentor does not monitor performance or get involved with complaints about the individual. Because of this, the mentor can help to establish a trusting relationship in which the individual can speak openly about how they feel without being judged.

As a mentor, you are a support; you will help the individual to take ownership of any problems or concerns they may have and try to point them in the right direction to overcome any issues. You are not the trainer, but you may identify and suggest training. Your relationship will be a professional one with appropriate boundaries. You are a trusted colleague with whom they feel safe.

What makes a good mentor?

Do:	Don't:
Maintain a professional relationship ✔ Discuss roles and responsibilities ✔ Establish boundaries ✔ Have regular contact with the individual ✔ Agree how you will work together ✔ Provide support as agreed ✔ Maintain confidentiality (except where the interest of the organisation or other individuals are compromised) ✔ Keep a record of the support you give as outlined by your organisation ✔	Get involved with personal matters ✘ Be a 24/7 helpline ✘ Get involved with complaints or performance (you could signpost to procedures though) ✘

Figure 10: What makes a good mentor?

When personalities clash

Sometimes the relationship between a mentor and mentee just does not work. This can simply be because of a difference of personalities. If this happens, the mentoring support is unlikely to be successful. However, it does not mean that you have failed as a mentor; you are just not compatible in that particular mentor/mentee relationship.

The important thing is to be professional and speak to your manager or supervisor so that a different mentor can support the individual.

Supervision

If you are a supervisor, you should have had training in how to supervise staff. **Supervision** is carried out by a more senior person to the individual. The supervisor will monitor how the individual is carrying out their role and support them in their personal and professional development in order for them to be competent in their work. The individual will be encouraged to discuss any areas of their work that get in the way of them doing their job well and together with their supervisor will explore strategies for dealing with them.

The process of supervision

There are certain agreed formalities for the process of supervision:

- A contract is set up and signed prior to supervision taking place; this outlines the responsibilities and expectations of both the supervisor and the **supervisee.**
- Regular supervision meetings are arranged (in a private place where there will be no interruptions).
- An agenda is set before the meeting, starting with a review of the previous supervision meeting and any agreed actions.
- Both parties should be fully prepared for the supervision meeting, as stated in the supervision contract.
- The supervisor documents the content of the meeting and any agreed actions. Both sign the record.
- The supervisee has a copy of the record and a copy is stored securely in the organisation.

What makes a good supervision meeting?

The relationship between the supervisor and supervisee needs to be a professional, supportive and trusting one. Both parties should feel that the supervision meeting has met the intended outcomes.

The following guidance will help you as a supervisor to get the most out of the meeting, both for you and your supervisee.

- Arrive on time and well prepared for the meeting.
- Display effective communication skills.
- Be supportive and empathetic.
- Give the individual your undivided attention.
- Keep focused on the agenda.
- Have a good knowledge of professional and organisational requirements.
- Record discussions and actions clearly and accurately.

Summary

Mentoring and supervision are important to support staff in doing their job well. Take a professional approach to these roles. This will help to raise standards of care and build your competence and confidence, as well as that of others.

Key terms

Supervision – one-to-one meeting with your supervisor to discuss how you are getting on at work

Supervisee – the person who is being supervised

Professional working

As a supervisor you should have a full understanding of the code of conduct as well as the organisation's aims and objectives. You can then support the supervisee in their understanding of them.

6Cs

Communication, care, compassion

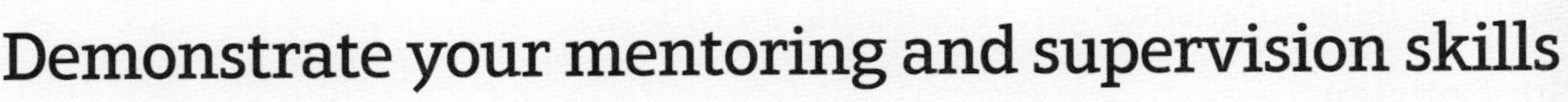

Demonstrate your mentoring and supervision skills

Mentoring and supervision are important to support staff in doing their job well and you must be able to demonstrate your skills in this area.

Activities

Qualification mapping

Unit 2 LO 1 AC 1.2, 1.3, LO 5 AC 5.1 and 5.2

Your role as a mentor

The manager of your organisation recognises that mentoring new members of staff helps to retain them and to raise standards. Mentors need to have good professional skills. Your manager has asked for staff to volunteer if they would like to mentor new members of the team. A training session has been organised but your manager wants to make sure that he recruits the right people for the role.

Make a list of reasons to present to your manager explaining why you would be a good mentor.

Supervising a new member of staff

You have been asked to supervise a new member of staff. They are new to adult care work and are unfamiliar with the process of supervision.

Put together a resource for use by a new member of staff that explains the following:

- the reason for supervision
- the procedure of supervision for them.

Mentoring and supervision are important aspects of your role as a lead adult care worker

Activity

Reflection on supervision

Reflect upon a recent mentor or supervision meeting. If possible, choose an example that you could improve upon.

- Using Kolb's model, reflect on the mentor or supervision meeting.
- Share your ideas for improvement with your assessor.

Practice for professional discussion

Prepare for a 10-minute professional discussion on the value of mentoring in adult care work.

You could include your responses to the following questions:

- What is the role of a mentor?
- What makes a good mentor?
- What are the benefits of mentorship to the mentee, the mentor and the organisation?
- Examples of when your mentoring skills were put to good use.

Qualification mapping

Unit 2 LO 2 AC 2.2

Case study: Niamh's supervision meeting

Niamh works in a unit that supports individuals who have eating disorders. Niamh is confident in her work when supporting individuals with disorders such as anorexia and bulimia. A new user to the service has pica, which is when an individual ingests substances that are not food, such as soil, hair and paper. Niamh has never supported an individual who has this disorder and she is finding it difficult. Niamh has seen the new user of the service eating her own faeces and hair. Gina, a lead adult care worker, is Niamh's supervisor and they have a supervision meeting booked for next week.

- How could supervision help support Niamh in her work?
- How can Niamh prepare for her supervision meeting?
- How can Gina support Niamh during and after the meeting?

Supervision is a good time to reflect on and evaluate how your own learning and experience has influenced your practice.

Activity

Witness testimony

As part of your lead adult care worker role, you will help to develop new colleagues to settle into their role.

Obtain a witness testimony from either a colleague who you have mentored or from your manager who has witnessed your mentoring skills.

The witness testimony will provide evidence that you have competently carried out the mentoring role.

Good practice: recruitment and induction

Qualification mapping

Unit 2 LO 1 AC 1.1, 1.2 and 1.3

How can you make sure that people with the right qualities and skills are employed in adult care and that they are supported when they start in their new role? A robust recruitment and induction process will help.

People working in adult care must have appropriate qualities and skills. If the wrong person entered the care sector, it could have damaging effects on the users of the service, the individual worker themselves and the team who work in the organisation. Having a strong recruitment process will help to bring the right people into the sector. A comprehensive and supportive induction process will help them on their way to becoming an effective adult care worker.

Professional working

Skills for Care provide statistics on the adult social care sector and its workforce. You can find information on national and regional trends and reports on how many people are employed, the recruitment and retention of staff, as well as pay rates and information about demographics and those who use the services. You can access useful information on their website at www.skillsforcare.org.uk – follow the links for workforce intelligence.

Why is there a growing need for adult care workers?

There are many different reasons why more adult care workers are needed:

- More people are living longer; as they grow older, they need more physical support.
- The incidence of dementia is rising as the population ages.
- Society is supporting individuals with more complex physical and mental health needs.
- There is a pressure to free up bed spaces in hospitals so more people are discharged from hospital with care needs.
- The existing workforce are getting older and retiring.
- There can be a high turnover of staff in some areas; staff may choose to leave the sector or gain promotion and move on.

The right person for the job

You know how rewarding a job in adult care is but not everyone does. Some people in our society have the right qualities to be a good adult care worker, yet have never thought of entering the profession.

Read Sophie's account in the following case study.

Case study: Sophie

'My name is Sophie. I am 17 years old and I am at college. When I was younger, I always wanted to be a midwife so I applied to study health and social care at my local college. For my course, I had to do some work experience in the sector and a placement in 'Active Lives' – a community hub for people who have learning disabilities. At first I really didn't want to go; I wanted a placement at my local hospital in the maternity department but this was not possible. But I have been at Active Lives for 6 months on a work placement and it has totally changed my future career plans. Now I want to work in social care, even though this was an option that I had never thought about before.'

- Why do you think that Sophie had not thought about a career in social care?
- What do you think it was about the Active Lives work placement that changed Sophie's mind about her future career plan?
- Why is it good for individuals like Sophie to gain some work experience in a social care setting?

The recruitment process

The process from a person being interested in a job in social care to being an effective member of the adult care workforce needs to be a structured and organised one. You may be asked to be involved in any part of the recruitment process. Your input will be valuable because you have an active working knowledge and understanding of the job itself.

Advertise

There are different ways of advertising, for example, via social media or posting an advert in your local newspaper. A closing date will be given for when completed applications must be submitted. An outline of the job role and responsibilities should be stated.

Applications

Individuals who wish to be considered for the post will complete an application to demonstrate their potential suitability. Each application should be carefully read and considered.

Short list and invite for interview

Each of the applications will be reviewed, and the strengths and weaknesses assessed. Those whose applications potentially meet the requirements of the role will be shortlisted and invited for an interview. The invitation should state what to expect on the day. For example, some organisations will ask for the person to present information about a specific topic.

Planning for the interview

Interviewers will plan in detail for the interviews; for example, selecting and agreeing questions that will be asked. The same questions should be asked of each applicant so as to give equal opportunities to everyone. Interviewers will also agree assessment criteria for the interview and produce recording forms to document the process.

The interview

You should be aware that the candidate may be very nervous so do your best to put them at ease; that way you will get a more accurate view of the person. Ask the same questions of each applicant, making it fair and equal to all. Open questions, that have been prepared and agreed beforehand with your manager, will help to draw out information from the person; questions should be related to the job description. Your interview notes should be kept securely in case an unsuccessful applicant asks you for feedback as to why they didn't get the job.

References and DBS

The next step is to get references for the successful applicant before they start in employment. Usually two references are required; one should be from their previous employer. A current disclosure and barring service (DBS) check will also be required. Some applicants will have subscribed to the DBS updating service, which will make the process quicker. They must not start work until references and DBS have been received.

When the most appropriate person has been selected and approved for the post, the unsuccessful applicants have to be told. This can be difficult as it is likely that they will be disappointed, so good communication skills are important. They may ask for feedback; remember to make sure your feedback is constructive.

Professional working

Many individuals have not thought about social care as a future career. Welcoming volunteers and work placement opportunities will give individuals an insight into what the job is like. This will help to bring new and enthusiastic people into the sector.

Professional working

You have to be very careful when recruiting new staff. Strictly follow equality law and make sure not to discriminate; for example, adverts must not say that you will not consider people who have a disability. You should be aware of the protected characteristics; do not ask if an individual is married or planning to have children.

Professional working

The recruitment process can differ between organisations. For example, some will have a panel of interviewers and require the applicant to carry out a presentation, whereas the interview for a post for a personal assistant, for example, may be more informal and base the interviews on questions alone. Whatever the interview type, it is advisable to have at least two interviewers where possible, as this will give a more balanced view.

6Cs

Competence, communication

Induct the new worker

Even if the new member of staff has had lots of experience in the social care sector, they will need to adapt to your work setting. All new staff should undertake an induction programme. This will help to ensure they have the essential knowledge and skills for safe working. Successful completion of each part of the induction programme should be recorded. The new member of staff must also undertake relevant training before carrying out an activity; for example, they should not participate in moving and handling activities without having had training.
Some organisations have an induction checklist. For example:

- aims and objectives of the service
- policies and procedures – fire and other emergencies, data protection, safeguarding, health and safety, and others specific to the organisation
- complaints and compliments
- orientation of the workplace including specific routines
- sickness recording, and holiday entitlement and booking procedure.

Summary

A structured and organised recruitment process will help to make sure that the right individuals enter the social care workforce. A robust induction programme will support new adult care workers to work in a safe and effective way.

Support the recruitment and induction process

As a lead adult care worker, you have a part to play in ensuring robust recruitment and induction processes so that the right people are employed to support individuals who need care.

Activities

Recruitment for adult care work

There is a growing need for individuals to join the social care workforce. There are many individuals with the right qualities who have not considered adult care work as a career; they should be encouraged to think about work in the adult care sector.

Produce a poster that would encourage individuals to join your area of work. Think about how you could promote and share the information.

Ask your assessor or manager if they think that your advertising poster would encourage new people to start a new career in social care.

Qualification mapping

Unit 2 LO 1 AC 1.1, 1.2 and 1.3, LO 5 AC 5.1

Drawing up a job description

Imagine that you have a vacancy for a position in your workplace and your manager has asked you to help design an advert for the job. Choose a position in your workplace and design a job description. Think about all the different points it must cover.

Ask your supervisor or manager to check it for you to see if it meets legal requirements.

Designing interview questions

Getting the right person for the job is crucial. It is very costly and time consuming if an individual starts a role and then leaves because the job is not what they thought it would be. The interview process helps to determine who the right person for the job is.

For the role that you chose in the above activity, create a list of five questions that you would ask the applicant at an interview.

Contributing to the induction process

When an individual is appointed for a new job, they will need to undergo a structured induction programme.

Create an induction programme for a new member of staff in your workplace.

Think about all the different aspects of induction that they should complete.

Ask your supervisor or manager to check it for you to see if it meets legal requirements.

It is essential to draw up the right questions for interviewing a prospective adult care worker

Qualification mapping

Unit 2 LO 2 AC 2.2

Reflection and witness testimony

If you have an opportunity to participate in a part of the recruitment process, use Kolb's model of reflection to demonstrate your learning after the event. See page v to remind you of the Kolb model.

You could also get a witness testimony to put into your portfolio of evidence.

Practice for professional discussion

The role of a lead adult care worker is a highly respected and trusted one; you will be expected to work in a professional way. Use the points below to help you to prepare for a 10-minute professional discussion on the importance of professional working.

You could include your response to the following points:

- What does working professionally mean to you?
- Give examples of professional boundaries in your work and why they are important.
- Evaluate the role of reflection in your work.

Situational judgement questions

1. Your manager has asked you to help them put together a disciplinary case for a colleague you are mentoring; as they are not meeting their targets. Your manager asks you to include comments from your mentoring discussions. Do you:
   a. Refer back to your mentoring notes and highlight areas that may be of use to support the disciplinary?
   b. Explain that you can't because it conflicts with the relationship that you have as a mentor?
   c. Give your manager all of the discussion notes so that she can select what she may find helpful?
   d. Apologise to your colleague (mentee) and explain that you had no option but to hand the information over?
2. You have worked hard to build up a relationship with a user of your service. He has now invited you to be a contact on social media. Do you:
   a. Accept; it has taken you a long time to build the bond and you want to maintain it?
   b. Accept but only to view their posts?
   c. Say no and explain that you are not allowed to because of your position?
   d. Ignore them and change the subject when it is brought up in conversation?
3. You are a lead adult care worker to a new user of your service. They have a specific need relating to an unusual medical condition. You and your team need accurate information on how best to support them in the event of a medical emergency. Do you:
   a. Ask them and note down their instructions?
   b. Post a question on social media?
   c. Find out information yourself from professional sources and ask a health professional for advice?
   d. Suggest a colleague does a research project on the subject and share her findings?
4. Your manager has asked you to help prepare for interviews for a new junior carer post. Do you:
   a. Prepare different questions for each applicant?
   b. Suggest that you could interview some applicants on your own to save time?
   c. Interview with your manager and use the same questions for each applicant?
   d. Only select applicants of the same ethnic background to the users of service?
5. You are key worker to a user of the service with a specific difficulty that you have not dealt with before. Your colleague says that she supported someone 20 years ago with the same problem. Do you:
   a. Use her advice from her experience 20 years ago and ask her to devise an information sheet and check list for the staff?
   b. Ask her to take charge in sharing her information during a team meeting?
   c. Leave it to sort itself out and respond to any specific needs as they arise?
   d. Listen to your colleague but do your own research by making contact with a specialist organisation?
6. An inexperienced junior colleague asks you for feedback after carrying out an activity. There were some parts that they did well, while some others could have been better. Do you:
   a. Tell her what she has done well and what she could improve upon, but finish on a positive note?
   b. Tell her what she has done well but don't upset her by telling her what she has done wrong?
   c. Tell her what she has done wrong and what she needs to try to do better next time?
   d. Tell her that you will explain to her mentor and they will give her feedback?
7. Work is getting pressured. You are leading the shift and some team members are off sick. Those who are on shift are saying that they are fed up. Do you:
   a. Agree with them and suggest that you all go to the pub after the shift to have a moan about work?
   b. Go to your manager on their behalf and say that something needs to be done immediately?
   c. Tell them to stop moaning and get on with the job they have agreed to do?
   d. Explain that there is nothing that can be done right now but you understand their frustrations, act positively and smile?

Answers to situational judgement questions

Topic A

1 b, 2 b, 3 c, 4 c, 5 a, 6 d, 7 b

Topic B

1 b, 2 d, 3 a, 4 d, 5 d, 6 b

Topic C

1 b, 2 b, 3 c, 4 d, 5 c, 6 c, 7 d, 8 b

Topic D

1 c, 2 b, 3 c, 4 c, 5 b, 6 c, 7 a and d, 8 c

Topic E

1 a, 2 d, 3 b, 4 c, 5 a, 6 b

Topic F

1 b, 2 c, 3 c, 4 c, 5 d, 6 a, 7 d

Topic E page 159 – answers to legislation activity

Actions to meet requirements of the law	Relevant law or regulation
You explain to a person that you can't take them to the toilet on your own as they have been assessed as needing two people to assist them.	Manual Handling Operations Regulations 1992
Someone slips over on a wet patch on the floor. This is recorded in the accident book, even though there are no apparent injuries.	RIDDOR
You read the moving and handling risk assessment for a new user of your service and use the recommended equipment to transfer her into a chair.	Management of Health and Safety at Work Regulations 1999
You are called to assess a member of the kitchen staff who has cut his finger, because you are the first aider on duty.	Health and Safety (First Aid) Regulations 1981
You move some cleaning fluid that the cleaner has left in the toilet and lock it in the cleaners' cupboard.	COSHH
You are provided with, and use, protective gloves to wash a user of services.	The Health and Safety at Work Act 1974
You encourage an individual to walk with a walking frame rather than pushing them in a wheelchair.	Manual Handling Operations Regulations 1992

Topic E page 182 – answers to fire safety activity

1b Close the door to stop the replacement of oxygen ✔

2d Make sure blankets are not touching radiators ✔

Glossary

Accountable – to be completely responsible for what you do and to be able to explain what you have done

Active listening – the 'active' part is using skills to gain information that someone might otherwise choose not to share

Advocacy – taking action to help people say what they want, secure their rights, represent their interests and obtain services they need

Advocate – someone who will act in the best interest of the individual

Barrier – a circumstance or obstacle that keeps people or things apart or prevents communication or progress

Body mass index (BMI) – a measure of body fat based on your weight in relation to your height, calculated by dividing a person's weight in kilograms by the square of their height in metres.

Breach of confidentiality – passing on confidential or sensitive information, for example, from a user of services

Calibration – checking that a monitor is working accurately

Confidentiality – the state of keeping or being kept secret or private

Constructive – helpful, useful

Delegate – give someone else the responsibility of doing a job or task

Dialect – a form of language that is specific to a particular geographical area or group of people

Disclosure – revelation of information that was previously kept secret

Discrimination – treating an individual unfairly or less well because they are different

Diversity – recognising differences and that each individual is unique

Duty of care – providing care and support for individuals within the law and within the policies, procedures and agreed ways of working of your employer; avoiding abuse and injury to individuals

Empathy – ability to understand and share the feelings and emotions of someone else

Employee – the workers at the setting are employees

Employer – the owner or manager of the setting acts as the employer

Equality – providing everyone with equal opportunities and chances, for example, access to services

Escalate – to bring any concerns to a more senior member of the team

Groomed / Grooming – when someone builds an emotional connection with a user of the service to gain their trust for the purpose of exploitation

Harm – the consequence if a hazard causes injury or illness

Hazard – something that could cause harm, such as illness or injury

Inclusion – placing individuals at the centre of planning and support, regardless of their circumstances or background

Informed choice – the person is given information so they understand the benefits and the risks

Infringing rights – when a person's entitlements are ignored through deliberate or accidental actions

Leading question – question expressed in such a way that it suggests what the answer should be

Least restrictive – allowing as much freedom as possible without risking harm

Linguistic – relating to language

Mental capacity – the ability to make decisions for yourself

Paraphrase – express the meaning of something using different words

Person-centred support – ensuring the user of service is at the centre of everything you do

Prejudice – forming a negative opinion about someone before you even know them (for example, where the person lives, age, sexuality or job they do); there is no firm evidence around the prejudiced judgement

Principle – an accepted or professed rule of action or conduct

Private – services that are run as a business and paid for by the user of the service, for example, private residential home, counsellor

Proximity – closeness

Reminiscence – activities to encourage older people to think about something familiar from their past

Risk – the likelihood that a hazard will cause harm

Self-esteem – confidence in yourself as an individual person

Sensory – relating to the five senses – sight, hearing, touch, smell, taste

Statutory – provided by the state, for example, National Health Service, school education

Spam – irrelevant or unsolicited messages sent over the Internet, typically to a large number of users, for the purposes of advertising, phishing, spreading malware etc.

Stereotyping – negatively judging groups of people (for example, because of their race, culture, sexuality); all individuals of that group will then be viewed unfavourably and often offensively

Supervisee – the person who is being supervised

Supervision – one-to-one meeting with your supervisor to discuss how you are getting on at work

Transcribed – written down

Transferable skills – different skills and abilities that you have and can use in various situations

Voluntary – services that are provided by charities or individuals and are not run for profit, for example, befriender, food banks

Vulnerable – an individual who is unable to protect themselves from others trying to abuse or take advantage of them

Whistleblowing – the act of telling the authorities or the public that an organisation is doing something immoral or illegal

Index